EXERCISES AND APPLICATIONS FOR

MICROECONOMIC ANALYSIS

Third Edition

Gary W. Yohe

Wesleyan University

W. W. Norton & Company · New York · London

For Linda, Mari, Courtney, and Bonne Belle

Table of Contents

iv

Introduction

There are times in virtually everyone's education when
he or she is asked to graduate from solving contrived
problems scribbled by some teacher on some blackboard
somewhere to answering what school children affectionately
call "word problems" drawn in some measure from the "real
world". In arithmetic, for example, students begin to be
asked not for the solution to questions like:

$$\{100 - (4 \times 10) - (6 \times 8)\} = ?,$$

but for answers to questions like: "How much change would
you have left over from one dollar if you went to the store
and purchased four 10 cent candies and six 8 cent chewing
gums?" In the calculus course that comes later, the same,
but older student might be asked to compute the dimensions
of the largest rectangular area which could be enclosed by
fence of fixed length if one side of the enclosure could
abut a river and would therefore need no fencing. A
question like this would be posed, however, only after the
student had become reasonably proficient at solving problems
like

$$\max_{X;Y} \{XY\}$$

$$\text{s.t.} \quad 2X + Y = \bar{L}.$$

Exactly the same process occurs when people turn to study economic theory. They are taught the fundamental concepts and lead to develop the skills necessary to exercise those concepts by doing a number of contrived problems. They might see fully specified utility functions, for example, and be asked to compute the corresponding demand schedules, to verify the Slutsky equation, or to maximize utility subject to a specified budget constraint. But just as it was not enough to become proficient at addition without learning how and when to apply it, it is not enough to become proficient at manipulating the basic principles of economic theory without learning how and when they might be applied. And even that is not enough, of course; a good researcher must also understand both the power of a theoretical argument and its limitation. So, just as young students must practice word problems to learn how to use arithmetic, more advanced students who want to apply their mathematical skills to support their understanding of economic theory must practice applied theory problems if they are to learn how to use that theory. This volume speaks to that need.

Problems using fundamental constructions and concepts presented in each of the various chapters of the Third Edition of Hal Varian's *Microeconomic Analysis* have been drawn from the literatures of public finance, economic systems, international trade, and industrial organization. They are meant to acquaint the reader not only with those literatures, but also with the wide variety of methodologies which can facilitate the application of the microeconomic principles found in their text to a diverse body of thought and inquiry.

Each problem begins with a brief introduction to the specific literature from which it was drawn. Each continues with a self-contained formal modeling of the problem, a rough sentence or so previewing the method of solution, a thorough solution, and finally a conclusion that places the solution in its proper context. Selected references are finally listed at the end of each in case the reader is interested in pursuing a topic further. Specific references to topics covered in *Microeconomic Analysis* are indicated within square brackets either by page number or by section.

It is expected that you will read these problems with a pencil and paper handy. Plenty of space is provided around the equations and graphs to encourage your working through the omitted steps even if you are short of paper. This is not the thinly veiled attempt by the author to thwart your eventual participation on the supply side of the used book market. The exercises offered here are meant to be "word problem" practice, and will be most valuable only if they are worked through thoroughly and not just read. There may, of course, be a variety of solution techniques for each question, but the solutions presented here are, for the most part, those chosen by the authors who did the original research.

My appreciation is extended to Hal Varian of the University of Michigan for his contributions, suggestions, and encouragement, particularly in earlier editions. I also wish to thank Marielle Yohe for preparing the figures. Pam Williams, Gloria Cone, and Jane Tozer did an outstanding job preparing the manuscript, and my debt to them is considerable, as well. Bonne Belle guarded my sanity with her zany interruptions and amusing hijinks; and I thank her, too.

Finally, thanks to Drake McFeely and Rich Rivellese at Norton for their patience and support. Also, thanks, but apologies as well, to a nameless copy editor who slaved over the manuscript as his or her Memorial Day weekend slipped away, trying to make it look perfect, only to run squarely into my limited abilities with Wordperfect 5.1. Had I been able to follow all of his or her suggestions, the manuscript would look much better ... and would be devoid of confusing notation. But I couldn't, and it isn't. I do not think, however, that the remaining inconsistencies should cause you too much trouble. If you will allow a career hint: never agree to deliver 500 pages of camera ready copy.

You should be warned that I am a notoriously bad proofreader, so you may find some errors as you work through the details of the answers provided here. The results quoted have, for the most part, stood the test of time, though, so any errors which you might find are mine and, most likely, typographical. If you are the first to send corrections for a problem at my address at Wesleyan, I will send you compensation equal to my royalty share of the cost of your purchase. Don't get too excited - that is likely to be something like 96 cents; but you will receive grateful acknowledgement if and when a Fourth Edition is produced.

On the whole, all of the people involved in this project hope that our work will help, in some small way, to foster a generation of students who find the transition from course work to research just a little easier than before.

G.W.Y.

June 14, 1993

PROBLEM 1

1. The Elasticity of Substitution[1]

The elasticity of substitution is defined to reflect the responsiveness of the employment ratios to changes in the corresponding technical rate of substitution [see page 13 for the definition]. Since cost minimization conditions will equate input price ratios (w_1/w_2) with the technical rate of substitution [see page 40 of Chapter 3], the elasticity of substitution can equally well be given by:

$$\sigma \equiv \partial \; \frac{\dfrac{x_1(\vec{w},y)}{x_2(\vec{w},y)}}{\partial(w_1/w_2)} \cdot \frac{(w_1/w_2)}{(x_1/x_2)} \; .$$

For CES production functions of the form

$$y = f(x_1,x_2) = (ax_1^{\rho} + (1-a)x_2^{\rho})^{1/\rho} \tag{1}$$

it has been demonstrated that [page 20]

$$\sigma = 1/(\rho-1). \tag{2}$$

The Cobb-Douglas case requires that equation (1) become [page 12]

$$f(x_1,x_2) = x_1^{a}x_2^{1-a}, \tag{3}$$

---

[1] Material found in Chapters 1 and 3 is applicable here.

1

but $\sigma = -1$ is consistent with (2) in the limit when $\rho = 0$.

Beyond being the special case of unitary elasticity, it will frequently be observed that Cobb-Douglas is a limiting condition of theoretical importance. The next question will exhibit this limiting property in two examples germane to growth and technical change. They follow a bit of simple geometry here which reveals another limiting property: the isoquants drawn by the Cobb-Douglas technology are the first not to intersect the axes.

Question:

Graph isoquants through $x_1 = x_2 = 1$ so that they illustrate the following possible cases allowed by equation (1), including the limiting Cobb-Douglas case of equation (3):

i.) $\rho = - \infty$ so $\sigma = 0$ (the Leontief technology);

ii.) $- \infty < \rho < 0$ so $- 1 < \sigma < 0$ (little substitution available);

iii.) $\rho = 0$ so $\sigma = -1$ (the Cobb-Douglas case);

iv.) $0 < \rho < 1$ so $- \infty < \sigma < - 1$ (large amounts of substitution available); and

v.) $\rho = 1$ so $\sigma = - \infty$ (perfect substitution).

PROBLEM 1

Suggested Solution:

You are on your own for the graphing. Notice before you start, however, that y = 0 for the Cobb-Douglas technology of equation (3) if either x_1 or x_2 equals zero (zero raised to any power is zero, and zero times any number is zero). Any isoquant associated with a positive y in a Cobb-Douglas technology cannot, as a result, be drawn to intersect either axis.

The Leontief technology, the limiting case for little substitution and $- 1 < \sigma < 0$, displays right angle isoquants which clearly cannot intersect either axis. Similarly, zero raised to a negative power for $\rho < 0$ and $- 1 < \sigma < 0$ is undefined, and the ioquants are asymptotic to both axes. For $\rho < 1$ and $- \infty < \sigma < - 1$, though, output can be positive with either x_1 or x_2 (but not both) set equal to zero (zero raised to any positive power is zero, and zero added to some strictly positive number is still strictly positive). It gets harder than this!

Reference

(1) Arrow, K.J., H.B. Chenery, B.S. Minhas, and R.M. Solow, "Capital-Labor Substitution and Economic Efficiency," *Review of Economics and Statistics*, 43:225-250, August 1961.

PROBLEM 2

2. The Limiting Nature of the Cobb-Douglas Technology[1]

Question 1 noted that the elasticity of substitution can be defined to reflect the responsiveness of the employment ratios to changes in the corresponding factor price ratios:

$$\sigma \equiv \frac{\partial \{x_1(\vec{w},y) / x_2(\vec{w},y)\}}{\partial \{w_1/w_2\}} \cdot \frac{(w_1/w_2)}{(x_1/x_2)}$$

Recall that

$$\sigma = 1/(\rho-1) \tag{1}$$

for CES production functions of the form

$$y = f(x_1,x_2) = (ax_1^{\rho} + (1-a)x_2^{\rho})^{1/\rho}. \tag{2}$$

The Cobb-Douglas case,

$$f(x_1,x_2) = x_1^a x_2^{1-a},$$

conforms with (1) and (2) in the limit as ρ approaches 0 so that σ approaches unity. This limiting property of the Cobb-Douglas technology is frequently important; this problem will illustrate why in two separate instances.

----

[1] Material found in Chapter 2 is applicable here.

PROBLEM 2

Questions:

(a) Show that the relative share paid to x_2 may rise or fall with an increase in the availability of x_2. The direction depends upon whether $\sigma < -1$ or $\sigma > -1$.

(b) Suppose that the production of y in period t were summarized by

$$y(t) = [a(E_1(t)x_1(t))^p + (1-a)(E_2(t)x_2(t))^p]^{1/p},$$

where the $x_i(t)$ represent employment of x_i in period t and the $E_i(t)$ represent efficiency units for x_i. The $E_i(t)$ reflect technological changes and are expressed in terms of the number of old units of x_i (in some base period) needed to replace one current unit $x_i(t)$. Show that the factor price ratio (w_1/w_2) increases or decreases over time along a balanced growth path (i.e., a path such that (x_2/x_1) is fixed so $\partial(x_2/x_2)/\partial t = 0$), depending on whether σ lies above or below -1 and the sign of

$$\left(\frac{\dot{E_1}}{E_1} - \frac{\dot{E_2}}{E_2}\right).$$

PROBLEM 2

Dot notation reflects time derivatives so the sign of

$$(\frac{\dot{E_1}}{E_1} - \frac{\dot{E_2}}{E_2})$$

shows whether labor-saving (conserving of x_1) or capital-saving (conserving of x_2) technological change is progressing faster.

Suggested Solutions:

(a) Let the relative share of x_2 be

$$R_2 \equiv \frac{w_2 x_2}{w_1 x_1} ;$$

the relevant partial is then

$$\frac{\partial R_2}{\partial (x_2/x_1)} = \frac{x_2}{x_1} \frac{\partial (w_2/w_1)}{\partial (x_2/x_1)} \frac{w_2}{w_1}$$

$$= [(1/\sigma) + 1] \frac{w_2}{w_1} . \qquad (3)$$

The sign of equation (3) depends, therefore, on the absolute magnitude of σ; i.e.,

PROBLEM 2

$$> 0 \quad \sigma < -1; \ \rho > 0$$

$$\frac{\partial R_2}{\partial (x_2/x_1)} \quad = 0 \quad \sigma = -1; \ \rho = 0$$

$$< 0 \quad \sigma > -1; \ \rho < 0$$

The smaller the possibility for substitution, the more a decrease in the relative scarcity of a factor will work toward reducing its share by lowering its relative price. Substitution below that allowed by the Cobb-Douglas case, in fact, actually causes a reduction in the relative share because (w_2/w_1) falls so much.

(b)   Begin by observing that

$$\frac{\partial (w_1/w_2)}{\partial t} = \frac{a}{1-a} \frac{\partial}{\partial t} \left\{ \frac{E_1^\rho x_1^{\rho-1}}{E_2^\rho x_2^{\rho-2}} \right\}$$

$$(4)$$

with (x_2/x_1) constant because

PROBLEM 2

$$\frac{w_1}{w_2} = \frac{\dfrac{\partial f(x_1, x_2)}{\partial x_1}}{\dfrac{\partial f(x_1, x_2)}{\partial x_2}} = \frac{a}{1-a} \cdot \frac{E_1^{\rho} x_1^{\rho-1}}{E_2^{\rho} x_2^{\rho-1}}$$

when profits are maximized [see page 26]. The sign of (4) clearly depends only on the sign of the bracketed term. Ignoring the constraint to form equation (5), that term equals:

$$(E_2^{\rho} x_2^{\rho-1})^{-2} [(E_2^{\rho} x_2^{\rho-1}) (E_1^{\rho} (\rho-1) x_1^{\rho-2} \dot{x}_1 + x_1^{\rho-1} E_1^{\rho-1} \dot{E}_1)$$

$$- (E_1^{\rho} x_1^{\rho-1}) (E_2^{\rho} (\rho-1) x_2^{\rho-2} \dot{x}_2 + x_2^{\rho-1} \rho E_2^{\rho-1} \dot{E}_2)]$$

$$= (E_2^{\rho} x_2^{\rho-1})^{-2} [E_2^{\rho} E_1^{\rho} (\rho-1) x_2^{\rho-2} x_1^{\rho} (\frac{x_2 \dot{x}_1}{x_1^2} - \frac{x_1 \dot{x}_2}{x_1^2})$$

$$+ E_2^{\rho} E_1^{\rho} \rho x_2^{\rho-1} x_1^{\rho-1} (\frac{\dot{E}_1}{E_1} - \frac{\dot{E}_2}{E_2})] .$$

The constraint requires that (x_2/x_1) remain fixed, though, so

8

PROBLEM 2

$$\left(\frac{\dot{x}_2}{x_1}\right) = \frac{x_1\dot{x}_2 - x_2\dot{x}_1}{x_1^2} = 0$$

and, as a result, the entire first term of (5) vanishes.
The sign of (4) is thus dependent upon the sign of

$$\rho\left(\frac{\dot{E}_1}{E_1} - \frac{\dot{E}_2}{E_2}\right)$$

$$> 0 \quad \rho > 0 \ \& \ \frac{\dot{E}_1}{E_1} > \frac{\dot{E}_2}{E_2} \quad or \quad \rho < 0 \ \& \ \frac{\dot{E}_1}{E_1} < \frac{\dot{E}_2}{E_2}$$

$$< 0 \quad \rho > 0 \ \& \ \frac{\dot{E}_1}{E_1} > \frac{\dot{E}_2}{E_2} \quad or \quad \rho > 0 \ \& \ \frac{\dot{E}_1}{E_1} < \frac{\dot{E}_2}{E_2}$$

because E_2, E_1, x_2, and x_1 are all nonzero.

When technological change proceeds more quickly for x_1
than x_2, then the relative factor prices (w_1/w_2) will
increase along a balanced growth path if and only if a great
deal of substitution is possible (i.e., if and only if
$\sigma < -1$). The reverse is true, too. If change favors x_2,
then (w_1/w_2) will fall if and only if substitution is
similarly easy and $\sigma > -1$. Since the effect of this type of
technological change is to increase the "effective"
availability of a factor, these observations are easily seen
to be consistent with those recorded above in part (a).

PROBLEM 2

Beyond their academic interest, these results hold a place of importance in the theory of economic growth and technological change. Allen (1) captures their intent in a catalog of growth models and various notions of factor-saving technological change. Our point is more basic, though; whenever economic actors are allowed to respond to growth or other changes, their response might undermine the most obvious effect. Here, for example, an increase in the relative efficiency or labor (say, x_1) can move the relative wage in either direction. These same observations can, in addition, be used to evaluate the truth of empirical estimates for the elasticity of substitution derived from time series data.

References

(1) Allen, R.G.D., *Macro-Economic Theory - A Mathematical Treatment*, New York, St. Martin's Press, 1966 (Chap. 5).

(2) Arrow, K.J., H.B. Chenery, B.S. Minhas, and R.M. Solow, "Capital-Labor Substitution and Economic Efficiency," *Review of Economics and Statistics*, 43:225-250, August 1961.

(3) Uzawa, H., "Production Functions with Constant Elasticities of Substitution," *Review of Economic Studies*, 29:291-299, Oct. 1962.

3. Per Capita Production Functions[1]

Linearly homogeneous production functions are expressed, quite frequently for the sake of convenience, in "per capita" terms. The trick is simple: one input is factored through the equation (that factor is usually labor, and hence the use of the "per capita" terminology). Consider, for example

$$y = f(x_1, x_2)$$

where $f(x_1, x_2)$ is homogeneous of degree one. It is possible to define a new function $\phi(X)$ by dividing through by x_2 so that

$$y = x_2 \, f((x_1/x_2), 1) \equiv x_2 \, \phi(\chi), \qquad (1)$$

where $\chi \equiv (x_1/x_2)$. Alternatively,

$$(y/x_2) = \phi(\chi),$$

is the per capita production function in terms of x_2. This problem will investigate several properties of $\phi(\chi)$ and will close with an illustration of how per capita functions are employed in growth theory.

Questions:

(a) Express the profit-maximizing conditions in terms of

_____

[1] Material found in Chapter 2 is again applicable.

PROBLEM 3

w_1, w_2, and $\phi(\chi)$ under the assumption that the price of output y is unity.

(b) Show that

$$\sigma = \frac{\phi'(\chi) [\phi(\chi) - \chi\phi'(\chi)]}{\chi\phi(\chi)\phi''(\chi)}.$$

$$(2)$$

(c) Show that if $f(x_1, x_2)$ were a standard CES production function of the form

$$y = (ax_1^\rho + (1-a)x_2^\rho)^{1/\rho},$$

then the expression offered in part (c) would be consistent with

$$\sigma = 1/(\rho-1). \qquad (2')$$

(d) Return now to the move general function defined in equation (1). Suppose that x_1 and x_2 were to represent capital and labor, respectively. Investment would then correspond simply to an increase in the stock of x_1. Assume further that labor "owned" no capital, and that it saved $s_2 \cdot 100\%$ of its wage earnings $(w_2 x_2)$. Let the capitalists, meanwhile, provide no labor while they save $s_1 \cdot 100\%$ of their income from capital $(w_1 x_1)$.

Consider now, an economy progressing along a steady state balanced growth path in macroeconomic equilibrium, so savings equals investment. That is to say, assume

12

PROBLEM 3

that

$$(\text{investment}) = \dot{x}_1 = s_1 w_1 x_1 + s_2 w_2 x_2 = (\text{savings})$$

and require that (x_1/x_2) remain fixed even though x_2 is growing at a rate n. Dot notation again denotes time derivatives, so the steady state requirement can be expressed

$$(\dot{x}_1/x_2) = 0.$$

Should the laborers encourage the capitalists to increase s_1; i.e., would their wage increase if s_1 were to climb? Show that the answer depends on both the size of the absolute value of σ and the sign of $(s_2 - s_1)$.

Suggested Solutions:

(a) With the prices properly normalized so that $p = 1$,

$$
\begin{aligned}
w_2 &= \frac{\partial f(x_1, x_2)}{\partial x_2} = \frac{\partial (x_2 \phi(\chi))}{\partial x_2} \\
&= -\phi'(\chi)(x_1/x_2) + \phi(\chi) \\
&= \phi(\chi) - \chi \phi'(\chi)
\end{aligned}
$$

(3)

PROBLEM 3

while

$$w_1 = \frac{\partial f(x_1, x_2)}{\partial x_1} = \frac{\partial(x_2 \phi(\chi))}{\partial x_1}$$

$$= x_2 \phi'(\chi) x_2^{-1}$$

$$= \phi'(\chi)$$

(4)

For any χ, then, $(w_1\ w_2)$ can be illustrated graphically.

Notice from Figure 3.1 and w_1 declines and w_2 increases as χ increases. To see this, observe first of all that the slope of the per capita production function $f[(x_1/x_2), 1]$ at (e.g.) point A is simply w_1; that is the message buried in equation (4). Equation (3) meanwhile instructs us that the intercept of the line tangent to the production schedule at point A is w_2. It is, then, clear that the intercepts of lines like the one tangent to the production function at point A [direct measures of w_2] climb while their slopes [equally direct measures of w_1] fall as χ increases.

(b)   In light of the representations of w_1 and w_2 produced in part (a), it is more convenient to consider

14

Figure 3.1

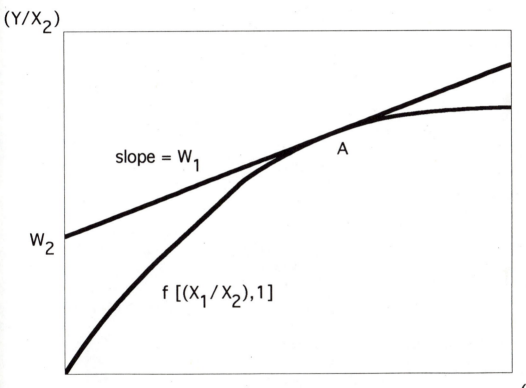

(Y/X_2)

(X_1/X_2)

slope = W_1

W_2

A

$f[(X_1/X_2),1]$

PROBLEM 3

$$\sigma^{-1} = \frac{\partial(w_1/w_2)}{\partial\chi} \quad \frac{\chi}{w_1/w_2}$$

$$= \frac{(\phi-\chi\phi')\,\phi''+\chi\phi'\phi''}{(\phi-\chi\phi')^2} \quad \frac{\chi(\phi-\chi\phi')}{\phi'}$$

$$= \frac{\chi\phi\phi''}{\phi'(\phi-\chi\phi')}$$

Clearly, then

$$\sigma = \frac{\phi'(\chi)\,[\phi(\chi)-\chi\phi'(\chi)]}{\chi\phi(\chi)\,\phi''(\chi)}$$

(5)

(c) For the standard CES function,

$$\phi(\chi) = [a\chi^\rho + (1-a)]^{1/\rho}$$

(6)

and so, from equations (3) and (4),

PROBLEM 3

$$w_1 = a(\phi(\chi)/\chi)^{1-\rho} \quad and$$

$$w_2 = \phi(\chi) - a\chi(\phi(\chi)/\chi)^{1-\rho}$$

so that

$$\frac{w_2}{w_1} = \frac{\phi - a\chi(\phi/\chi)^{1-\rho}}{a(\phi/\chi)^{1-\rho}}$$

$$= (\frac{\chi^{1-\rho}}{a})\phi^\rho - \chi.$$

Finally, using equation (6), it can be seen that

$$\frac{w_2}{w_1} = (\frac{\chi^{1-\rho}}{a})a\chi^\rho + (\frac{\chi^{1-\rho}}{a})(1-a) - \chi$$

$$= \frac{(1-a)}{a}\chi^{1-\rho}.$$

(7)

Furthermore, since

17

PROBLEM 3

$$\phi'' = a\left(\frac{\phi}{\chi}\right)^{-\rho}\left(\frac{\chi\phi'-\phi}{\chi^2}\right)(1-\rho),$$

notice that

$$\phi\phi''\chi = a(\phi/\chi)^{1-\rho}(\phi-\chi\phi')(\rho-1)$$

and equation (2) predictably reveals that

$$\sigma = \frac{\phi'(\phi)-\chi\phi')}{\phi\phi''\chi} = \frac{1}{\rho-1}.$$

(d)   The macro equilibrium condition stated in the problem requires that savings equal investment; notationally,

$$\dot{x}_1 = S = s_1 w_1 x_1 + s_2 w_2 x_2.$$

(8)

As a result,

$$\frac{\dot{x}_1}{x_1} = s_1 w_1 + s_2 w_2 (1/\chi).$$

The requisite of steady state growth in equilibrium also holds that (x_1/x_2) be constant over time, so

18

PROBLEM 3

$$\frac{\delta(x_1/x_2)}{\delta t} = (\frac{x_1}{x_2})(\frac{\dot{x}_1}{x_1} - \frac{\dot{x}_2}{x_2})$$

$$= s_1 w_1 \chi + s_2 w_2 - n\chi = 0.$$

(8')

Recalling (3) and (4), equation (8) mandates that the impact on w_2 of a change in s_1 must be traced along a growth path such that

$$s_1\phi'\chi + s_2(\phi-\chi\phi') - n\chi = 0.$$

Consider, then

$$\frac{dw_2}{ds_1} = \frac{dw_2}{d\chi}\frac{d\chi}{ds_1}$$

(9)

along such a path. It is immediately clear from equation (3) that

$$\frac{dw_2}{d\chi} = \phi' - \phi' - \phi''\chi > 0.$$

The second term of (9) is thus the critical expression, as it can be evaluated by implicitly differentiating (8') with respect to s_1:

19

PROBLEM 3

$$-s_2\chi\phi''\left(\frac{d\chi}{ds_1}\right) + \phi'\chi + s_1(\phi' + \chi\phi'')\frac{d\chi}{ds_1} - n\frac{d\chi}{ds_1} = 0.$$

Clearly, then,

$$\frac{d\chi}{ds_1} = \frac{\chi\phi'}{[\chi\phi''(s_2 - s_1) - (s_1\phi' - n)]}.$$

(10)

Two observations will now facilitate the evaluation of (10). First of all, equations (2) and (3) combine to show that

$$\frac{\chi\phi''}{\phi'} = \left(\frac{\phi-\chi\phi'}{\phi}\right)\left(\frac{\phi\phi''\chi}{\phi'(\phi-\chi\phi')}\right) = \frac{w_2}{\phi\sigma} < 0.$$

(11)

In addition, it is seen from (8') and (3) that

$$s_1\phi' - n = - s_2w_2/\chi < 0;$$

(12)

i.e., $(s_1\phi' - n)/f' < 0$. Equations (11) and (12) therefore conspire to show that the sign of (9) is the sign of

PROBLEM 3

$$\frac{d\chi}{ds_1} = \frac{\chi}{[(s_2 - s_1) w_2/\phi\sigma - (s_1\phi' - n)/f']}$$

and can be negative only when $s_1 < s_2$ and σ is small in magnitude. Otherwise, the second term in the denominator either dominates, or it is joined when $s_1 > s_2$ to guarantee that the overall effect is positive.

To conclude, then,

$$\frac{dw_2}{ds_1} \quad \begin{array}{l} > 0, \quad s_1 > s_2 \text{ or } s_1 < s_2 \text{ and } |\sigma| \text{ large} \\ \\ < 0, \quad s_1 < s_2 \text{ and } |\sigma| \text{ small.} \end{array}$$

The careful reader will observe that even though $\sigma = -1$ is not the critical point upon which the sign turns, the qualitative result is consistent with those of Problem 2. The availability of substitution is still crucial, and increases in supply of one factor (x_1) through increased investment will push the wage of the other factor up except when substitution is severely limited.

The conversion of linearly homogeneous production functions into per capita schedules is a common technique

21

with which theorists have attacked a multitude of problems.
Growth theory is but one area in which it is used
extensively [see Posinetti (2), Solow (3), and Stiglitz (4
and 5) for a few examples]. The idea is to simplify the
mathematics by reducing the number of variables by one.
Extra care should be taken, however, when the mathematics
stops and the economics ultimately derived in terms of the
simplification is interpreted. It is hoped that the simple
growth-theoretic exercise outlined in (d) successfully
illustrates this point even though it lies outside the
traditional boundaries of microeconomics. A more thorough
presentation of the per capita representation can be found
in Allen (1), and part (d) is derived in part from Stiglitz
(4).

References

(1) Allen, R.G.D., *Macro-Economic Theory - A Mathematical
Treatment,* New York, St. Martin's Press, 1966 (Chapter 3).
(2) Posinetti, L.L., "Rate of Profit and Income Distribution
in Relation to the Rate of Economic Growth," *Review of
Economic Studies*, 29:267-279, 1962.
(3) Solow, R.M., "A Contribution to the Theory of Economic
Growth," *Quarterly Journal of Economics,* 70: 65-94, 1956.
(4) Stiglitz, J.E., "A Two-Sector Two Class Model of
Economic Growth," *Review of Economic Studies,* 34:227-234,

PROBLEM 3

1967.

(5) Stiglitz, J.E., "Distribution of Income and Wealth Among Individuals," *Econometrica*, 37:382-397, 1969.

4. The Cost and Timing of Land Development[1]

An article by Arnott and Lewis (1) has analyzed the timing decision of a real estate investor using little more than the theory of production and the notion that costs should be minimized. This problem will present that analysis in its simplest form. It is assumed that a developer will maximize the present value of the land with respect to time of development and density. Present value is introduced in Chapter 19 of Varian, but it is a common concept from principles.

Agricultural rents are assumed to be zero, the price of capital (X) is constant at p, depreciation and property taxes are zero, and housing rents are assumed to increase at a constant rate from an arbitrary r_0 according to:

$$r(t) \ = \ r_0 e^{\eta t}.$$

(1)

Investment in housing will be made through a "per capita" production function f(x) that converts capital per unit of land into housing per unit of land. Investment at time T will therefore show a present discounted cost pxe^{-it} if i is the interest rate, and return a stream of discounted

---

[1] Material found in Chapter 4 is applicable here. The fundamental notion of present value is introduced in Chapter 19, but only its rudimentary definition is employed here.

PROBLEM 4

rents valued at

$$\int_{t}^{\infty} r(t) f(x) e^{-it} \, dt.$$

(2)

Assume, finally, that $df/dx > 0$ and $d^2f/dx^2 < 0$.

Questions:

(a) Characterize the optimal timing T* and investment x* that maximize the developer's objectives. Explain these characterizations.

(b) Show that optimal development must satisfy the condition that (η/i) equal the ratio of discounted land value to discounted property value (land plus housing).

(c) Argue that $d\varepsilon(x^*)/(dx^*) \leq 0$ is necessary for (T^*, x^*) to be a maximum where

$$\varepsilon(x) \equiv \frac{df}{dx} \frac{x}{f(x)}$$

is defined to be the "elasticity of housing with respect to capital."

(d) Show that the results of part (c) are sufficient to show that the elasticity of substitution between land and

25

PROBLEM 4

capital in the production of housing must be greater than
-1; i.e., it must be impossible to produce housing from
land or capital alone [remember the shapes of the
isoquants in Problem 1].

Suggested Solutions:

(a) Notice first of all that equations (1) and (2) combine
to show that the present value of developed land, net of the
cost of that development, is

$$P(s) \; = \; \int_{s}^{\infty} r(0) f(x) e^{\eta t} e^{-i(t-s)} \; dt$$

$$(3)$$

for $s \geq T$. After some algebra, then,

$$P(T) \; = \; \frac{r(T) f(x)}{(i-\eta)} \; .$$

$$(4)$$

The first-order conditions of the developer's decision
are now tractable. The developer chooses to maximize the
present value of land to be developed at time T with a
capital investment of x that produces $f(x)$ housing at that
time; i.e., the developer's problem is

PROBLEM 4

$$\max \ \{\int_T^{\infty} r(t) f(x) e^{-it} \ dt \ - \ pxe^{-iT}\} \ \equiv \ \max \ L(T,x)$$

(5)

The first-order condition associated with the timing

decision is thus

$$-r(T^*) f(x) e^{-iT^*} \ + \ ipxe^{-iT^*} = 0$$

regardless of the investment chosen. Rearranging,

$$\frac{px}{r(T^*) f(x)} \ = \ \frac{1}{i}$$

(6)

so that, from equation (4),

$$\frac{px}{P(T^*)} \ = \ \frac{i-\eta}{i}.$$

(6')

The left-hand side of equation (6') is the ratio of the
cost of capital and the value of the property at the optimal
time T^*. It must equal a ratio that compares the interest
rate with the rate of growth of housing rents. Writing (6')
to look like

27

PROBLEM 4

$$ipx = (1-\eta)P(T^*)$$

brings forth a more intuitive interpretation: a developer
waits to invest until the interest saved by postponing
investment (ipx) equals the rent forgone $((1-\eta)P(T^*) =$
$r(T^*)f(x))$.

Differentiating with respect to x produces the other
first-order condition:

$$\int_T^\infty r(t) \; \frac{df}{dx} \; e^{-it} \; dt - pe^{-iT} = 0.$$

(7)

Denoting (df/dx) by f'(x) and recalling (1), one sees that
equation (7) reduces to

$$\frac{r(T) f'(x^*)}{i-\eta} \; e^{-iT} - pe^{-iT} = 0.$$

Applying (4) and multiplying through by x^*,

$$\frac{px^*}{P(T)} = \frac{f'(x^*) x^*}{f(x^*)} \equiv \varepsilon(x^*).$$

(8)

Even though $\varepsilon(x^*)$ has been introduced primarily to simplify
notation, it does have a natural interpretation. It can be

28

PROBLEM 4

thought of as the output elasticity of housing with respect
to optimal investment. In any case, equation (8) instructs
the developer to invest to the point where the cost (p) of
providing one more unit of x equals the (discounted) value
of the rents that unit would provide $(P(T)f'(x^*)/f(x^*) =$
$r(T)/(i-\eta))$.

(b) Equations (6) and (8) combine to show that optimal
development at the optimal time requires that

$$\varepsilon(x^*) = \frac{px^*}{P(T^*)} = \frac{i-\eta}{i}.$$

(9)

It is possible to use equation (9) to show that the ratio of
the value of the property at T^* to the value of the land
(net of property) at T^* must equal the ratio of the interest
rate to the growth rate of rents. To see this, note that
the value of the land is simply $P(T^*) - px^*$. Clearly, then,

$$\frac{P(T^*)-px^*}{P(T^*)} = 1 - \frac{px^*}{P(T^*)} = (\eta/i).$$

(c) It is possible to show that $[d\varepsilon(x^*)/dx^*]$ must be
nonpositive from convexity assumptions on the developer's
objective function that guarantee a maximum. It is,
however, more instructive to proceed intuitively. Suppose
that $[d\varepsilon(x^*)/dx^*] > 0$. For $x_1 < x^*$ where x^* is characterized

29

by

$$\varepsilon(x^*) = px^*/P(T^*) = (i-\eta)/i,$$

it must be true that

$$\varepsilon(x_1) < px_1/P(T^*).$$

That would, in turn, require that

$$\frac{f'(x_1^*)x_1^*}{f(x_1^*)} < \frac{px_1^*}{P(T^*)}$$

so that

$$p > \frac{P(T^*)f'(x_1^*)}{f(x_1^*)} = \frac{r(T^*)}{(i-\eta)}.$$

The (marginal) cost of x^* would exceed the discounted value of its possible rents, and investment would fall to zero. Similarly, starting at $x_2 > x^*$, one can argue that investment would increase because the discounted rents would exceed costs. A positive value for $[d\varepsilon(x^*)/dx^*]$ would make (T^*, x^*) a minimum, therefore, so a necessary condition for maximization is that

$$[d\varepsilon(x^*)/dx^*] \le 0.$$

(10)

PROBLEM 4

(d) The f(x) function is really a "per capita" production

function similar to the ones discussed in Problem 3.   The

variable x reflects "capital invested per unit of land" and

f(x) reflects "housing per unit land."   The elasticity of

substitution between land and capital in the production of

housing can thus be defined as it was in Problem 3:

$$\sigma \; = \; \frac{f'(x) \, [f(x) \, - \, xf'(x)]}{xf(x) \, f''(x)} \, .$$

(11)

In the meantime, condition (10) expands to

$$\frac{f(x) \, [f'(x) \, + \, xf''(x)] \, - \, xf'(x) \, f'(x)}{[f(x)]^2} \; \leq 0$$

(12)

from the definition alone.   Collecting terms in (12), one

sees that

$$\frac{xf''(x)}{f(x)} \, \{1 \, + \, \frac{f(x) \, f'(x) \, - \, x[f'(x)]^2}{xf(x) \, f''(x)}\} \, \leq 0 \, .$$

(13)

In light of equation (11) and the fact that f"(x) < 0,

therefore, the necessary condition for a maximization

translates into

31

PROBLEM 4

$$(1 + \sigma) \geq 0; \; i.e., \; \sigma \geq -1.$$

The Arnott and Lewis piece (1) goes on to include some comparative statics, a weakening of some of the assumptions, and a small empirical section. The Canadian data seem to fit the more general model quite well, so the intuitive notions behind the conclusions garner some additional support. The authors also suggest some further extension, and the interested reader is referred to their concluding remarks for that discussion.

References

(1)   Arnott, R., and F.D. Lewis, "The Transition of Land to Urban Use," *Journal of Political Economy*, 87:161-169, 1979.

(2)   Shoup, D., "The Optimal Timing of Urban Land Development," *Papers of the Regional Science Association*, 25:33-44, 1970.

5. Constant Elasticity of Substitution Production Functions with Two or More Inputs[1]

The first few problems reviewed and exploited the general form for a production function based on only two inputs and characterized by constant elasticity of substitution. When there are three of more factors, however, things become more complicated. First of all, a standard definition of exactly what is meant by the elasticity of substitution has not been well established. Instead, three different definitions have been advanced in the literature.

The most popular definition is the logical extension of the two-factor definition. It was first proposed by Hicks, extended by Allen (1), and later analyzed by Uzawa (8). It holds that the (partial) elasticity of substitution between two factors of production is given by:

$$\sigma_{ij} \equiv \frac{x_1 f_1 + \ldots + x_n f_n}{x_i x_j} \frac{F_{ij}}{F},$$

(1)

where

$$y = f(x_1, \ldots, x_n),$$

___

[1] Material found in Chapters 4 and 5 is applicable here.

PROBLEM 5

$$f_i \equiv \partial f/\partial x_i,$$

$$f_{ij} \equiv \partial^2 f/\partial x_i \partial x_j,$$

and F_{ij} is the cofactor in the bordered Hessian matrix for the production function associated with f_{ij} [see page 479]. Fortunately, Allen [(1), page 508] has simplified the definition embodied in equation (1) to a more usable form:

$$\sigma_{ij} = \frac{\lambda(\vec{w}) \; \partial x_i/\partial w_j}{x_i x_j},$$

(2)

where

$$\vec{w} = (w_1, \ldots, w_n)$$

is the vector of factor prices for

$$\vec{x} = (x_1, \ldots, x_n) \text{ and } \lambda(\vec{w})$$

and

$$\lambda(\vec{w}) \equiv c(\vec{w}, 1)$$

is the unit cost schedule corresponding to the production $f(x_1, \ldots, x_n)$ is the dual of the original production schedule.

A second definition, called direct partial elasticity

of substitution [DES in McFadden's (6) terminology], applies

equation (1) to each pair of factors, holding fixed the

employment of the remaining factors.   The shadow partial

elasticity (SES) finally applies equation (1) pairwise,

holding the imputed prices and the total cost of the other

factors fixed.

This problem will explore constant elasticity of

substitution production functions under the Allen-Uzawa

definition for more than two factors.   Since these partial

elasticities are potentially important, constant elasticity

schedules allow a theorist a convenient arena in which to

investigate their import.   Despite the structural

restrictions that severely hamper their applicability to

many empirical studies [as noted in Chapter 12 and explored

here in a later problem], the theoretical power of these

constant elasticity functions is potentially quite potent.

Questions:

(a) Define

$$\Lambda(\vec{w}) \;=\; \log \; \lambda(\vec{w}).$$

Using Shephard's lemma [page 74] and equation (2), show

that

PROBLEM 5

$$\frac{\partial^2 \Lambda}{\partial w_i \partial w_j} = - (1 + \sigma_{ij}) \frac{\partial \Lambda}{\partial w_i} \frac{\partial \Lambda}{\partial w_j}.$$

(b) Consider

$$y = f(x_1, x_2, x_3, x_4) = (ax_1^\rho + (1-a) x_2^{\rho^{\alpha/\rho}} (bx_3^r + (1-b) x_4^r)^{(1-\alpha)/r}.$$

(3)

Show that

$$\sigma_{12} = \sigma = 1/\rho - 1,$$

$$\sigma_{34} = \sigma' = 1/r - 1, \text{ and}$$

$$\sigma_{13} = \sigma_{14} = \sigma_{23} = \sigma_{24} = -1.$$

Suggested Solutions:

The solution to part (a) is simply manipulative; Shephard's lemma provides a convenient substitution. Given (what will become) equation (7), part (b) can also be accomplished by straightforward manipulation. The solution provided will, however, break the problem down into parts that will both simplify the algebra and provide the basis for the discussion that evolves in a later problem. There

36

is, in particular, a natural dichotomy of the factors that allows known cost schedules to be applied directly.

(a) The unit cost schedule solves the problem

$$\min \sum_{i=1}^{n} w_i x_i$$
$$\text{s.t. } f(x_1, \ldots, x_n) = 1.$$

(4)

It is clear, therefore, that

$$\lambda(\vec{w}) = c(\vec{w}, 1).$$

Shephard's lemma is then immediately applicable, so

$$\frac{\partial \lambda(\vec{w})}{\partial w_i} = \frac{\partial c(\vec{w}, 1)}{\partial w_i} = x_i(\vec{w}, 1).$$

for any $i = 1, \ldots, n$. Equation (2) thus becomes

$$\sigma_{ij} = - \frac{\lambda \dfrac{\partial x_i}{\partial w_j}}{x_i x_j} = - \frac{\lambda \dfrac{\partial^2 \lambda}{\partial w_i \partial w_j}}{\dfrac{\partial \lambda}{\partial w_i} \dfrac{\partial \lambda}{\partial w_j}}$$

(5)

for any $i \neq j$ because

$$\frac{\partial x_i(\vec{w}, 1)}{\partial w_j} = \frac{\partial \left(\frac{\partial \lambda}{\partial w_i} \right)}{\partial w_j} = \frac{\partial^2 \lambda}{\partial w_i \partial w_j} .$$

Turning now to $\Lambda(\vec{w}) \equiv \log(\lambda(\vec{w}))$, observe that

$$\frac{\partial \Lambda}{\partial w_i} = \frac{1}{\lambda} \frac{\partial \lambda}{\partial w_i} ,$$

$$\frac{\partial \Lambda}{\partial w_j} = \frac{1}{\lambda} \frac{\partial \lambda}{\partial w_j} , \text{ and}$$

$$\frac{\partial^2 \Lambda}{\partial w_i \partial w_j} = \frac{1}{\lambda} \frac{\partial^2 \lambda}{\partial w_i \partial w_j} - \frac{1}{\lambda^2} \frac{\partial \lambda}{\partial w_i} \frac{\partial \lambda}{\partial w_j}$$

for any $i \ne j$. These forms combine with equation (5) to reveal that

$$\frac{\frac{\partial^2 \Lambda}{\partial w_i \partial w_j}}{\frac{\partial \Lambda}{\partial w_i} \frac{\partial \Lambda}{\partial w_j}} = \frac{\frac{1}{\lambda} \frac{\partial^2 \lambda}{\partial w_i \partial w_j} - \frac{1}{\lambda^2} \frac{\partial \lambda}{\partial w_i} \frac{\partial \lambda}{\partial w_j}}{\frac{1}{\lambda^2} \frac{\partial \lambda}{\partial w_i} \frac{\partial \lambda}{\partial w_j}} = -(1 + \sigma_{ij})$$

(6)

and, as claimed,

$$\frac{\partial^2 \Lambda}{\partial w_i \partial w_j} = - (1 + \sigma_{ij}) \frac{\partial \Lambda}{\partial w_1} \frac{\partial \Lambda}{\partial w_j} .$$

(7)

(b) Computing the unit cost schedule for (3) can be accomplished by brute force by solving (7) directly. There is, however, a simpler way that employs a few of the results in the text. Start by rewriting $y = f(x_1, x_2, x_3, x_4)$ in parts:

$$y = z_1^\alpha z_2^{1-\alpha},$$

where

$$z_1 = (ax_1^\rho + (1-a) x_2^\rho)^{1/\rho} \text{ and}$$

$$z_2 = (bx_3^r + (1-b) x_4^r)^{1/r}.$$

(8)

The long-run unit cost schedule for y in terms of the unit costs for z_i (noted ω_i) is then [see page 55]

$$\lambda(\omega_1, \omega_2) = K\omega_1^\alpha \omega_2^{1-\alpha} = c(\omega_1, \omega_2, 1) .$$

(9)

Since K is a positive constant, all that is required, now, is the proper specification of the ω_i. To that end,

PROBLEM 5

consider

$$\min \quad \omega_1 z_1 + \omega_2 z_2$$

$$\text{s.t.} \quad 1 = z_1^\alpha z_2^{1-\alpha} \equiv g(z_1, z_2);$$

(10)

the resulting first-order condition is familiar:

$$\frac{\dfrac{\partial g}{\partial z_1}}{\dfrac{\partial g}{\partial z_2}} = \frac{\omega_1}{\omega_2}.$$

(11)

Suppose, on the other hand, that the firm were to produce z_i along cost schedules $c_i(z_i)$; the problem corresponding to (10) would then be

$$\min \quad c_1(z_1) + c_2(z_2)$$

$$\text{s.t.} \quad 1 = z_1^\alpha z_2^{1-\alpha} \equiv g(z_1, z_2).$$

The first-order condition that

$$(12)$$

subsequently requires that the ratio of marginal products
equal the ratio of marginal costs instead of factor prices.
Equation (12) would be satisfied, of course, if

$$\frac{\partial c_i(z_i)}{\partial z_i} = \omega_i \qquad (13)$$

so the search for the appropriate ω_i is reduced to a search
for $c_i(z_i)$.

These schedules are, however, well known. By
consulting the end of the general CES example [pages 55 and
56] and adjusting the notation slightly to conform with
equation (8), it is seen, for example, that

$$c(w_1, w_2, z_1) = \{a^{-1/\rho-1}w_1^{\rho/\rho-1} + (1-a)^{-1/\rho-1}w_2^{\rho/\rho-1}\}^{\rho-1/\rho}z_1$$

$$= \{a^{-\sigma}w_1^{1+\sigma} + (1-a)^{-\sigma}w_2^{1+\sigma}\}^{1/(1+\sigma)}z_1,$$

i.e., that

PROBLEM 5

$$\frac{\partial c_1(z_1)}{\partial z_1} = \{a^{-\sigma}w_1^{1+\sigma} + (1-a)^{-\sigma}w_2^{1+\sigma}\}^{1/(1+\sigma)}. \qquad (14a)$$

By symmetry, then

$$\frac{\partial c_2(z_2)}{\partial z_2} = \{b^{-\sigma'}w_3^{1+\sigma'} + (1-b)^{-\sigma'}w_4^{1+\sigma'}\}^{1/(1+\sigma')}. \qquad (14b)$$

Substituting equations (14a) and (14b) into (13) and then into (9) finally reveals the unit cost schedule in terms of (w_1, w_2, w_3, w_4):

$$\lambda(\vec{w}) = K[\{a^{-\sigma}w_1^{1+\sigma} + (1-a)^{-\sigma}w_2^{1+\sigma}\}^{\alpha/(1+\sigma)}$$

$$\cdot \{b^{-\sigma'}w_3^{1+\sigma'} + (1-b)^{-\sigma'}w_4^{1+\sigma'}\}^{(1-\alpha)/(1+\sigma')}.$$

The logarithmic form is then

$$\Lambda(\vec{w}) = \log (K) + [\alpha/(1+\sigma)] \log \{a^{-\sigma}w_1^{1+\sigma} + (1-a)^{-\sigma}w_2^{1+\sigma}\}$$

$$+ [(1-\alpha)/(1+\sigma)]\{b^{-\sigma'}w_3^{1+\sigma'} + (1-b)^{-\sigma'}w_4^{1+\sigma'}\} . \qquad (15)$$

Equation (7) can now be employed to compute the elasticities of substitution between the factors. Consider, first of all, the elasticities across the additive blocks of equation (15). Since the left-hand side of (7) is certainly zero, in these cases,

PROBLEM 5

$$\sigma_{13} = \sigma_{23} = \sigma_{14} = \sigma_{24} = -1.$$

Within the blocks, though, some more computation is necessary. In computing σ_{12}, for example, the following partials are required:

$$\frac{\partial \Lambda}{\partial w_1} = \alpha \left[a^{-\sigma} w_1^{1+\sigma} + (1-a)^{-\sigma} w_2^{1+\sigma} \right]^{-1} a^{-\sigma} w_1^{\sigma},$$

$$\frac{\partial \Lambda}{\partial w_2} = \alpha \left[a^{-\sigma} w_1^{1+\sigma} + (1-a)^{-\sigma} w_2^{1+\sigma} \right]^{-1} (1-a)^{-\sigma} w_2^{\sigma}, \text{ and}$$

$$\frac{\partial \Lambda}{\partial w_1 \partial w_2} = -\alpha^2 \left[a^{-\sigma} w_1^{1-\sigma} + (1-a)^{-\sigma} w_2^{1+\sigma} \right]^{-2} \left[a(1-a) \right]^{-\sigma} (w_1 w_2)^{\sigma}.$$

Combine these partials with equation (7) to see immediately that $\sigma_{12} = \sigma$. Similarly, $\sigma_{34} = \sigma'$.

The Allen-Uzawa definition was chosen here because it is the most popular among those whose work requires three or more factors [see, for a few examples, Batra and Cases (2), Binswanger (3), Brendt and Wood (4), and Casas (5)]. The functional form of (3) is, furthermore, an example of the most general constant (Allen) elasticity of substitution production schedule. Uzawa (8) has, in fact, proven that a function

43

PROBLEM 5

$$y = f(x_1, \ldots, x_n)$$

displays constant elasticities of substitution between each pair of factors if and only if there exists a partition of the factors and their prices,

$$(\vec{x}^{(1)}, \ldots, \vec{x}^{(s)}) \quad \text{and} \quad (\vec{w}^{(1)}, \ldots, \vec{w}^{(s)})$$

for which $f(x_1, \ldots, x_n)$ can be written

$$y = \prod_{k=1}^{s} \{ \sum_{x_i \epsilon x^{(k)}} a_i^k x_i^{\rho k} \}^{\alpha k / \rho k} = f(\vec{x}^{(1)}, \ldots, \vec{x}^{(s)})$$

$$(16)$$

where

$$\sum_i a_i^k = 1, \quad \sum_k \alpha_k = 1, \quad \text{and} \quad 1 > \rho_k > -\infty$$

for all k. Given (16), in addition

$$\sigma_{ij} = \begin{array}{ll} 1/(\rho_s - 1) & x_i \epsilon x^{(k)} \quad \text{and} \quad x_j \epsilon x^{(k)} \\ 1 & x_i \epsilon x^{(k)} \quad \text{and} \quad x_j \epsilon x^{(k')}; \quad k' \neq k. \end{array}$$

The reader should feel, at the very least, that this theorem is reasonable because the method of proof used by Uzawa in the sufficiency direction provided the template for this

44

question. Necessity was shown by creating an equivalence relation based on repeated use of (7).

A similar theorem emerges when constant (DES and SES) elasticity of substitution schedules are considered. The impact of all of these theorems is that to have constant elasticity, a research must be content with one of two cases:

(a) the elasticities between all pairs of factors are equal; or

(b) the elasticities can differ, but there must be at least one pair between which the elasticity is -1.

The effect on theoretical studies of this observation is obvious; the restrictions it places on empirical studies are explored later.

References

(1) Allen, R.G.D., *Mathematical Analysis for Economists*, London, Macmillan & Co., 1938 (pages 503-509).

(2) Batra, R.N., and Casas, F.R., "A Synthesis of the Hecksher-Ohlin and the Neoclassical Models of International Trade," *Journal of International Economics*, 6:27-38, February 1976.

(3) Binswanger, H.P., "The Measurement of Technical Change Biases with Many Factors of Production," *American Economic*

PROBLEM 5

Review, 64:964-976, December 1974.

(4) Berndt, E.R. and Wood, D.O., "Technology, Prices and the Derived Demand for Energy," *Review of Economics and Statistics*, 57:259-268, August 1975.

(5) Casas, F.R., "The Theory of Intermediate Products, Technical Change and Growth," *Journal of International Economics*, 2:189-200, May 1972.

(6) McFadden, D., "Constant Elasticity of Substitution Production Functions," *Review of Economic Studies*, 30:73-83, February 1963.

(7) Murota, T., "On the Symmetry of Robinson Elasticities of Substitution: A Three Factor Case," *Review of Economic Studies,* 41:173-176, February 1974.

(8) Uzawa, H., "Production Functions with Constant Elasticities of Substitution," *Review of Economic Studies,* 29:291-299, October 1962.

6. Approximation Results for CES Production Functions[1]

This problem examines two approximation results that have come to the aid of applied researchers. The functional forms of CES production functions specified by the Uzawa-McFadden Theorem [see Problem 5 above] can put restrictions on applied research that the practitioner might not like. The simplicity of specifying a CES schedule is, in particular, offset by the requirement that either (1) all of the elasticities of substitution must be equal or (2) the elasticity between at least one pair of factors must be set equal to -1. In some cases, the resulting loss of simplicity caused by graduating to variable elasticity schedules is the inevitable cost of looking more closely at a complicated system. In others, however, the cost can be more severe. The usefulness of the research might be sacrificed if the production function becomes so complicated that the researcher is unable to trace observed effects to their ultimate sources. This problem examines a way out of this dilemma for dynamic modelers.

Questions:

(a) Consider a general production function given over time by:

_____

[1] Material found in Chapters 1, 4, and 6 is applicable here.

PROBLEM 6

$$Y(t) = f((x_1(t), x_2(t), x_3(t)).$$

Suppose that you would like to specify a production structure within which the elasticity of substitution between $x_2(t)$ and $x_3(t)$ were equal to $(1-\rho)^{-1}$ while the elasticity of substitution between $x_1(t)$ and an aggregate $x(t) = x_2(t) + x_3(t)$ were equal to $(1-r)^{-1}$. Look at CES - CD nested schedule conforming to one of the options of the Uzawa result to devise a method of adjusting the share of Y devoted to paying $x_1(t)$ over time so that you can approximate the desired structure.

(b) Look at a two-input simplification of the production function to support both the geometric intuition behind your solution to part (a) and its technical grounds of convergence.

Suggested Solutions:

(a) The idea is to represent

$$Y(t) = x_1(t)^{a(t)} \{bx_2(t)^\rho + (1-b)x_3(t)^\rho\}^{[1-a(t)]/\rho}$$

(1)

during any single period while adjusting a(t), the share paid to $x_1(t)$, over time so that the elasticity of

48

PROBLEM 6

substitution between $x_1(t)$ and $x(t) = x_2(t) + x_3(t)$ across time equals $(1-r)^{-1}$. From Varian [page 20], it is clear that the elasticity of substitution between $x_2(t)$ and $x_3(t)$ equals $(1-\rho)^{-1}$ for any time period. Consider, therefore,

$$Y(t) = \{bx_1(t)^r + (1-b)x(t)^r\}^{1/r}.$$

Applying some of the analysis of Chapter 4 [notably, page 55], it is clear after some algebra that

$$\frac{x(t)}{x_1(t)} = \{\frac{(1-b)}{b}\}^{1/(r-1)}\{\frac{w(t)}{w_1(t)}\}^{1/(r-1)}.$$

Consequently,

$$\frac{w(t)x(t)}{w_1(t)x_1(t)} = \{\frac{(1-b)}{b}\}^{1/(r-1)}\{\frac{w(t)}{w_1(t)}\}^{r/(r-1)}.$$

(2)

Notice, however, that the left-hand side of (2) is simply the ratio of the share of $Y(t)$ paid to $x(t)$ and the share of $Y(t)$ paid to $x_1(t)$; i.e.,

$$\frac{(1-a(t))}{a(t)} = \{\frac{(1-b)}{b}\}^{(1/r-1)}\{\frac{w(t)}{w_1(t)}\}^{r/(r-1)}$$

(3)

49

and

$$a(t) = \frac{1}{\{\frac{(1-b)}{b}\}^{1/r-1}\{\frac{w(t)}{w_1(t)}\}^{r/r-1} + 1}.$$

The procedure is now defined. Manipulating $a(t)$ over time according to equation (3) guarantees an implicit elasticity of substitution between $x_1(t)$ and the aggregate employment of $x_2(t)$ and $x_3(t)$ equal to the desired $\sigma' = (1-r)^{-1}$.

It should be emphasized that the entire construction is based upon equilibrium input prices $w_i(t)$. There must, therefore, be a supply structure operating in the background against which the derived demand schedules developed above can react. With such a structure in place, though, the approximation procedure is an iterative procedure that begins in period t with $a(t)$ in equation (1), generates $w_i(t)$ and $x_i(t)$ and thus $y(t)$, and then finishes by computing a new $a(t+1)$. To begin with, of course, there must be initial conditions for both the share of x_1 (i.e., $a(0)$) and the (x_1, w_1). To comply with equation (3), moreover, these initial values must satisfy

$$a(0) = \frac{1}{\{\frac{(1-b)}{b}\}^{1/r-1}\{\frac{w(0)}{w_1(0)}\}^{r/r-1} + 1}$$

but that, too, is easily guaranteed by manipulating b.

50

PROBLEM 6

(b) Let the general CES schedule be represented by its
derived demands [see Chapter 6]:

$$\ln (x_1/x_2) = (1/(\rho-1)) \ln ((1-b)/b) + (1/(\rho-1)) \ln (w_1/w_2)$$

$$(4)$$

and let the Cobb-Douglas special case be similarly
represented by

$$\ln (x_1/x_2) = \ln (a/(1-a)) - \ln (w_1/w_2)$$

Figure 6.1 displays both with the Cobb-Douglas case
exhibiting the steeper slopes because $\rho > 0$.

Starting at point C, it is clear that the employment
response defined along the CES schedule can be approximated
by movement along the Cobb-Douglas schedule for small
changes in $\{w_1/w_2\}$. The schedule defined in equation (4)
can, in other words, be used to approximate the schedule
recorded in (5) according to the strict definition of
convergence (i.e., within an open neighborhood of point C).
The issue, therefore, is what to do when changes in $\{w_1/w_2\}$
move that ratio outside of this open interval of
convergence.

Suppose, for instance, that $\{w_1/w_2\}$ were to rise to a
level reflected on the log scale by point J. The procedure
proposed here will call for an adjustment in the intercept

51

Figure 6.1

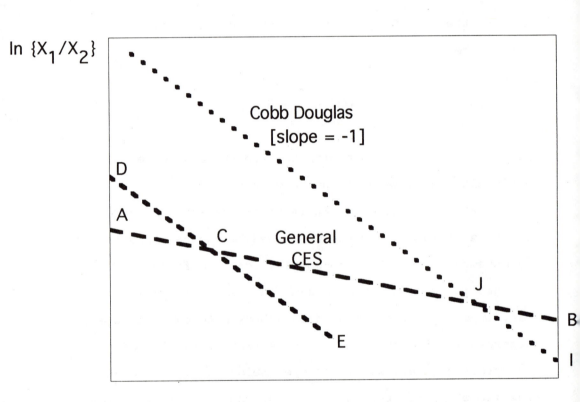

of the Cobb-Douglas formula to be accomplished by manipulating the α parameter. In that way, a different Cobb-Douglas schedule can be used to approximate (4) in the neighborhood of J. This is shown in Figure 6.1 by line JI with the intercept $\{\ln [b/(1-b)]\}$ increased to produce a new interval of convergence around J; only an appropriate increase in α, the share paid to x_1, is required.

Approximation of this type depends upon technical notions of convergence, of course, but that is guaranteed by the continuity of the logarithm function. Suppose, for example, that it were necessary to guarantee that approximation errors were less than some arbitrarily selected $\epsilon > 0$. There exists and $\epsilon' > 0$ such that deviations of less an $\epsilon' > 0$ in $\ln \{x_1/x_2\}$ would generate deviations of less than $\epsilon > 0$ in $\{x_1/x_2\}$. Meanwhile, there exists $\delta' > 0$ such that deviations in $\ln \{w_1/w_2\}$ guarantee movement of less than $\epsilon' > 0$ in $\ln \{x_1/x_2\}$. Finally, a $\delta > 0$ exists such that movement in $\{w_1/w_2\}$ of less than $\delta > 0$ means movement in $\ln \{w_1/w_2\}$ of less than $\delta' > 0$. The technicalities of convergence are thus handled.

The procedure outlined in part (a) has been employed in a long-range projection project concerning carbon dioxide emissions and atmospheric concentrations [see Nordhaus and Yohe (2)]. One of the objectives of that work was to underscore the contributions of various sources of uncertainty to our general level of uncertainty about concentrations through the year 2100. Constrained by the Uzawa-McFadden theorem, one significant source of uncertainty would have been missed.

References

(1) McFadden, D., "Constant Elasticity of Substitution Production Functions," *Review of Economic Studies*, 30: 73–83, 1963.

(2) Nordhaus, W., and G. Yohe, "Future Carbon Dioxide Emissions from Fossil Fuels," Chapter 2 in *Changing Climate: Report of the Carbon Dioxide Assessment Committee*, National Research Council, 1983.

(3) Uzawa, H., "Production Functions with Constant Elasticities of Substitution," *Review of Economic Studies*, 29: 291–299, 1962.

PROBLEM 7

7. Approximating Elasticities of Substitution with the Price Elasticity of Derived Demand[1]

It is frequently easier to obtain estimates of the price elasticities of derived factor demand than it is to estimate elasticities of substitution. This problem suggests when the two are approximately equal.

Question:

Let production be given by

$$Y = (bx_1^\rho + (1-b)x_2^\rho)^{1/\rho},$$

Show that the elasticity of substitution between x_1 and x_2 can be approximated by the price elasticity of derived demand for x_1 if the share paid to x_1 is relatively small.

Suggested Solution:

Assume that the output price of Y is normalized to unity. Given the standard CES representation recorded in the question, then,

---

[1] Material found in Chapters 3, 4, and 6 is applicable here.

55

PROBLEM 7

$$w_1 = b(Y/x_1)^{\rho-1}$$

(1)

is a cost minimizing first-order condition [see page 50].
Rewriting equation (1) in terms of logarithms therefore
reveals that

$$\ln w_1 = \ln b + (\rho-1) [\ln Y - \ln x_1]; \text{ i.e.,}$$

$$\ln x_1 = \frac{-\ln w_1 + \ln \alpha}{\rho - 1} + \ln Y.$$

As a result, the elasticity of demand for x_1 is

$$\frac{\delta \ln x_1}{\delta \ln w_1} = - \frac{1}{\rho - 1} + \frac{\ln Y}{\ln w_1}.$$

(2)

The key to the approximation, therefore, is that the ratio
$\{\delta \ln (Y)/\delta \ln (w_1)\}$ is guaranteed to be small when the
share of x_1 is kept small.

To see why this is so, recall Euler's theorem [page 481
and Chapter 3] applied to a constant returns-to-scale
production function when the price of output is normalized
to unity:

PROBLEM 7

$$Y = w_1 x_1 + w_2 x_2$$

and note that

$$\frac{\delta Y}{\delta w_1} = x_1 + w_2 \frac{\delta x_2}{\delta w_1} \approx x_1$$

when x_2 is fixed. As a result,

$$\frac{\delta \ \ln \ x_1}{\delta \ \ln \ w_1} \approx - \frac{1}{\rho - 1} = \sigma$$

when the share of y devoted to x_1 (i.e., $w_1 x_1 / y$) is small.
Equation (2) then produces the desired result.

The approximation procedure reviewed here has been
employed throughout the literature; Hogan and Manne (1)
offered its original substantiation.

References

(1) Hogan, W., and A. Manne, "Energy-Economy Interactions,"
in C.J. Hitch (ed.), *Modeling Energy-Economic Interactions*,
Resources for the Future, 1977.

(2) McFadden, D., "Constant Elasticity of Substitution
Production Functions," *Review of Economic Studies*, 30: 73-
83, 1963.

PROBLEM 8

8. Optimal Commodity Taxes[1]

Consider an economy in which welfare is represented by $u(x)$, where x represents not only commodities demanded but also factors of production supplied. Let there be $(n+1)$ commodities and factors of production other than labor, and denote labor by x_0. If people derive no income independent of the factors they supply to production, then the appropriate budget constraint for all individual decisions is

$$p \cdot x \leq 0$$

for any set of prices p. Assume that there are m firms in the economy operating along production frontiers given (for the jth firm) by $F^j(z^j) = 0$ [see page 339 for a more complete definition and Figure 8.1 for a graphical depiction]. The vectors y^j are input-output vectors, and the economy's resource constraints are

$$\sum_{j=i}^{m} z_i^j \leq x_i; \ i = 0, 1, \ldots, n.$$

Question:

Characterize the set of commodity taxes that raises

---

[1] Material found in Chapters 7 and 8 is applicable here. Refer to Chapter 18, particularly to Section 18.8, for coverage of the production possibility frontier. Section 22.3 introduces the notion of optimal commodity taxation.

an amount of revenue R most efficiently without taxing wage payments to labor.

Suggested Solution:

The solution will have two parts. Efficiency will be characterized first in the absence of any taxes by allowing the government to choose prices $p*$ and production vectors $(z^j)*$ that maximize welfare; this benchmark characterization is developed in Part A below. The efficiency conditions will correspond precisely to those analyzed in Chapter 18, and they would be achieved automatically by a competitive economy.

A wedge between producer and consumer prices will represent the taxes in the second part of the solution. The discussion recorded in Part B below will make extensive use of some basic consumer theory results [found in Chapters 7 and 8] to show that the best taxes reduce the consumption of all goods along their (Hicksian) compensated demand schedule [see page 105] by the same proportion.

A. Nontax Optimization

Solving the basic allocation problem,

PROBLEM 8

$$\max u(\mathbf{x})$$

$$\text{s. t. } (\mathbf{p} \cdot \mathbf{x}) \leq 0$$

generates an indirect utility function which can be represented by $v(\mathbf{p}, y)$ [see pages 102-103] where y denotes independently derived income; it is fixed by assumption at zero. The government's problem, therefore, is to select a vector of prices $\mathbf{p}^*$ and a set of production vectors $(\mathbf{z}^j)^*$ that solve

$$\max v(\mathbf{p}, y)$$

$$\text{s. t. } F^j(\mathbf{z}^j) \leq 0; \quad j = 1, \ldots, m, \text{ and}$$

$$\sum_{j=1}^{m} z_k^j \leq x_i; \quad i = 0, 1, \ldots, n.$$

The appropriate Lagrangian is then

$$L(p, z) = v(p, y) + \sum_{k=0}^{n} \lambda_k \left(\sum_{j=1}^{m} z_k^j - x_k \right) + \sum_{k=1}^{m} \mu_k F^k(z^k)$$

for which the first-order conditions are

$$\frac{\partial L}{\partial p_i} = \frac{\partial v_i}{\partial p_i} - \sum_{k=0}^{n} \lambda_k \frac{\partial x_k}{\partial p_i} = 0; \quad i = 0, 1, \ldots, n, \text{ and}$$

(1)

PROBLEM 8

$$\frac{\partial L}{\partial z_k^j} = \lambda_k + \mu_j \frac{\partial F^j}{\partial z_k^j} = 0; \quad \begin{array}{l} k = 0, 1, \ldots, n \\ \\ j = 1, \ldots, m. \end{array}$$

(2)

Equation (2) characterizes productive efficiency, requiring that the marginal rate of transformation between any two vector components be equal across all firms; i.e., equation (2) requires that

$$\frac{\partial F^j}{\partial z_k^j} \Big/ \frac{\partial F^j}{\partial z_k^e} = \frac{\lambda_k}{\lambda_e}$$

(3)

regardless of which firm is considered ($j = 1, \ldots, m$). Equation (1) characterizes consumption efficiency; the utility impact of a price change, on the margin, equals the weighted (by their shadow prices) sum of the marginal changes in the consumption or provision of all $(n+1)$ goods that affect utility.

B. Commodity Tax Optimization.

Now let p represent consumer prices, q represent producer prices, and t represent the vector of taxes wedged in between; i.e., let

$$p - t = q.$$

61

PROBLEM 8

The structure built into the problem also suggests a natural normalization of these prices: let

$$q_0 = p_0 = 1 \text{ and } t_0 = 0$$

summarize the situation in the labor market. Rewriting (1) in light of the identification rendered by equation (3) that the λ_k are productive shadow prices, it follows that

$$\frac{\partial v}{\partial p_i} = \lambda_0 \sum_{k=0}^{n} \left(\frac{\lambda_k}{\lambda_0}\right) \frac{\partial x_k}{\partial p_i}$$

$$= \lambda_0 \sum_{k=0}^{n} q_k \frac{\partial x_k}{\partial p_i}$$

$$= \lambda_0 \sum_{k=0}^{n} (p_k - t_k^*) \frac{\partial x_k}{\partial p_i} \quad .$$

(4)

Differentiating two constraints, $\mathbf{p} \cdot \mathbf{x} = 0$ and $\mathbf{t} \cdot \mathbf{x} = R$, meanwhile reveals that

$$x_i + \sum_{k=0}^{n} p_k \frac{\partial x_k}{\partial p_i} = 0 \text{ and}$$

(5)

PROBLEM 8

$$\frac{\partial R}{\partial t_i} = x_i + \sum_{k=0}^{n} t_k \frac{\partial x_k}{\partial t_i} \cdot$$

(6)

Combining equations (4), (5), and (6),

$$\frac{\partial v}{\partial p_i} = \frac{\partial R}{\partial t_i} \lambda_0 \cdot$$

(7)

The marginal impact on utility of a (tax-created) price change must equal the marginal value of the resulting revenue if it is to be most efficient.

Translating equation (7) into an optimal tax structure requires some standard results from consumer theory. Roy's identity [pages 106-107] holds that

$$\frac{\partial v}{\partial p_i} = - x_i \frac{\partial v}{\partial y},$$

(8)

while the usual Slutsky equation [page 119] requires that

$$\frac{\partial x_j}{\partial p_i} = \frac{\partial x_j}{\partial p_i} \bigg|_{\bar{u}} - x_i \frac{\partial x_j}{\partial y},$$

(9)

and the symmetry of the substitution matrix [property 2, page 123],

$$\left(\frac{\partial x_j}{\partial p_i}\right) \bigg|_{\bar{u}} = \left(\frac{\partial x_i}{\partial p_j}\right) \bigg|_{\bar{u}},$$

(10)

PROBLEM 8

will all be employed. Recalling (5), equations (8), (9),
and (10) allow equation (4) to be expressed in an expanded,
more illuminating form:

$$0 = - x_i \frac{\partial v}{\partial y} + \lambda_0 \{ x_i + \sum_{k=0}^{n} t_k^* \; [(\frac{\partial x_k}{\partial p_i}) \Big|_{\bar{u}} - x_i \frac{\partial x_k}{\partial y} \,] \}$$

$$= - x_i \frac{\partial v}{\partial y} + \lambda_0 \{ x_i + \sum_{k=0}^{n} t_k^* \; (\frac{\partial x_u}{\partial p_i}) \Big|_{\bar{u}} - x_i \sum_{k=0}^{n} \frac{\partial x_k}{\partial y} \}.$$

Put another way,

$$\sum_{k=0}^{n} \frac{t_k^*}{x_i} \; (\frac{\partial x_i}{\partial p_k}) \Big|_{\bar{u}} = \{ \frac{1}{\lambda_0} \frac{\partial v}{\partial y} - 1 + \sum_{k=0}^{n} t_k^* \frac{\partial x_k}{\partial y} \} \qquad (11)$$

holds for all i = 0, 1, ..., n. The right-hand side of
equation (11) does <u>not</u> depend on i, though, so it can be
considered a constant across all goods; i.e.,

$$\sum_{k=0}^{n} \frac{t_k^*}{x_i} \; \frac{\partial x_i}{\partial p_k} \Big|_{\bar{u}} \equiv \theta, \; i = 0, 1, ..., n \; . \qquad (12)$$

Meanwhile, the left-hand side of (12) is the percentage
change in the (compensated) consumption or provision of x_i.
To see this final point, observe that

64

PROBLEM 8

$$\frac{dh_i(\mathbf{p},y)}{x_i(\mathbf{p},y)} = \frac{1}{x_i(\mathbf{p},y)} \sum_{k=0}^{n} \frac{\partial h_i}{\partial p_k} dp_k , \qquad (13)$$

where $x_i = h_i(\mathbf{p},y)$ is the compensated (Hicksian) demand schedule. Equation (13), showing the percentage change in x_i, replicates the left-hand side of (12) because the change in p_k is simply the tax rate. The percentage decrease in the consumption or provision of x_i along the compensated schedule is θ for all possible $i = 0, 1, \ldots, n$.

This question has reproduced some of the results produced originally by Boiteux (3) and updated by Atkinson and Stiglitz (1). The analysis has not stopped there, however. There have been more general equilibrium treatments of indirect taxation [see, e.g., Diamond and Mirrlees (4)] in which the revenue generated by the taxes is used to provide public goods [Chapter 23]. There have also been analyses of optimal income taxation [see Mirrlees (5) on Sheshinski (7)] and attempts to determine when they have the same effect. It has been discovered that no indirect taxes are necessary if a general income tax function is available to the government and utility is separable between labor and all other commodities [Atkinson and Stiglitz (2)]; marginal cost pricing under optimal income taxation then guarantees maximum welfare.

One potentially fruitful line of continued questioning

can now be suggested by casting the results of this problem in the light of the labor research cited above. Much has been made of the efficiency-equity trade-off that is buried in (12); necessities must bear higher taxes to achieve the proportional decrease in consumption mandated by efficiency. Optimal income taxes have, meanwhile, been thought of as a tool for achieving the best distributional position within that trade-off. If the best income tax were to decrease (compensated) consumption by the same proportion, would not the optimal commodity tax also achieve the same best position? What circumstances would guarantee that the income-tax impact would be proportional?

References

(1) Atkinson, A.B., and Stiglitz, J.E., "The Structure of Indirect Taxation and Economic Efficiency," *Journal of Public Economics*, 1: 97-120, 1972.

(2) Atkinson, A.B., and Stiglitz, J.E., "The Design of Tax Structure: Direct Versus Indirect Taxation," *Journal of Public Service*, 6: 55-75, 1976.

(3) Boiteux, M., "Le 'Revenue Distribuable' et les Pertes Économiques," *Econometrica*, 19: 112-33, 1956.

(4) Diamond P.A., and Mirrlees, J.A., "Optimal Taxation and Public Production," *American Economic Review*, 61: 8-27 and 261-278, 1970.

(5) Mirrlees, J.A., "An Exploration in the Theory of Optimal Income Taxation," *Review of Economic Studies*, 38: 175-208, 1971.

(6) Sandmo, A., "Optimal Taxation -- An Introduction to the Literature," *Journal of Public Economics*, 6: 37-54, 1976.

(7) Sheshinski, E., "The Optimal Linear Income Tax," *Review of Economic Studies*, 39: 297-302, 1972.

9. Selected Applications of the Expenditure Function[1]

The expenditure function has proven to be an extremely useful tool in the public finance literature. Diamond and McFadden (2) have catalogued several of these applications in a piece that includes some illuminating geometry. This problem will reproduce a few optimal commodity tax results produced in Problem 8 by using compensated expenditures in an unusual way. The deadweight loss of a tax structure will (under constant producer prices) be the difference between compensated expenditures and tax revenues that would be achieved if that compensation were provided. Since this is not a standard definition of welfare loss, replication of results derived by more traditional techniques will be reassuring. It will, in addition, provide an introduction to a potentially fruitful analytical method with which to tackle welfare analysis.

Let $\vec{x} \equiv (x_1, \ldots, x_n)$ represent the vector of commodities available. Reflect consumer prices with $\vec{q} \equiv (q_1, \ldots, q_n)$, producer prices with $\vec{p} \equiv (p_1, \ldots, p_n)$, and the tax wedge in between with

$$\vec{t} \equiv (t_1, \ldots, t_n) \equiv \vec{q} - \vec{p}.$$

---

[1] Material found in Chapters 3 and 7 is applicable here. Deadweight loss introduces the notion of consumer surplus [Chapter 10]; optimal taxes are discussed in Section 22.3.

PROBLEM 9

Questions:

(a) According to the definition suggested in the introduction to this problem, let the deadweight loss associated with $\vec{t}$ be given by

$$L(\vec{q}, \vec{p}, \bar{u}) \equiv E(\vec{q}, \bar{u}) - T(\vec{q}, \vec{p}, \bar{u}) \qquad (1)$$

where $\bar{u}$ indicates the pretax level of utility. Of course,

$$E(\vec{q}, \bar{u}) \equiv \sum_{i=1}^{n} q_i h_i(\vec{q}, \bar{u})$$

is the compensated expenditure function, the $h_i(\vec{q}, \bar{u})$ are the Hicksian demand schedules for the x_i, and compensated tax revenues are

$$T(\vec{q}, \vec{p}, \bar{u}) \equiv \sum_{i=1}^{n} (q_i - p_i) h_i(\vec{q}, \bar{u}) = \sum_{i=1}^{n} t_i h_i(\vec{q}, \bar{u}).$$

Show that

$$\frac{\partial L}{\partial q_K} [\vec{q}, \vec{p}, \bar{u}] = - \sum_{i=1}^{n} t_i \frac{\partial j_i(\vec{q}, \bar{u})}{\partial q_K}.$$

(b) When producer prices are allowed to adjust, a semblance of general equilibrium can be achieved. Let good 1 be the numéraire and define units so that $p_l \equiv 1$.

69

PROBLEM 9

Profits available to the producers facing $\vec{p}$ can be denoted $\pi(\vec{p})$, and are equal to whatever is left of total expenditures after tax revenues and the necessary compensation are paid. Show that if supply equals demand after taxes are imposed, then

$$\frac{\partial L}{\partial q_k}[\vec{t},\bar{u}] = - \sum_{i=1}^{n} t_i\{ \frac{\partial h_i}{\partial t_k} [\vec{p}(\vec{t})+\vec{t},\bar{u}]\}.$$

The $\pi(\vec{p})$ schedule is a perfectly good profit function to which the standard properties [see Chapter 3] can be attributed.

(c) A set of commodity taxes is efficient if the marginal burden of the last dollar raised is the same for all goods. You can see this by looking at equation (7) of Problem (8), but it should make sense in terms of standard micro-theory results. Use this condition to show that a constant tax rate $\tau = (q_i - p_i)/p_i$ $(i=1,\ldots,n)$ is efficient only if the compensated demand schedules for the x_i depend only on their own price q_i $(i=1,\ldots,n)$ and have the same price elasticities, even when producer prices can move.

Suggested Solutions:

The solutions follow fairly quickly from the

70

PROBLEM 9

definitions of losses and profits in (a) and (b),
respectively. The efficiency condition in (c) simply
requires that

$$\frac{\partial L(\vec{t},\bar{u})/\partial t_k}{\partial T(\vec{t},\bar{u})/\partial t_k} = \text{constant}$$

for all $k = 1, \ldots, n$.

(a)   Marginal deadweight burden is computed for x_k by
      looking at

$$\frac{\partial L(\vec{q},\vec{p},\bar{u})}{\partial q_k} = \frac{\partial E(\vec{q},\bar{u})}{\partial q_k} - \frac{\partial T(\vec{q},\vec{p},\bar{u})}{\partial q_k} \; .$$

From the properties of the expenditure function [number 5 on
page 105], though,

$$\frac{\partial E(\vec{q},\bar{u})}{\partial q_k} = h_k(\vec{q},\bar{u}) ;$$

compensated tax revenues are meanwhile given by

$$T(\vec{q},\vec{p},\bar{u}) = \sum_{i=1}^{n} (q_i - p_i) h_i(\vec{q},\bar{u}), \text{ so}$$

$$\frac{\partial T(\vec{q},\vec{p},\bar{u})}{\partial q_k} = h_k(\vec{q},\bar{u}) + \sum_{i=1}^{n} t_i \frac{\partial h_i(\vec{q},\bar{u})}{\partial q_k}.$$

The required result is then immediate:

$$\frac{\partial L(\vec{q},\vec{p},\bar{u})}{\partial q_k} = -\sum_{i=1}^{n} t_i \frac{\partial h_i(\vec{q},\ \bar{u})}{\partial q_k}. \tag{2}$$

Relating the marginal burden of each tax to the marginal revenue it produces, it can also be noted that

$$\frac{\partial L(\vec{q},\vec{p},\bar{u})/\partial q_k}{\partial T(\vec{q},\vec{p},\bar{u})/\partial q_k} = -\frac{\displaystyle\sum_{i=1}^{n} t_i \frac{\partial h_i(\vec{q},\vec{p},\bar{u})}{\partial q_k}}{h_i(\vec{q},\bar{u}) + \displaystyle\sum_{i=1}^{n} t_i \frac{\partial h(\vec{q},\vec{p},\bar{u})}{\partial q_k}}. \tag{2'}$$

Together with the intuitive notion that an efficient set of commodity taxes arranges things so that the marginal burden of the last dollar raised is constant over all goods, (2') can produce a result that will emerge from more standard welfare treatments: if compensated demand for x_k depends only on its own price, then, in fact, setting $[(\partial L/\partial q_k)/\partial T/\partial q_k)]$ shown in (2') equal to some θ for all $k = 1,\ldots,n$ reproduces equation (12) in Problem 8.

PROBLEM 9

(b) Losses plus tax revenues plus profits must add up to compensated expenditures in terms of the numéraire; i.e.,

$$E(\vec{q},\bar{u}) = L(\vec{q},\vec{p},\bar{u}) + T(\vec{q},\vec{p},\bar{u}) + \pi(\vec{p}).$$

The market clears for all but the numéraire in which compensation is made, so

$$\frac{\partial E(\vec{q},\bar{u})}{\partial q_k} = h_k(\vec{q},\bar{u}) = \frac{\partial \pi(\vec{p})}{\partial p_k} = x_k^s(\vec{p}), \quad k = 2,\ldots,n \quad (3)$$

where $x_k^s(\vec{p})$ is the supply of x_k; the last equality in equation (3) is the derivative property of Hotelling's lemma [see page 43]. Noting that

$$\vec{q}(\vec{t}) = \vec{p}(\vec{t}) + \vec{t}$$

and choosing units for the numéraire so that $p_1 = 1$, the loss function can be written

$$L(\vec{t},\bar{u}) = E[(\vec{p}(\vec{t})+\vec{t}),\bar{u}] - \sum_{i=1}^{n} t \; h \; [(\underset{\sim}{p}(t)+t),\bar{u}] - \pi[\vec{p}(\vec{t})].$$

Differentiating with respect to t, then

73

$$\frac{\partial L(\mathfrak{E},\bar{u})}{\partial t_k} = h_k[(\vec{p}(\mathfrak{E})+\mathfrak{E}),\bar{u}] + \sum_{i=1}^{n} h_i[(\vec{p}(\mathfrak{E})+\mathfrak{E}),\bar{u}] \frac{\partial p_i}{\partial t_k}$$

$$- h_k[(\vec{p}(\mathfrak{E})+\mathfrak{E}),\bar{u}] - \sum_{i=1}^{n} t_i \{\frac{\partial h_i}{\partial t_k} [(\vec{p}(\mathfrak{E})+\mathfrak{E}),\bar{u}]\}$$

$$- \sum_{i=1}^{n} \frac{\partial \pi}{\partial p_i} \frac{\partial p_i}{\partial t_k} . \tag{4}$$

Consolidating terms and using equation (3) reduces (4) to

$$\frac{\partial L(\mathfrak{E},\bar{u})}{\partial t_k} = - \sum_{i=1}^{n} t_i \{\frac{\partial h_i}{\partial p_i} [(\vec{p}(\mathfrak{E})+\mathfrak{E}),\bar{u}]\}. \tag{5}$$

Finally, then

$$\frac{\partial L(\mathfrak{E},\bar{u})/\partial t_k}{\partial T(\mathfrak{E},\bar{u})/\partial t_k} = - \frac{\sum_{i=1}^{n} t_i \frac{\partial h_i}{\partial t_k} [(\vec{p}(\mathfrak{E})+\mathfrak{E}),\bar{u}]}{h_k[(\vec{p}(\mathfrak{E})+\mathfrak{E}),\bar{u}] + \sum_{i=1}^{n} t_i \frac{\partial h_i}{\partial t_k} [(\vec{p}(\mathfrak{E})+\mathfrak{E}),\bar{u}]} \tag{6}$$

nearly reproduces (2').

(c) Since $\vec{p}(1+\tau) = \vec{q}$, $\mathfrak{E} = \tau\vec{p}$ and (5) can be written

$$\frac{\partial L(\tau,\vec{q},\bar{u})}{\partial t_k} = - \frac{\tau}{1+\tau} \sum_{i=1}^{n} q_i \frac{\partial h_i}{\partial t_k} . \tag{7}$$

Meanwhile, and for the same reason,

$$\frac{\partial T(\tau, \vec{q}, \bar{u})}{\partial t_k} = h_k(\vec{q}, \bar{u}) + \frac{\tau}{1-\tau} \sum_{i=1}^{n} q_i \frac{\partial h_i}{\partial t_k} . \qquad (8)$$

The conditions on the compensated demand schedule finally imply that

$$\frac{\partial h_i}{\partial t_k} = \begin{cases} \dfrac{1+\tau}{\tau} \dfrac{\partial h_i}{\partial q_k} & \text{for } i = k \\ \\ 0 & \text{for } i \neq k. \end{cases} \qquad (9)$$

As a result, equations (7), (8), and (9) combine with (6) to show that

$$\frac{\partial L(\vec{t}, \bar{u})/\partial t_k}{\partial T(\vec{t}, \bar{u})/\partial t_k} = \{ \frac{h_k(\vec{t}, \bar{u}) + q_k[\partial h/\partial q_k]}{q_k(\partial h_k/\partial q_k)} \}^{-1} \qquad (10)$$

for all k. If (10) is to be equal to some θ' for all k = 1,...,n, then

$$q_k(\partial h_k/\partial q_k) = (1 + \theta')^{-1} h_k(\vec{t}, \bar{u})$$

for all k. Clearly, then, it is required that

PROBLEM 9

$$\varepsilon_k(q_k) = \theta = (1 + \theta')^{-1}, \quad k = 1, \ldots, n.$$

The results demonstrated in Part (c) are also true if the p_k are fixed; the proof is exactly the same. Beyond illustrating some familiar tax results, the problem was included here to exhibit one of the more exotic ways in which expenditure functions have been applied. Replication of the tax results was, in fact, planned to help skeptics to believe that the application was appropriate. Equations (2) and (5) also appear in Harberger (3). The reader is referred to Diamond and McFadden (2) for some geometric support and other applications.

References

(1) Baumol, W., and D. Bradford, "Optimal Departures from Marginal Cost Pricing," *American Economic Review*, 69:265–283, 1970.

(2) Diamond, P.A., and D.L. McFadden, "Some Uses of the Expenditure Function in Public Finance," *Journal of Public Economics*, 3:3–21, 1974.

(3) Harberger, A., "Measurement of Waste," *American Economic Review*, 54:58–76, 1964.

(4) McFadden, D.L. (ed.), *An Econometric Approach to Production Theory*, Amsterdam, North Holland, 1975.

10. **Negative Income Taxation and the Labor-Leisure Decision**[1]

Both the optimal income tax and traditional negative income tax literatures have long included studies of the incentive impacts of income redistribution. The political stakes surrounding these impacts are immense, and there are empiricists who have actually designed and conducted social experiments to observe these impacts. While no evaluation of these studies will be attempted here, the implications of one commonly reported result will be explored. This problem will, in particular, trace immediate implications of a negatively sloped labor supply curve.

It will, first of all, be argued that leisure must be a normal good [i.e., it must have a positive income effect as defined on page 120] if there is any chance for the labor supply curve to bend backward. Secondly, the effect on the labor supplied under a typical negative income tax structure will be partially quantified and applied to a capital-based growth model.

Questions:

(a) Let a person's utility depend on consumption (x) and

---

[1] Material presented in Chapters 8 and 9 is applicable here. The discussion of labor supply recorded early in Chapter 9 is particularly germane.

leisure (ℓ), and allow him a fixed amount of time (k) to devote either to leisure or to labor (L). A wage rate (w) is paid for each unit of labor provided, and a nonwage income (a) is also received. The labor-leisure choice therefore involves solving

$$\max \quad u(x,\ell) \tag{1}$$
$$\text{such that} \quad k = \ell + L$$
$$x = wL + a.$$

Show that if the labor supply curve that emerges from (1) is negatively sloped, then leisure must be a normal good in $u(x,\ell)$.

(b) In the context of the problem recorded in equation (1), suppose that a negative income tax were arranged to redistribute income and to provide for governmental services. Let $\bar{x}$ be the mean income across the population and define τ as the proportional tax rate applied to all income that would generate just enough revenue to cover all nondistributive governmental costs. Let t be the redistributive proportional tax rate applied to all income to finance a lump sum $t\bar{x}$ to everyone. After-tax nonwage income would then be

$$a' \equiv (1-t-\tau)a + t\bar{x}, \tag{2a}$$

PROBLEM 10

and after-tax wage income would be

$$w' \equiv (1-t-\tau)w. \tag{2b}$$

For the person described in part (a), show that an increase in t (the redistribution effort) can reduce the work effort of only those whose before-tax income is well below $\bar{x}$ if leisure is normal.

(c) Now consider a production function in capital (K) and labor (L):

$$y = f(K,L) \tag{3}$$

and a labor supply function given by

$$L = g(w). \tag{4}$$

Assume a perfectly competitive labor market with a negatively sloped supply schedule. Use the Walrasian stability condition [that the supply schedule is less steeply sloped than demand – see Samuelson (3), page 263] to show that increases in the capital stock will produce lower employment levels; i.e., output will increase slower than the marginal product of capital.

Suggested Solutions:

(a) Maximizing $u(x, \ell)$ subject to $x = w(k-\ell) + a$ is equivalent to maximizing

$$u[w(k-\ell)-a,\ell]$$

with respect to ℓ. The first- and second-order conditions
are

$$-\frac{\partial u}{\partial x} w + \frac{\partial u}{\partial \ell} = 0 \text{ and} \tag{5}$$

$$\frac{\partial^2 u}{\partial \ell^2} - 2w \frac{\partial^2 u}{\partial x \partial \ell} + w^2 \frac{\partial^2 u}{\partial x^2} \equiv D < 0, \tag{6}$$

respectively. To see how the optimal provision of leisure
(ℓ^*) changes with w and a, totally differentiate (5):

$$d\ell^* = \frac{\frac{\partial u}{\partial x} - (k-\ell)[\frac{\partial^2 u}{\partial x \partial \ell} - w \frac{\partial^2 u}{\partial x^2}]}{D} dw - \frac{\frac{\partial^2 u}{\partial x \partial \ell} - w \frac{\partial^2 u}{\partial x^2}}{D} da. \tag{7}$$

The slope of the labor supply function can now be computed.
From the time constraint and (7),

$$\left.\frac{\partial L^*}{\partial w}\right|_{a \text{ fixed}} = \left.\frac{\partial \ell^*}{\partial w}\right|_{a \text{ fixed}}$$

$$= -\frac{\partial u/\partial x}{D} - \frac{L^*}{D} [(\partial^2 u/\partial x \partial \ell) - w(\partial^2 u/\partial x^2)]$$

PROBLEM 10

$$= - \frac{\partial u / \partial x}{D} - L* \frac{d\ell*}{da} \bigg|_{\text{w fixed.}} \tag{8}$$

Equation (8) is very much like a Slutsky equation [Section 8.2]. The first term, nonnegative from (6), reflects a substitution effect away from leisure when its opportunity cost (w) increases. The second term is an income effect. If the labor supply schedule is to be negatively sloped, equation (8) asserts emphatically that the second term must be strictly negative. This can only happen if leisure is normal; i.e.,

$$\frac{d\ell*}{da} \bigg|_{\text{w fixed}} > 0.$$

From the tax schedules,

$$a' = (1-\tau-t)a + t\bar{x} \text{ and} \tag{2a}$$

$$w' = (1-\tau-t)w, \tag{2b}$$

holding $\bar{x}$ and the governmental cost tax τ fixed produces

$$da' = (1-\tau-t) da + (\bar{x}-a) dt \text{ and} \tag{9a}$$

$$dw' = (1-\tau-t) dw - w dt. \tag{9b}$$

Looking at changes in L* caused by a change in t through

81

(7), it is seen that

$$
\frac{dL^*}{dt} = - \frac{\frac{\partial u}{\partial x} - L^*[\frac{\partial^2 u}{\partial x \partial \ell} - w \frac{\partial^2 u}{\partial x^2}]}{D} \frac{dw}{dt} + \frac{[\frac{\partial^2 u}{\partial x \partial \ell} - w \frac{\partial^2 u}{\partial x^2}]}{D} \frac{da}{dt}
$$

$$
= - \frac{\frac{\partial u}{\partial x} - L^*[----]}{D} \frac{dw}{dw'} \frac{dw'}{dt} + \frac{[----]}{D} \frac{da}{da'} \frac{da'}{dt} \quad . \quad (10)
$$

Applying equations (2a), (2b), (9a), and (9b) to (10) term by term, it is seen that

$$
\frac{dL^*}{dt} = (1-t-\tau)^{-1}\{\frac{W}{D} \frac{\partial u}{\partial x} + \frac{\bar{x}-a-wL^*}{D} (\frac{\partial^2 \hat{u}}{\partial x \partial \ell} - w \frac{\partial^2 \hat{u}}{\partial x^2})\}
$$

$$
= (1-t-\tau)^{-1}\{\frac{W}{D} \frac{\partial u}{\partial x} + (\bar{x}-a-wL^*) \frac{d\ell^*}{da} \Big|_{w \text{ fixed}} \}. \quad (11)
$$

Since the first term in (11) is nonpositive and from (a),

$$
\frac{d\ell^*}{da} \Big|_{w \text{ fixed}} > 0,
$$

(dL*/dt) can be positive only when $\bar{x} > a-wL^*$. The normality of leisure causes a decrease in the work effort in response to a redistributive negative income tax for everyone but (possibly) those whose before tax incomes fall well short of the mean.

PROBLEM 10

(c) With labor paid its marginal revenue product and p = 1 [recall Chapter 2],

$$w = \frac{\partial f}{\partial L} (K,L).\tag{12}$$

Totally differentiating equations (3), (4), and (12) with respect to K,

$$\frac{\partial f}{\partial K} + \frac{\partial f}{\partial L} \frac{dL}{dK} = \frac{dy}{dK},\tag{13a}$$

$$\frac{dL}{dK} = \frac{\partial g}{\partial w} \frac{dw}{dK}, \text{ and}\tag{13b}$$

$$\frac{dw}{dK} = \frac{\partial^2 f}{\partial L^2} \frac{dL}{dK} + \frac{\partial^2 f}{\partial L \partial K}.\tag{13c}$$

Combining the last two conditions,

$$\frac{dL}{dK} = \frac{dw}{dK} - \frac{\partial^2 f}{\partial L \partial K} \Big/ \frac{\partial^2 f}{\partial L^2}$$

$$= \frac{\partial L}{\partial K} \Big/ \frac{\partial g}{\partial w} \frac{\partial^2 f}{\partial L^2} - \frac{\partial^2 f}{\partial L \partial K} \Big/ \frac{\partial^2 f}{\partial L^2},$$

so that

$$\frac{dL}{dK} = \frac{\partial g}{\partial w} \frac{\partial^2 f}{\partial L \partial K} \Big/ (1 - \frac{\partial g}{\partial w} \frac{\partial f}{\partial L^2}) < 0$$

83

when $(\partial g/\partial w) < 0$ and

$$1 > \frac{\partial g}{\partial w} \frac{\partial^2 f}{\partial L^2}$$

to satisfy Walrasian stability conditions. As a result, growth in the capital stock can actually elicit a reduction in the amount of labor supplied and then dampen the anticipated output expansion. This point can be made emphatically by noting that the second term in the relation

$$\frac{\partial y}{\partial K} = \frac{\partial g}{\partial K} + \{\frac{\partial f}{\partial L} \frac{\partial g}{\partial w} \frac{\partial^2 f}{\partial L \partial K} \ / \ (1 - \frac{\partial g}{\partial w} \frac{\partial f}{\partial L^2})\}$$

(computed from (13a), (13b), and (13c), as well) is nonpositive and output expansion is _less_ than the marginal product of capital.

The reader is referred to Sheshinski (4) for an introduction to optimal linear income taxes, Green (1) and Tobin (5) for traditional treatments of negative income taxes, and the work by Watts et al. (6) for analysis of the experiments in New Jersey and Indiana. These are important contributions, but do not relate directly to the central point of this exercises: the inferences garnered from empirical study can reduce the number of possible cases and otherwise aid the explanatory power of an alert theorist. The possible cases allowed by equation (11) are doubled, for example, if leisure cannot be assumed to be a normal good. The conclusions recorded in part (c), first published by Krueger (2), can help explain the mystery of slower growth rates in more developed economies. They, too, are based on an empirical result.

References

(1) Green, C., *Negative Taxes and the Poverty Problem,* Washington, Brookings Institution, 1967.

(2) Krueger, A.O., "The Implications of a Backward Bending Supply Curve," *Review of Economic Studies*, 29:327-328, 1962.

(3) Samuelson, P.A., *Foundations of Economic Analysis,* New York, Atheneum, 1970 (first published by Harvard University Press in 1947.)

(4) Sheshinski, E., "The Optimal Linear Income Tax," *Review of Economic Studies*, 39:297-302, 1972.

(5) Tobin, J.T., *National Economic Policy*, New Haven, Yale University Press, 1966.

(6) Watts, H., et al., *The New Jersey Income Maintenance Experiment,* Vols. I, II, III, New York, Harcourt, Brace, Jovanovich and Academic Press, 1977-78.

11. Separable Utility and Conditional Demand[1]

Consider a utility schedule in three goods represented by

$$u = u(x_1, x_2, x_3). \tag{1}$$

The Marshallian demand schedules associated with (1) can be represented

$$x_i(\vec{p}, y) = x_i,$$

where $\vec{p} \equiv (p_1, p_2, p_3)$ are commodity prices and y is income [see page 105 and subsequent sections in Chapter 7. Suppose now that the consumption of x_3 were fixed at x_3; expenditures on x_3 would then be fixed at $p_3 x_3$. Conditional demand schedules for x_1 and x_2 could therefore be defined as solutions to [see Pollak (3 and 4)]:

$$\max \quad u(x_1, x_2, \bar{x}_3)$$

$$\text{s.t.} \quad p_1 k_1 + p_2 x_2 \le A$$

---

[1] Material found in Chapters 7, 8, and 9 is applicable here. Marshallian demand curves and supporting Slutsky equations are explored in the context of weak separability; an early section of Chapter 9 introduces separability more generally.

PROBLEM 11

for some net income A. Represent these schedules

$$\bar{x}_i = g_i(p_1, p_2, A, \bar{x}_3) \ . \tag{2}$$

It is possible to be more precise. Suppose that $\bar{x}_3$ were precisely the amount the consumer would have selected in an unrestricted maximization of (1) subject to $\vec{p} \cdot \vec{x} \leq y$; i.e., let

$$\bar{x}_3 = x_3(\vec{p}, y) \ .$$

If $[y - p_3 x_3(\vec{p}, y)]$ then remains, then the consumption of x_1 and x_2 would also maximize (1) subject to

$$p_1 x_1 + p_2 x_2 \leq y - p_3 x_3(\vec{p}, y) \tag{3}$$

because (3) actually repeats $\vec{p} \cdot \vec{x} \leq y$. Clearly, then

$$g_i(p_1, p_2, \ [y - p_3 x_3(\vec{p}, y)], x_3(\vec{p}, y)) = x_1(\vec{p}, y) \tag{4}$$

relates ordinary Marshallian demand schedules with their conditional counterpart.

Now assume that utility can be written:

$$u(\vec{x}) = U(w(x_1, x_2), x_3). \tag{1'}$$

87

PROBLEM 11

It is intuitively appealing that, under this condition, (x_1, x_2) be separable in $u(\vec{x})$ from x_3. This problem will explore that notion.

Questions:

(a) Show that equation (1') satisfies the conventional definition of (weak) separability; i.e., show that the marginal rate of substitution between x_1 and x_2 is invariant to changes in x_3.

(b) Show that the demand schedules for x_1 and x_2 depend only on p_1, p_2, and the amount spent on x_1 and x_2. Use this to show that a change in the consumption of either x_1 or x_2 in response to a change in p_3 is proportional to the change in x_1 in response to a change in y.

(c) Show that a change in the compensated (Hicksian) consumption of either x_1 or x_2 in response to a change in p_3 is proportional to the compensated change in x_1 in response to a change in y.

(d)   Consider two possible forms for (1')

$$u(\vec{x}) = [\alpha x_1^{\rho} + (1-\alpha)x_2^{\rho}]^{a/\rho} \, x_3^{1-a} \text{ and} \qquad (1'a)$$

$$u(\vec{x}) = \{\alpha[\alpha x_1^{\rho} + (1-\alpha)x_2^{\rho}]^{r/\rho} + (1-a)x_3^{r}\}^{1/r}. \qquad (1'b)$$

PROBLEM 11

Show that while demands for x_1 and x_2 are both totally independent of p_3 (i=1,2) for (1'a), demands for both depend implicitly on p_3 for (1'b) by virtue of changes in expenditures devoted to x_1 and x_2.

Suggested Solutions:

(a)   Notice simply that [see page 98]

$$mrs_{1,2} = \frac{(\partial u/\partial x_1)}{(\partial u/\partial x_2)} = \frac{(\partial U/\partial w)(\partial w/\partial x_1)}{(\partial U/\partial w)(\partial w/\partial x_2)} = \frac{(\partial w/\partial x_1)}{(\partial w/\partial x_2)}$$

does not depend on x_3, since $w(x_1,x_2)$ does not depend on x_3.

b. Consider the problem

$$\max \quad U(w(x_1,x_2),\bar{x}_3)$$

$$s.t. \quad p_1 x_1 + p_2 x_2 \leq y - p_3,\bar{x}_3) \equiv A. \tag{5}$$

Solutions to (5) satisfy

$$\frac{(\partial w/\partial x_1)}{(\partial w/\partial x_2)} = \frac{p_1}{p_2} \quad \text{and}$$

$$p_1 x_1 + p_2 x_2 = A;$$

they do not depend explicitly on $\bar{x}_3$ and so can be represented by

89

$$x_i = g_i(p_1, p_2, A), \quad i = 1, 2.$$

From equation (4) then,

$$\bar{x}_i(\vec{p}, y) = g_i(p_1, p_2, A), \quad i = 1, 2 \qquad (6)$$

does not depend explicitly on $\bar{x}_3$ [there is an implicit dependence, though, through A, which will be illustrated in part (d)]. Rather, $x_i(\vec{p}, y)$ depends on p_1, p_2, and total expenditure devoted to (x_1, x_2).

From equation (6), meanwhile, notice that

$$\frac{\partial x_i(\vec{p}, y)}{\partial p_3} = \frac{\partial g_i}{\partial A} \cdot \frac{\partial A}{\partial p_3} \quad \text{and} \qquad (7a)$$

$$\frac{\partial x_i(\vec{p}, y)}{\partial y} = \frac{\partial g_i}{\partial A} \cdot \frac{\partial A}{\partial y} \quad . \qquad (7b)$$

Combining (7a) and (7b) by eliminating $(\partial g_i / \partial A)$, then

$$\frac{\partial x_i(\vec{p}, y)}{\partial p_3} = k \frac{\partial x_i(\vec{p}, y)}{\partial A} \frac{}{\partial y} \qquad (8)$$

where $k \equiv [(\partial A/\partial p_3)/(\partial A/\partial y)]$ depends on x_3.

(c) From the Slutsky equation [page 119],

PROBLEM 11

$$\frac{\partial h_i(\vec{p},\bar{u})}{\partial p_3} = \frac{x_i(\vec{p},y)}{\partial p_3} + x_3(\vec{p}_3,y)\frac{\partial x_i(\vec{p},y)}{\partial y}$$

for $i = 1, 2$; as usual, $h_i(\vec{p},\bar{u})$ represents the Hicksian demand schedule for x_i. From equation (8), then

$$\frac{\partial h_i(\vec{p},u)}{\partial p_3} = [k + x_3(\vec{p},y)]\frac{\partial x_i(\vec{p},y)}{\partial y}$$

$$\equiv k'\frac{\partial x_i(\vec{p},y)}{\partial y}, \quad i = 1,2.$$

Of course, k' depends on x_3, too.

(d) For a Cobb-Douglas utility function of the form

$$u(z_1,z_2) = z_1^a \, z_2^{1-a},$$

total expenditure on z_1 equals (ay) regardless of how much z_2 costs per unit. To see this, recall that the demand for z_1 can be written [see the example on page 111]

$$z_1 = (ay)/p_1$$

so that

$$p_1 z_1 = ay.$$

PROBLEM 11

Clearly, then, the demand schedules for x_1 and x_2 in

$$u(\vec{x}) = [\alpha x_1{}^\rho + (1-\alpha)x_2{}^\rho]^{a/\rho} \; x_3{}^{(1-a)}$$

solve

$$\max = [\alpha x_1{}^\rho + (1-\alpha)x_2{}^\rho]^{1/\rho}$$

$$\text{s.t.} \quad p_1 x_1 + p_2 x_2 \le ay.$$

From the properties of the general CES function, then [see the example on page 112],

$$x_1(p_1, p_2, ay) = \frac{p_1{}^{s-1} ay}{(p_1^s + p_2^s)} \qquad \text{and}$$

$$x_2(p_1, p_2, ay) = \frac{p_2{}^{s-1} ay}{(p_1^s + p_2^s)}$$

where $s = \rho/(1-\rho)$. Meanwhile,

$$x_3(p_3, (1-a)y) = \frac{(1-a)y}{p_3} \;,$$

and the demand schedules for x_1 and x_2 (x_3) do not even implicitly depend on p_3 $(p_1$ or $p_2)$.

For the utility of the form

$$u(\vec{x}) = \{a[\alpha x_1^{\rho} + (1-\alpha)x_2^{\rho}]^{r/\rho} + (1-a)x_3^{r}\}^{1/r},$$

however, the story is different. In that case, expenditures on x_1 and x_2 are y minus expenditures on x_3; i.e.,

$$y - \frac{p_3^{\sigma} y}{(p_3^{\sigma} + c^{\sigma})} \equiv A(p_3, y),$$

where c is the shadow price of $z = [\alpha x_1^{\rho} + (1-a)x_2^{\rho}]^{1/\rho}$ and σ is the usual elasticity of substitution. As a result,

$$x_1(p_1, p_2, A(p_3, y)) = \frac{p_1^{s-1} A(p_3, y)}{(p_1^{s} + p_2^{s})},$$

$$x_2(p_1, p_2, A(p_3, y)) = \frac{p_2^{s-1} A(p_3, y)}{(p_1^{s} + p_2^{s})},$$

and the demand for x_i depends on p_3 implicitly through $A(p_3, y)$.

This problem was intended to explore the concept of separability in utility. Even though the results are cast in terms of three goods, they are perfectly generalizable. The two most important are recorded below.

(a) See Goldman and Uzawa (1) to see that a utility function $u(x_1, \ldots, x_n)$ weakly separable (defined with the marginal rate of substitution) along a partition of goods

$$(x_1,\ldots,x_n) = (\{x_{11},\ldots,x_{1r_1}\},\ldots,\{x_{m_1},\ldots,x_{mr_m}\})$$

if and only if it can be written

$$u(\vec{x}) = U(w_1(x_{11},\ldots,x_{1r_1}),\ldots,w_m(x_{m_1},\ldots,x_{mr_m})). \quad (9)$$

(b) If $u(\vec{x})$ can be represented as indicated by equation (9), then both Hicksian and Marshallian demand schedules for any good can be written as a function of the prices of only the other goods in the partition and the total expenditure made on goods in that partition. Changes in prices of goods outside the partition therefore have effects proportional to the impact of changes of income [see Pollak (4)].

The implications of these results on empirical work are immense. A future problem will explore a method of testing for separability in production functions with an eye toward property specifying the derived demand schedules for factors.

References

(1) Goldman, S.M., and H. Uzawa, "A Note on Separability in Demand Analysis," *Econometrica*, 32: 387-398, 1964.

(2) Gorman, W.M., "Separable Utility and Aggregation," *Econometrica*, 28:469-481, 1960.

(3) Pollak, R.A., "Conditional Demand Functions and Consumption Theory," *Quarterly Journal of Economics*, 83:60-78, 1969.

(4) Polak, R.A., "Conditional Demand Functions and the Implication of Separable Utility," *Southern Economic Journal*, 37:423-433, 1971.

12. **Random Income Taxation**[1]

The concept of horizontal equity - equal treatment of
equals - has long been revered in both legal and economic
circles. It holds the same high place in the annals of
public finance as it does in the Constitution of the United
States through its "equal protection under the law" clause.
Against such formidable firepower, it would appear to be
imprudent, at best, to treat identical individuals randomly.
But is that really the case?

Consider the possibility of a random income tax. As
long as identical citizens faced identical distributions of
tax bills, such a random tax would be, _ex ante_, horizontally
equitable; everyone's expected taxes would be identical even
though their _ex post_ tax burdens might be dramatically
unequal. But is _ex post_ horizontal equity the appropriate
measure? Most economists would say so, agreeing with
Musgrave (5). Others would argue that the Constitution says
so, too. But what about the draft lottery for selective
service? Was that not a "random tax" on a clearly defined
subset of the population?

The purpose of this exercise is not to answer these
questions. It is, instead, to explore a little bit of what

[1] Material found in Chapters 7 and 11 is applicable here.
This problem uses the measure of relative risk aversion
introduced in Section 11.8; it is, quite formally, the
income elasticity of the marginal utility of income.

PROBLEM 12

might be considered a relevant sideshow to the horizontal

equity issue - the possibility that random taxation might

improve social welfare over a system of horizontal equity.

This possibility is not an illusion. It is not the product

of "slight of minus sign" calculation or hidden vacuous

assumption. It is the product of a noncavity of the type

that can cause problems for the economist who is overly

comfortable with convexity.

Questions:

(a)   Begin with an exercise that explores the intuitive

foundation of horizontal equity. Consider two

individuals (1 or 2) with identical utility schedules;

i.e., let $U(C_1) = U(C_2)$ whenever $C_1 = C_2$ represents a

common level of consumption. Assume, further, that these

levels of consumption are defined by $C_j = Y_j - T_j$ where Y_j

= Y represents income for individual $j = 1,2$ and T_j

represents the tax bill faced by individual $j = 1,2$.

Show that if the government must raise R from T_1 and T_2,

then

$$T_1^* = T_2^* = .5R$$

must maximize a Benthamite social objective function of

the form:

PROBLEM 12

$$w = U(C_1) + U(C_2).$$

The remainder of this exercise will look at the simplest of indirect taxation problems. Let there be two individuals (A and B this time) whose utilities depend upon consumption C^j ($j=A,B$) and labor L^j ($j=A,B$). Income to finance consumption is generated by providing labor services; the wage rate is unity because of normalization. Appropriate delineation of units also lets the pretax price of consumption goods be unity so that

$$P^j = 1 + \tau^j, \qquad j = A,B,$$

represents the price paid by individual j given indirect tax rate τ^j. The point will be whether or not $P^A \neq P^B$ can ever maximize

$$w = U^A(C^A,L^A) + U^B(C^B,L^B) \ .$$

Let individuals choose their consumption-labor combination _after_ they know their tax rates by defining an indirect utility schedule [see page 102]

$$v^j = v^j(P^j,0) \equiv \max U^j(C^j,L^j), \qquad j = A,B,$$

$$\text{s.t. } P^j C^j \geq L^j + 0$$

98

for j = A,B. Of course,

$$v_1^j (p^j,0) < 0 \text{ and } v_{11}^j (p^j,0) > 0.$$

We will consider maximizing

$$w = v^A (p^A,0) + v^B(p^B,0) \tag{1}$$

subject to the government's need to raise tax revenue R by taxing c^A and c^B; i.e.,

$$R = \tau^A c^A + \tau^B c^B$$

$$= (p^A-1) c^A(p^A,0) + (p^B-1) c^B(p^B,0). \tag{2}$$

Parts (b) through (e) will lead you to the conclusion that $\tau^A = \tau^B$ need not necessarily maximize welfare.

(b)   Show that social welfare indifference curves defined by equation (1) are concave and that the budget constraint defined by equation (2) can be either concave or convex.

(c)   Show that the maximization problem in (p^A, p^B) space defined by equations (1) and (2) has a critical point where $p^A = p^B$, but that that point can be either a maxima of (1) or a minima of (1).

(d)   Express the curvature of the welfare indifference

curve at the critical point where $P^A = P^B = P$ in terms of the Pratt measure of relative risk aversion [see page 188],

$$R^j = - Y^j \ V_{22}^j(P,0)/V_2^j(P,0) \ ;$$

the price elasticity of the demand for consumption, and the income elasticity of that demand, where $Y^j = PC^j(P,0)$. Similarly express the curvature of the budget constraint at $P^A = P^B = P$ in terms of the price elasticity of demand and the curvature of that demand,

$$v^j = PC_{11}^j \ (P,0)/C_1^j(P,0) \quad .$$

(e) Argue how relative risk aversion, the curvature of the demand for consumption, and the government's need for revenue influence the likelihood that unequal taxes maximize (1).

Suggested Solutions:

(a) Consider the problem

$$\max_{T_1,T_2} \ \{U(Y-T_1) \ + \ U(Y-T_2)\}$$

$$(3)$$

$$\text{s.t.} \quad T_1 + T_2 = R \quad .$$

Working with the appropriate Lagrangian,

PROBLEM 12

$$L = U(U-T_1) + U(Y-T_2) + \lambda(R-T_1-T_2) \quad .$$

produces three first-order conditions that characterize the optimal taxes (T_1^*, T_2^*) that solve (3):

$$- U'(Y-T_1^*) - \lambda = 0 \ ,$$

$$- U'(Y-T_2^*) - \lambda = 0 \ , \quad \text{and}$$

$$T_1^* + T_2^* = R.$$

These conditions can only be satisfied by equal taxes, and so some support for the equalitarian foundation of horizontal equity is demonstrated.

(b)   The maximand of this problem generates social indifference curves defined implicitly by

$$w = V^A(P^A,0) + V^B(P^B,0) \quad .$$

Along each indifference curve, therefore,

$$dw = 0 = V_1^A(-) \ \frac{dP^A}{dP^B} + V_1^B(-) \quad ; \ \text{i.e.} \qquad (4)$$

$$\frac{dP^A}{dP^B}\bigg|_{\overline{w}} = \frac{v_1^A(-)}{v_1^B(-)} < 0 \quad .$$

Furthermore, continued differentiation of (4) reveals that

$$0 = v_1^A(-) \frac{d^2P^A}{d(P^B)^2}\bigg|_{\overline{w}} + \frac{dP^A}{dP^B}\bigg|_{\overline{w}} v_{11}^A(-) \frac{dP^A}{dP^B}\bigg|_{\overline{w}} + v_{11}^B(-) \quad .$$

As a result,

$$\frac{d^2P^A}{d(P^B)^2}\bigg|_{\overline{w}} = \frac{1}{v_1^A(-)} \left\{ \frac{[v_1^B(-)]^2 \, v_{11}^A(-)}{[v_1^A(-)]^2} + v_{11}^B(-) \right\}$$

$$= \frac{v_1^B(-)}{v_1^A(-)} \left\{ \frac{v_1^B(-) \, v_{11}^A(-)}{[v_1^A(-)]^2} + \frac{v_{11}^B(-)}{v_1^B(-)} \right\} < 0 \quad .$$

Social indifference curves must, therefore, be concave as drawn in Figure 12.1.

The budget constraint,

$$(P^A-1) \, c^A(P^A,0) + (P^B-1) \, c^B(P^B,0) = R$$

can be manipulated similarly to show that

Figure 12.1

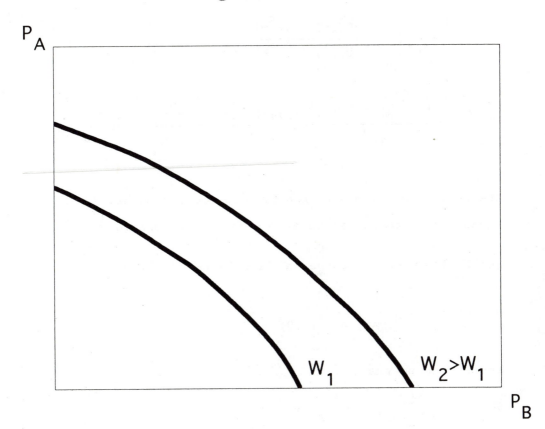

$$\left.\frac{dP^A}{dP^B}\right|_{\underline{R}} = - \frac{c^B(-) + (P^B-1)\ c_1^B(-)}{c^A(-) + (P^A-1)\ c_1^A(-)} < 0 \qquad (5)$$

and that

$$\left.\frac{d^2P^A}{d(P^B)^2}\right|_{\underline{R}} = \frac{2c_1^B(-) + (P^B-1)\ c_{11}^B(-)}{c^A(-) + (P^A-1)\ c_1^A(-)} \ +$$

$$\frac{[2c_1^A(-) + (P^A-1)\ c_{11}^A(-)]\ [c^B(-) + (P^B-1)\ (c_1^B(-)]}{[c^A(-) + (P^A-1)\ c_1^A(-)]^2}. \qquad (6)$$

The last expression has an ambiguous sign, however, and the revenue constraint can be either convex or concave.

(c) Notice that along the 45° line in (P^A, P^B) space,

$$v^A(P<0) \equiv v^B(P,0)$$

for $P^A = P^B$ so that

$$\left.\frac{dP^A}{dP^B}\right|_{\underline{w}} = \left.\frac{dP^A}{dP^B}\right|_{\underline{R}} = -1.$$

A maxima or minima must therefore occur along the 45° locus. As shown in Figure 12.2a, this critical point must be a

Figure 12.2a

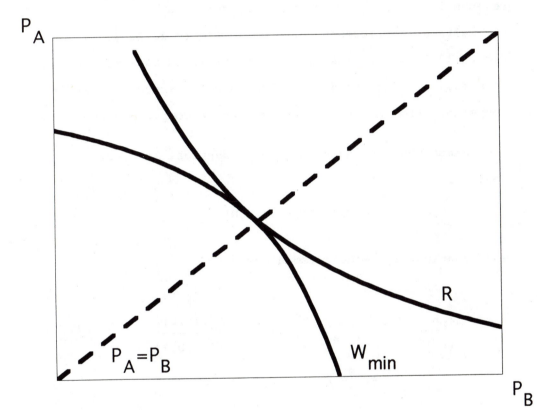

minima if the revenue constraint were convex. Should it be concave, however, Figures 12.2b and 12.2c show that it could be either a minima or a maxima depending upon the relative curvatures of the two schedules. If, in particular, the revenue constraint were more (less) curved at $P^A = P^B$ than the welfare indifference curve as in Figure 12.2c (as in Figure 12.2b), then the critical point would be a maxima (minima). The key to determining which, therefore, lies in comparing terms in the second derivative computed above.

(d)   Since the two individuals are identical in every respect,

$$V_1^A(P,0) = V_1^B(P,0) \quad,$$

and equation (5) reduces immediately to

$$\left. \frac{d^2 P^A}{d(P^B)^2} \right|_{\substack{\overline{w} \\ P^A = P^B = P}} = \frac{V_{11}^A(P,0)}{V_1^A(P,0)} \quad \frac{V_{11}^B(P,0)}{V_1^B(P,0)} \quad . \qquad (7)$$

To continue, appeal to Roy's lemma [page 106]:

$$- c^j(P,0) \; V_2^j(P,0) = V_1^j(P,0)$$

for j = A and B.   Clearly, therefore,

Figure 12.2b

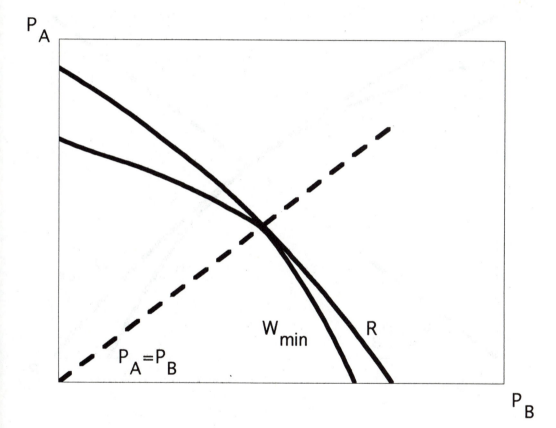

Figure 12.2c

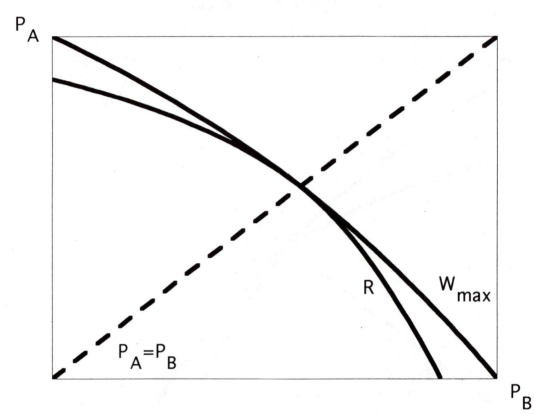

$$v_{12}^j(-) = - c^j(-) \ v_{22}^j(-) - v_2^j(-) \ c_2^j(-) \quad \text{and}$$

$$v_{11}^j(-) = - c^j(-) \ v_{12}^j(-) - v_2^j(-) \ c_1^j(-) \ .$$

Through substitution and collection of terms, then,

$$\frac{v_{11}^A(-)}{v_1^A(-)} = - \frac{c^A(-) \ v_{12}^A(-) - c_1^A(-) \ v_2^A(-)}{-c^A(-) \ v_2^A(-)}$$

$$= \frac{1}{P} \{- \frac{PC^A(-) \ v_{22}^A(-)}{v_2^A(-)} - \frac{PC_2^A(-) \ c^A(-)}{c^A(-)} + \frac{PC_1^A(-)}{c^A(-)}\} \ .$$

Given the specified measure of relative risk aversion

$$R^A \equiv - Y^A v_{22}^A(-)/v_2^A(-) \quad > 0$$

with $Y^A = PC^A(-)$, an income elasticity of demand for consumer goods

$$\varepsilon_Y^A = [d \ \ln \ c^A(-)/d \ \ln \ Y^A] > 0$$

and the corresponding price elasticity of demand

$$\varepsilon_P^A = [d \ \ln \ c^A(-)/d \ \ln \ P \ ] < 0 \ ,$$

then

PROBLEM 12

$$\frac{V_{11}^A(-)}{V_1^A(-)} = \frac{1}{P} \{R^A - \varepsilon_Y^A + \varepsilon_P^A\} \; .$$

and from equation (7),

$$\frac{d^2P^A}{d(P^B)^2} \bigg|_{\substack{\bar{w} \\ P^A = P^B = P}} = \frac{1}{P} \{R^A - \varepsilon_Y^A - \varepsilon_P^A + R^B - \varepsilon_Y^B - \varepsilon_P^B\}$$

$$= \frac{2}{P} \{R^A - \varepsilon_Y^A - \varepsilon_P^A\} \; .$$

The more risk averse society becomes, therefore (i.e., the larger R^A and R^B measured where $P^A = P^B = P$), the less negative is the second derivative of the social indifference curve; i.e., the flatter it is in the neighborhood of the $P^A = P^B = P$ critical point.

Manipulating the revenue constraint at that point can produce a similar type of simplification. Assuming identical individuals allows an immediate reduction to

$$\frac{d^2P^A}{d(P^B)^2} \bigg|_{\substack{\bar{R} \\ P^A = P^B = P}} = \frac{2c_1^B(-) + (P-1) \; c_{11}^B(-)}{c^A(-) + (P-1) \; c_1^A(-)} \quad \frac{2c_1^A(-) + (P-1) \; c_{11}^A(-)}{c^A(-) + (P-1) \; c_1^A(-)}$$

110

$$= 2 \left\{ \frac{2c_1^A(-) + (P-1) \ c_{11}^A(-)}{c^A(-) + (P-1) \ c_1^A(-)} \right\}$$

$$= 2 \left\{ \frac{2c_1^B(-) + (P-1) \ c_{11}^B(-)}{c^B(-) + (P-1) \ c_1^A(-)} \right\} .$$

But if $v^A \equiv Pc_{11}^A(-)/c_1^A(-)$ is the curvature of the demand schedule and $\tau = (P-1)/P$ is the percentage tax rate, then

$$\left. \frac{d^2p^A}{d(p^B)^2} \right|_{\substack{\bar{R} \\ p^A = p^B = P}} = 2 \left\{ \frac{c_1^A(-)}{c^A(-)} \right\} \frac{[2 + (\tau \ Pc_{11}^A(-)/c_1^A(-))]}{[1 + (\tau \ Pc_1^A(-)/c^A(-))]}$$

$$= - \frac{2\varepsilon_P^A \ [2 + \tau \ v^A]}{P \ [1 + \varepsilon_P^A\tau]} .$$

(e)   Figures 12.2a and 12.2b illustrate two circumstances for which the $p^A = p^B = P$ critical point represents a local minimum.   In Figure 12.2a, notice that

$$\left. \frac{d^2p^A}{d(p^B)^2} \right|_{\substack{\bar{R} \\ p^A = p^B = P}} > 0 > \left. \frac{d^2p^A}{d(p^B)^2} \right|_{\substack{\bar{W} \\ p^A = p^B = P}} ;$$

in Figure 12.2b, meanwhile

$$0 > \left. \frac{d^2 P^A}{d(P^B)^2} \right|_{\substack{\bar{R} \\ P^A = P^B = P}} > \left. \frac{d^2 P^A}{d(P^B)^2} \right|_{\substack{\bar{w} \\ P^A = P^B = P}} \cdot$$

Only when

$$0 < \left. \frac{d^2 P^A}{d(P^B)^2} \right|_{\substack{\bar{w} \\ P^A = P^B = P}} > \left. \frac{d^2 P^A}{d(P^B)^2} \right|_{\substack{\bar{R} \\ P^A = P^B = P}} ,$$

in fact, can the critical point be a maximum. Minimization is assured therefore, if

$$\frac{2}{P} \{R^A - \varepsilon_Y^A - \varepsilon_P^A\} < - \frac{2\varepsilon_P}{P} \frac{[2 + \tau v]}{[1 + \varepsilon_P \tau]} \quad ; \ i.e.,$$

$$v^A < - \{[R^A - \varepsilon_Y^A - \varepsilon_P^A] - \frac{R^A - \varepsilon_Y^A + \varepsilon_P^A}{\varepsilon_P^A \tau}\} .$$

The larger the curvature of the demand schedule, therefore, the less likely it is that the critical point is a maximum. Because

$$[R^A - \varepsilon_Y^A + \varepsilon_P^A] > R^A - \varepsilon_Y^A - \varepsilon_P^A > 0,$$

larger values of τ (larger revenue requirements) and smaller
values of R^A (smaller societal risk aversion) have the same
effect. The possibility that equal treatment of equals
might reduce welfare below a level that might be achieved by
unequal treatment of equals cannot, therefore, be dismissed
without strong evidence of serious risk aversion, relatively
small revenue needs, and concave or weakly convex demand.
Figure 12.3 shows how the existence of a minimum at equal
prices (equal taxes) produces a maximum somewhere else.

This exercise is derived from a working paper on
random taxation by Joseph Stiglitz. It suggests that
notions of horizontal equality, utilitarianism, and pareto
optimality need to be reconsidered in their mutual contexts
with an eye toward discovering internal contradiction. This
suggestion is obscure, perhaps, and certainly philosophical.
From a practical perspective, its results are probably
vacuous; no random taxation will be written into law in the
United States in the near future.

From a logical perspective, however, it is not
mysterious. Random taxation was seen to be desirable
whenever the labor response to taxation caused the revenue
raised by the tax to increase more than proportionately to
the tax rate. As a result, the average tax rate could be
raised by skewing different tax burdens onto different
individuals of identical economic standing. In this final

Figure 12.3

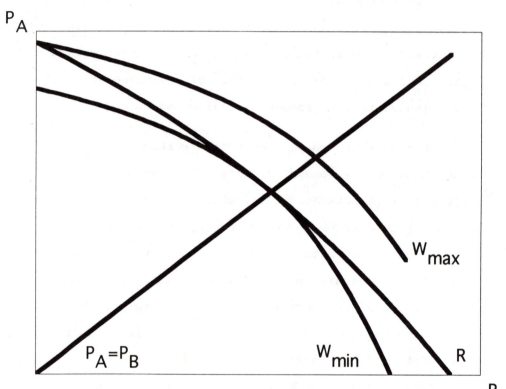

context, the lesson of general equilibrium is viewed once again - in simplifying a problem to its apparent foundation [as in part(a) of this problem], some important elements in the foundation can be missed.

References

(1) Atkinson, A.B., and J.E. Stiglitz, "The Structure of Indirect Taxation and Economic Efficiency," *Journal of Public Economics*, 1: 97-119, 1972.

(2) Atkinson, A.B., and J.E. Stiglitz, "The Design of Tax Structure: Direct Versus Indirect Taxation," *Journal of Public Economics*, 6: 55-75, 1976.

(3) Diamond P.A. and J.A. Mirrlees, "Optimal Taxation and Public Production," *American Economic Review*, 61: 8-27 and 261-278, 1971.

(4) Diamond, P.A., and J.E. Stiglitz, "Increases in Risk and in Risk Aversion," *Journal of Economic Theory*, 9: 337-360, 1974.

(5) Musgrave, R.A., "ET, OT and SBT," *Journal of Public Economics*, 6: 3-16, 1975.

(6) Stiglitz, J.E., and P.S. Dasgupta, "Differential Taxation, Public Goods, and Economic Efficiency," *Review of Economic Studies*, 38: 151-174, 1971.

(7) Stiglitz, J.E., and P.S. Dasgupta, "Random Taxation," *Stanford Report No. 214*, Stanford University, 1976.

PROBLEM 13

13. Risk Aversion with Many Commodities[1]

The significance of various measures of risk aversion
extends well beyond those topics which are easily handled
with utility functions of one variable. This exercise will
illustrate the potential of such extension by reproducing a
rather fundamental result: if an individual displays a
degree of relative risk aversion that is constant over all
incomes, then his or her underlying preferences for
commodities produce a homothetic indifference mapping.

Represent income by y and suppose there are n goods,

$$\vec{x} \equiv (x_1, \ldots, x_n),$$

whose prices are given by

$$\vec{p} \equiv (p_1, \ldots, p_n).$$

Consider three distinct utility functions in income and
prices:

$$u^1(\vec{p}, y) = a(\vec{p})y + b(\vec{p}), \tag{1}$$

$$u^2(\vec{p}, y) = w(\vec{p}) \ln y + v(\vec{p}), \text{ and} \tag{2}$$

$$u^3(\vec{p}, y) = w(\vec{p})y^{v+1} + z(\vec{p}), \quad v \neq 1. \tag{3}$$

---

[1] Material found in Chapters 7, 8, and 11 is applicable
here. Much of the analysis depends again on the Pratt-Arrow
measure of relative risk aversion defined on page 188.

116

PROBLEM 13

Questions:

(a) Show that if (1) represents utility, then the individual is risk neutral in the sense that relative (and actually absolute, as well) risk aversion is zero. Recall that the appropriate measure of relative risk aversion is defined by [see page 188]:

$$r(y) \equiv - \{ y \frac{\partial^2 u}{\partial y^2} \} / \{ \frac{\partial u}{\partial y} \}. \tag{4}$$

Show further that the utility functions given in equations (2) and (3) exhibit constant relative risk aversions equal to unity and v, respectively.

(b) Take each $u^i(\vec{p}, y)$ individually and argue that their underlying indifference mappings are homothetic. Notice that the $u^i(\vec{p}, y)$ are, in fact, indirect utility functions [see page 102], and recall that observing linear income expansion paths passing through the origin for every set of prices is sufficient to conclude homotheticity [page 116].

Suggested Solutions:

(a) Algebraic manipulation of equation (4) in light of

117

equations (1) through (3) proves the claims.

(b) While the details become more involved for (2) and (3), the method of analysis will persist throughout this section. Special care will therefore be taken in dealing with (1). Differentiating

$$\bar{u}^{1} = u^{1}(\vec{p}, y) \tag{5}$$

with respect to p_i is the key if one makes two observations:

(i)   the expenditure function $e(\vec{p}, u)$ plots minimum expenditure, and thus the minimum income required to maintain utility at u for all $\vec{p}$ [see page 103]; and

(ii) the compensated demand curve for x_i is the simple partial of $e(\vec{p}, u)$ with respect to p_i [property 5, page 105].

Implicitly differentiating equation (5) in light of the first observation reveals that

$$0 = a(\vec{p}) \frac{\partial e}{\partial p_i} + y \frac{\partial a(\vec{p})}{\partial p_i} + \frac{\partial b(\vec{p})}{\partial p_i}, \tag{6}$$

while rearranging (6) in light of the second produces the relationship that

$$x_i^c \approx -y_i a(\vec{p})/a(\vec{p}) - b_i(\vec{p})/a(\vec{p}). \tag{7}$$

118

Notationally,

$$a_i(\vec{p}) \equiv \frac{\partial a(\vec{p})}{\partial p_i} \quad \text{and} \quad b_i(\vec{p}) \equiv \frac{\partial b(\vec{p})}{\partial p_i} \ .$$

For small values of y, therefore

$$x_i^c = - \ b_i(\vec{p})/a(\vec{p}) \ .$$

To guarantee that $x_i^c > 0$, then $b_i(\vec{p})$ must be nonnegative if $a(\vec{p}) < 0$; but it must be nonpositive, otherwise. Indirect utility functions are homogeneous of degree zero in $(\vec{p},y)$, though [see page 102; property 2], and

$$\sum_{i=1}^{n} p_i b_i = 0$$

as a result (to see this, differentiate $b(t\vec{p}) = v(\vec{p})$ with respect to t). Since the $b_i(\vec{p})$ can never have mixed signs across the commodities, there is no possibility of cancellation in (7) regardless of the sign of $a(\vec{p})$. It must be true, then, that $b_i(\vec{p}) = 0$ for all $i = 1, \ldots, n$. As a result,

$$x_i^c = - \ y(a_i(\vec{p})/a(\vec{p})), \quad i = 1, \ldots, n. \tag{8}$$

PROBLEM 13

Equation (8) parameterizes the income expansion paths for $u^1(\vec{p}, y)$, and they are thereby seen both to be linear and to pass through the origin of commodity space. Homotheticity is thus proven.

The procedures that were applied to (1) can also be used to approach (2) and (3). Implicit differentiation of

$$\bar{u}^2 = u^2(\vec{p}, y)$$

in light of observation (i) reveals that

$$0 = \frac{w(\vec{p})}{y} \frac{\partial e}{\partial p_i} + (\ln y)(w_i(\vec{p})) + v_i(\vec{p}). \qquad (6')$$

Rearranging with the help of (ii),

$$x_i^C = -y (\ln y)(w_i(\vec{p})/w(\vec{p})) - (y/w(\vec{p}))v_i(\vec{p}).$$

Now, x_i^C must still always be positive, even where y assumes very large and/or very small values and

$$x_i^C \approx -y (\ln y)(w_i(\vec{p})/w(\vec{p})).$$

If $(w_i(\vec{p})/w(\vec{p})$ were strictly negative (positive) though, small (large) values of y would drive $x_i^C < 0$. It must be true, therefore, that

$$w_i(\vec{p})/w(\vec{p}) = 0$$

120

and

$$x_i^c = - (v_i(\vec{p})/w(\vec{p}))y.$$ (9)

Homotheticity is thereby assured because equation (9) looks exactly like equation (8).

Implicit differentiation of

$$\bar{u}^3 = u^3(\vec{p}, y)$$

yields similar results. Adding the simple division of both sides of the resulting equation by $(v + 1)$ to the procedure produces the relationship that

$$x_i^c = - \frac{y}{v+1} \frac{w_i(\vec{p})}{w} - \frac{\bar{y}^v}{w(v+1)} z_i.$$ (6")

The linear homogeneity of $z(p)$ requires that

$$\sum_{i=1}^{n} p_i z_i(\vec{p}) = 0$$ (10)

and provides the basis for neglecting the second term in (6"). Whenever $v < -1$ (or, alternatively, $v > -1$),

PROBLEM 13

$$x_i^C \approx - \frac{\bar{y}}{w(v+1)} \; z_i(p)$$

for large (small) values of y; it must be true, then that $[w(v+1)]^{-1} z_i \leq 0$ is required for all $i = 1, \ldots, n$ to assure that $x_i^C > 0$. Combining this observation with (10) allows the conclusion that $z_i = 0$ and that

$$x_i^C = - \frac{w_i(p)}{w(v+1)} \; y \qquad\qquad (11)$$

for all i. Equation (11) looks like (8), too, and homotheticity is assured again.

This problem reproduces several of the results proven in Stiglitz (9). They are, however, more than academic exercises. Various studies [see Prais and Houthakker (6), for example] have observed that linear income expansion paths do not fit the data as well as some of the other forms tested. The contrapositive of the problem would apply, of course, if the expansion paths were typically not linear: people would not react to risk independently of their incomes. This conclusion follows because the three cases listed above cover all of the ways that relative risk aversion can be constant.

The impact of such a conclusion could be immense; one example will close this exercise. Consider individual

122

investment as a form of risk taking that is necessarily conducted in the face of various forms of taxation. What impacts do these taxes have on risk taking? It can be shown that a proportional wealth tax will increase, decrease, or leave unchanged the demand for a risky asset if the investor displays increasing, decreasing, or constant relative risk aversion, respectively. Investor responses to more complicated tax structures (income taxation with and without loss offset, capital gains taxation, etc.) also depend, in less obvious ways, on how risk aversion moves with income. The interested reader is referred to Domar and Musgrave (2), Hall (3), Mossin (4), Richter (8), and Stiglitz (10) for extensive discussions of these questions and more, but the potential importance of allowing risk aversion to change with income should be clear to all.

References

(1) Arrow, K., *Essays in the Theory of Risk Bearing*, Chicago, Markham, 1970.

(2) Domar, E. and R. Musgrave, "Proportional Income Taxation and Risk Taking," *Quarterly Journal of Economics*, 56: 388–422, 1944.

(3) Hall, C., *Fiscal Policy for Stable Growth*, New York, Holt, Rinehart & Winston, 1965.

(4) Mossin, J., "Taxation and Risk-Taking: An Expected

Utility Approach," *Economica*, 35: 74-82, 1968.

(5) Musgrave, R., *Theory of Public Finance*, New York, McGraw-Hill, 1959.

(6) Prais, S. and H. Houthakker, *The Analysis of Family Budgets*, Cambridge, Cambridge University Press, 1955.

(7) Pratt, J., "Risk Aversion in the Small and in the Large," *Econometrica*, 32: 122-36, 1964.

(8) Richter, M., "Cardinal Utility, Portfolio Selection, and Taxation," *Review of Economic Studies*, 27: 152-66, 1960.

(9) Stiglitz, J., "Behavior Towards Risk with Many Commodities," *Econometrica*, 34: 660-67, 1969.

(10) Stiglitz, J., "The Effects of Income, Wealth, and Capital Gains Taxation on Risk-Taking," *Quarterly Journal of Economics*, 81: 263-283, 1969.

PROBLEM 14

14. Risk Aversion and Product Liability[1]

Discussions of product quality and the informational structures that produce consumers' perceptions of that quality do not appear until the last chapter. A model involving product failure published by Spence (4) can nonetheless be used now as an extremely rich illustration of how to apply the notion of insurance presented in Chapter 11 [see the example on page 180]. To that end, let

y = ex ante consumer income,

s = the probability a product will perform as promised,

$r(s)$ = consumer perceptions of s, and

$c(s)$ = marginal cost of producing a good with safety s.

Assume that both $\partial c/\partial s$ and $\partial^2 c/\partial s^2$ are nonnegative, that the consumers overestimate product safety ($r(s) > s$), and that this perception is imperfectly responsive ($\partial r/\partial s < 1$). Let m be the producer's liability to the consumer if the product fails and assume that the producer averages zero profits.

Questions:

(a) First presume risk neutrality in income and designate the cost of product failure to the consumer by ℓ. The

_____

[1] Material found in the beginning of Chapter 11 is applicable here. The entire problem is driven by the notion of expected utility introduced there.

PROBLEM 14

only possible liability here is m, so the zero expected
profits constraint is

$$p = c(s) + (1-s)m. \qquad (1)$$

Given consumer perceptions of s, characterize the
expected utility maximizing levels for s and m ($\hat{s}$ and $\hat{m}$).
Given the correct perceptions of s, characterize the
optimal levels for s and m (s* and m*). Show that safety
is underprovided by the unregulated market; i.e., show
that $\hat{s} < s^*$. Finally, demonstrate that devising a system
of liability whereby m = ℓ will elicit s* even with
consumer misperceptions.

(b) Instead of assuming risk neutrality, now let u(x)
represent utility if the product does not fail and v(x)
represent utility if the product does fail. Show that
when r(s) > s, insurance is undersupplied by the
unregulated industry. Furthermore, unless consumer
perceptions respond perfectly to changes in product
safety (i.e., unless $\partial r/\partial s = 1$), product safety will also
be misspecified.

(c) In the context of part (b), show that there is a way
of achieving the optimal level of product safety (s*).
In particular, add to the usual insurance policy (paid as

a liability by the firm to the consumer of a product that failed) a per unit subsidy paid to the consumer upon the purchase of the product (k). Finance that subsidy entirely through a liability f paid upon product failure to the government. Characterize this two pronged policy in such a way that the market chooses the optimal s*.

Suggested Solutions:

The general technique employed here will compare the optimum with the best zero-profit equilibrium that can be supported with consumers' misperceptions of the safety risks. The policy choices then come from setting parameters the government can reasonably alter so that the zero-profit equilibrium duplicates the optimum. In part (a), the government's policy is easily noted. In part (c), however, the usual technique of two-stage maximization is employed.

(a) Since risk neutrality implies that the consumer's utility is linear in income [see Section 11.5], the zero-expected profit condition designated in equation (1) allows expected consumer utility to be written

$$Eu_c = r(s)[y-p] + [1-r(s)][y-p+m-\ell]$$

$$= (y-c(s)-(1-s)m) + [1-r(s)](m-\ell]$$

PROBLEM 14

$$= y - c(s) - [1-r(s)]\ell + [s-r(s)]m. \tag{2}$$

Maximization of (2) with respect to m and s is now revealing.

If m cannot be negative, then $\hat{m} = 0$ maximizes expected utility when $r(s) > s$. The first-order condition for s is then simply

$$\frac{\partial c(s)}{\partial s} = \ell \frac{\partial r(s)}{\partial s}. \tag{3}$$

The optimum meanwhile looks at setting s to maximize

$$E_u = s(y-p) + (1-s)(y-p+m-\ell).$$

The zero-profit condition again comes into play so

$$E_u = s[y-c(s)-(1-s)m] + (1-s)[y-c(s)-(1-s)m+m-\ell]$$

$$= y - c(s) - (1-s)\ell. \tag{4}$$

The level of insurance is again insignificant since it does not enter (4), and s* maximizes E_u when

$$\frac{\partial c(s)}{\partial s} = \ell. \tag{5}$$

PROBLEM 14

Comparing equations (3) and (5), it is seen that if $[\partial r(s)/\partial s] < 1$, then $\hat{s} < s*$ and the zero-profit solution undersupplies safety even with no insurance.

If m were used as a policy tool, though, and set equal to ℓ by the government, then the first-order condition for the maximization in equation (2) with respect to s would read

$$\frac{\partial c(s)}{\partial s} = \ell \, \frac{\partial r(s)}{\partial s} + (1 - \frac{\partial r(s)}{\partial s}) \, \ell = \ell.$$

The optimum condition would be satisfied, therefore, by a rule that set the firm's liability equal to the consumer's loss measured in dollars. The government needs to know only ℓ to construct the optimal policy regardless of consumer misperceptions.

(b) Without risk neutrality,

$$Eu_c = r(s)u[y-p] + [1-r(s)]v[y-p+m]$$

$$= r(s)u[y - c(s) - (1-s)m] +$$

$$(1-r(s))v[y - c(s) + sm]. \tag{6}$$

The first-order conditions for maximizing (6) with respect to m and s are then

$$-r(\hat{s})u'(1-\hat{s}) + (1-r(\hat{s}))v'\hat{s} = 0 \text{ and} \tag{7a}$$

$$u\frac{\partial r}{\partial s} + r(\hat{s})u'(-\frac{\partial c}{\partial s} + \hat{m}) - v\frac{\partial r}{\partial s} + (1-r(\hat{s}))v'(-\frac{\partial c}{\partial s} + \hat{m}) = 0, \tag{7b}$$

respectively; notationally $u' \equiv \partial u/\partial x$ and $v' \equiv \partial v/\partial x$.
Rearranging (7a) yields the marginal condition for m:

$$\frac{v'(\ )}{u'(\ )} = \frac{(1-\hat{s})r(\hat{s})}{\hat{s}[1-r(\hat{s})]} . \tag{7a'}$$

Collecting terms in (7b) meanwhile shows that

$$\frac{\partial c}{\partial s} = \hat{m} + \frac{u(x) + v(x)}{su' + (1-s)v'} \frac{\partial r}{\partial s} . \tag{7b'}$$

Turning now to the optimum, consider

$$Eu = su[y-p] + (1-s)v[y-p+m]$$

$$= su[y - c(s) - (1-s)m] + (1-s)v[y - c(s) + sm]. \tag{8}$$

Maximizing (8) with respect to m and s now requires that

$$-s*u'(1-s*) + (1-s*) v's* = 0 \text{ and} \tag{9a}$$

$$u + s*u'(-\frac{\partial c}{\partial s} + m*) - v + (1-s*)v'(-\frac{\partial c}{\partial s} + m*) = 0. \tag{9b}$$

PROBLEM 14

Rearranging again (9a) shows that optimality is characterized by

$$u'(x^*) = v'(x^*) \text{ and} \tag{9a'}$$

$$\frac{\partial c}{\partial s} = m^* + \frac{u(\ ) + v(\ )}{u'} = m^* + \frac{u(\ ) + v(\ )}{v'} . \tag{9b'}$$

Equation (9a') restates a familiar result that insurance optimally equalizes the marginal utility of income over all states of nature.

Clearly, from equation (7a),

$$u'(y-c(\hat{s})\hat{m}) < v'(y-c(\hat{s}) + \hat{s}\hat{m})$$

when $r(s) > s$,. For the given $\hat{s}$, therefore, $\hat{m}$ must rise to increase u' and decrease v' into satisfying (9a'). Unless $\partial r/\partial s = 1$, furthermore, equation (7b') cannot replicate equation (9b'), but it is difficult to tell whether s* is larger or smaller than $\hat{s}$.

(c) The competitive industry would choose $\hat{s}$ by maximizing

$$Eu_c = r(s)u[y-p] + \{1-r(s)\}v[y-p+m])$$

subject to the new zero expected profit constraint that the price paid to the producer (p+k) equal marginal product costs (c(s)) plus the expected liability to the government and the consumer in case of an accident $[(1-s)f + (1-s)m]$. Plugging that constraint into (10), the industry maximizes

$$Eu_c = r(s)u[y+k-c(s)-(1-s)(m+f)]$$

$$+ (1-r(s))v[y+k-c(s)-(1-s)f+sm] \qquad (10)$$

with respect to s, taking m, f, and k as given. The first-order condition for this problem requires that

$$\frac{\partial c}{\partial s} = m + f + \frac{u(\ ) + v(\ )}{r(s)u' + (1-r(s)v')} \frac{\partial r}{\partial s} \qquad (11)$$

and acts as a constraint on the government's choices.

The government meanwhile maximizes

$$Eu - su[y-p] + (1-s)v(y-p+m)$$

subject to (11) as well as to the constraint that both the subsidy program and the firm break even in expected value, i.e., that

$$k = (1-s)f \text{ and}$$

$$p + k = c(s) + (1-s)(m+f).$$

PROBLEM 14

These combine to require that

$$p = c(s) + (1-s)m$$

so that the government would actually like to maximize

$$Eu = su[y-c(s)-(1-s)m] + (1-s)v[y-c(s)+sm]$$

subject to (11) with respect to s, f, and m. Since f enters only the constraint, though, the shadow price of (11) is zero. The government can therefore set m* so that

$$u' = v' \qquad (12)$$

and would set s* so that

$$\frac{\partial c}{\partial s} = m* + \frac{u-v}{u'} = m* + \frac{u-v}{v'}. \qquad (13)$$

By setting

$$f* = (1 - \frac{\partial r}{\partial s}) \frac{u-v}{u'} = (1 - \frac{\partial r}{\partial s}) \frac{u-v}{v'}, \qquad (14)$$

however, the government would be sure that the firm would select $\hat{s} = s*$ through (11); i.e., it could guarantee that

133

PROBLEM 14

$$\frac{\partial c}{\partial s} = m* + f* + \frac{u(x) + v(x)}{r(s)u' + (1-r(s))v'} \frac{\partial r}{\partial s}$$

duplicates equation (13) given equations (12) and (14). Its two policy tools, m and f, are thus sufficient to elicit optimal behavior from the firm.

The implications of this model seem to go well beyond the nominal statements of the results. In the first case of risk neutrality, for example, it would appear that requiring money-back guarantees is a good policy. Requiring producers to compensate a consumer dollar for dollar if the product fails generates the optimal provision of safety regardless of consumer perceptions of risk. Risk neutrality is a severely restrictive condition, though, and this result may only apply, therefore, when the potential losses are very small (like the 25¢ refund you can get if your cat does not eat a particular brand of food).

When the consumer is risk averse, the story is more complicated. An unregulated market again underprovides insurance and incorrectly sets product safety, but it now takes two policy tools to correct the situation. A second tool is required because consumers now need _more_ insurance against a product failure, and a single tool designed to bring forth optimal safety will _not_ necessarily provide that extra insurance. The informational requirements for this

policy are, however, enormous. The specifications for m*
and f* (and therefore k*) include not only the loss suffered
by a product failure (the ℓ from part (a)), but also how
consumers value income in both states of nature (u(x) and
v(x)) and how quickly consumers' perception of risk respond
to changes in risk ($\partial r(s)/\partial s$).

Direct regulation may be a preferred option, then, but
it merely trades the need for information on $\partial r(s)/\partial s$ for
information on technology (c(s)). Even so, direct
regulation should be imposed where the fine for failure
exceeds the ability of the firm to pay (like the infinite
loss that must be paid if a child dies playing with a
defective toy). To see that this could happen, let

$$v(x) = u(x) - \ell.$$

Then

$$f^* = (1 - \frac{\partial r(s)}{\partial s})\frac{\ell}{u'(x)}$$

and f* → ∞ when ℓ → ∞.

References

(1) Akerlof, G., "The Market for 'Lemons': Qualitative
Uncertainty and the Market Mechanism," *Quarterly Journal of
Economics*, 84: 488-500, 1970.

(2) Calibresi, G., *Costs of Accidents*, New Haven, Conn.,

Yale University Press, 1970.

(3) Oi, W., "The Economics of Product Safety," *Bell Journal of Economics*, 4: 3-29, 1973.

(4) Spence, M., "Consumer Misperceptions, Product Failure, and Producer Liability," *Review of Economic Studies*, 44: 561-572, 1977.

15. **Planning, Bonus Structures, and Truthful Information**[1]

Extending an analysis based on risk neutrality to include the possibility of risk aversion usually causes at least some of the original conclusions to falter. This problem will present an incentive example of such an extension.

Martin Weitzman's initial modeling of the then new Soviet bonus structure (3) assumed that the risks facing an enterprise manager were small enough to permit risk neutrality. Snowberger (2) extended the Weitzman modeling a year later to allow for risk averse managers. He found that some of Weitzman's results survived in tact, but others did not.

The new bonus scheme was devised to elicit truthful information from the enterprises. Planners, faced with immense data problems, depended upon enterprise managers reporting their true potential. Under the old setup, a manager knew that he would probably get a lower target that would be easier to satisfy if he underestimated his potential when he reported to the planner. Since his bonus hinged on his (over)fulfilling the specified target, there was a clear incentive for him to lie. The new scheme

---

[1] Material found in Chapter 11 is applicable here. The importance of incorporating risk aversion into individual decision-making processes is investigated explicitly.

encouraged higher, presumably more accurate, reporting by
linking the manager's bonus to the size of his target as
well as his actual performance.

The theoretical mechanism to be considered is most
easily summarized using some simple (Weitzman's) notation:

(y,B) = actual performance and bonus,

$(\bar{y},\bar{B})$ = preliminary target and bonus set by the planners,

$(\hat{y},\hat{B})$ = final target and bonus fund set by managers, and

(α,β,γ) = incentive parameters set by planners such that
$$0 < \alpha < \beta < \gamma.$$

The scheme then has three steps:

(1) Planners set $\bar{y}$, $\bar{B}$, α, β, and γ.

(2) A manager sets $\hat{y}$, and thus $\hat{B}$ defined

$$\hat{B} = \bar{B} + \beta(\hat{y}-\bar{y}).$$

(3) For performance y, the manager receives

$$B = \begin{cases} \hat{B} - \gamma(\hat{y}-y) & y \leq \hat{y} \\ \hat{B} + \alpha(y-\hat{y}) & y \geq \hat{y}. \end{cases}$$

It should be clear intuitively at least that step (2) should
encourage the manager to set a high target, while step (3)
should keep it from being excessive. Part (a) will explore
precisely why.

PROBLEM 15

Questions:

(a) Suppose that the manager could accurately identify y^* as the maximum, achievable performance of the enterprise. What level would be chosen for $\hat{y}$ in Step (2) above?

(b) Suppose, instead, that the manager knew only that the enterprise's actual performance was distributed by $f(y)$. Let the manager be risk averse in maximizing personal utility and let utility depend on the size of the bonus that might actually be received. Derive the first- and second-order conditions that would then characterize the manager's best $\hat{y}$.

(c) Show that increases in both α and β would decrease the manager's best $\hat{y}$ regardless of the degree of risk aversion. Also demonstrate that the effect of β on $\hat{y}$ would be ambiguous unless the manager were risk neutral. Provide some intuition to support all of these results.

Suggested Solutions:

(a) In a world of perfect information and absolute certainty, a manager would always set $\hat{y}$ equal to the enterprises's full potential (y^*). To see this, note that the actual formula can be written

139

PROBLEM 15

$$\bar{B} + \beta(\hat{y}-\bar{y}) - \gamma(\hat{y}-y) \quad \text{for } y \leq \hat{y}, \text{ and}$$

$$B =$$

$$\bar{B} + \beta(\hat{y}-\bar{y}) + \alpha(y-\hat{y}) \quad \text{for } y \geq \hat{y}.$$

The enterprise manager could, by assumption, be able to meet any target up to y^*. Since $\alpha < \beta$, the manager would want to set a target as high as possible because each unit of output would be worth more as part of a satisfied target than it would be as part of an overfulfillment. As a result, y^* is the lowest target the manager would consider setting.

Setting a target that is too high would be costly, though, because $\gamma > \beta$; shortfalls return a net per unit bonus equal to $(\beta-\gamma) < 0$. Since y^* is the maximum output, y^* must therefore also be the highest target the manager would consider. As long as marginal utility were positive, therefore, $\hat{y} = y^*$.

(b) One would expect that the manager would choose $\hat{y}$ so that the expected marginal utility of the bonus to be received across all possible "bad states of nature" (when the manager would be forced by circumstances to produce output less than $\hat{y}$) would equal the expected marginal utility that would be generated across the "good states of nature" (when more than $\hat{y}$ can be produced). This condition emerges from the usual maximization procedure.

To see why, define

$$B_1(y,\hat{y}) \equiv \hat{B} + \beta(\hat{y}-\bar{y}) + \gamma(y-\hat{y}) \text{ and}$$

$$B_2(y,\hat{y}) \equiv \hat{B} + \beta(\hat{y}-\bar{y}) + \alpha(y-\hat{y}).$$

The manager's problem can therefore be represented:

$$\max_{\hat{y}} \ \{\int_{-\infty}^{\hat{y}} u[B_1(s,\hat{y})]f(s) \ ds + \int_{\hat{y}}^{\infty} u[B_2(s,\hat{y})]f(s) \ ds\}. \quad (1)$$

Differentiating (1) with respect to y generates the appropriate first-order condition:

$$(\beta-\gamma) \int_{-\infty}^{\hat{y}} u'[B_1(s,\hat{y})]f(s) \ ds + (\beta-\alpha) \int_{-\infty}^{\hat{y}} u'[B_2(s,\hat{y})]f(s) \ ds$$

$$- u[B_1(\hat{y},\hat{y})]f(\hat{y}) + u[B_{\{1}(\hat{y},\hat{y})]f(\hat{y}) = 0. \quad (2)$$

Notice, though, that $B_1(\hat{y},\hat{y}) = B_2(\hat{y},\hat{y}) = \bar{B} + \beta(\hat{y}-\bar{y})$, so that equation (2) reduces immediately to

$$(\beta-\gamma) \int_{-\infty}^{\hat{y}} u'[B_1(s,\hat{y})]f(s) \ ds + (\beta-\alpha) \int_{\hat{y}}^{\infty} u'[B_2(s,\hat{y})]f(s) \ ds = 0.$$
$$\quad (2')$$

The anticipated condition is thus verified.

The associated second-order condition will also be

useful.   Differentiating (2'), one finds that

$$\Delta \equiv (\beta-\gamma)^2 \int_{-\infty}^{\hat{y}} u''[B_1(s,\hat{y})]f(s)ds + (\beta-\alpha)^2 \int_{\hat{y}}^{\infty} u''[B_2(s,\hat{y})]f(s)ds$$

$$- (\beta-\gamma)u'[B_1(s,\hat{y})]f(\hat{y}) + (\beta-\alpha)u'[B_2(s,\hat{y})]f(\hat{y}) \le 0. \quad (3)$$

The second line of equation (3) collapses to

$$(\gamma-\alpha)u'[B_1(\bar{B} + \beta(\hat{y}-\bar{y}))]f(\hat{y})$$

for the same reason that equation (2) simplified, but the
sign of Δ is the important implication.

(c) Comparative statistics can now be attempted.   Consider,
first of all, the effect of changes in α on the selected
target $\hat{y}$.   Totally differentiating in (2') with respect to $\hat{y}$
and α only, one sees that

$$\Delta d\hat{y} + \{(\beta-\alpha) \int_{\hat{y}}^{\infty} u''[B_2(s,\hat{y})](s-y)f(s)\ ds$$

$$- \int_{\hat{y}}^{\infty} u'[B_2(s,\hat{y})]f(s)\ ds\} \ d\alpha = 0. \quad (4)$$

Since $\beta > \alpha$, $u''(--) < 0$, $u'(--) > 0$, and $(s-\hat{y}) > 0$ in the

142

region of integration,

$$\frac{d\hat{y}}{d\alpha} = - \frac{N_1}{\Delta} \quad < 0$$

because N_1, the term in the {-} brackets of equation (4), is negative and equation (3) holds that Δ is nonpositive. Increases in the cost of underfulfilling an announced target should cause the manager to lower his target.

Similarly, differentiating (2') with respect to $\hat{y}$ and γ shows that

$$\Delta d\hat{y} + (\beta - \gamma) \{ \int_{-\infty}^{\hat{y}} u''[B_1(s,\hat{y})](s-\hat{y}) f(s) ds - \int_{-\infty}^{\hat{y}} u'[B_1(s,\hat{y})] f(s) ds \} d\gamma$$

must also equal zero. Now $\beta < \gamma$ and $(s-\hat{y}) \leq 0$ in the region of integration, so

$$\frac{d\hat{y}}{d\gamma} = - \frac{N_2}{\Delta} \quad < 0$$

because the comparably defined N_2 is also negative. Increases in the extra bonus of overfulfilling an announced target are seen to reduce the target, as well.

Risk aversion has, thus far, altered nothing but the size of the effects (increasing them because the u"(--) terms amplify the u'(--) terms in N_1 and N_2). That story

143

changes, though, when β is considered. Differentiating (2')

once more

$$\Delta d\hat{y} + \{\int_{-\infty}^{\hat{y}} u'[B_1(s,\hat{y})]f(s)\ ds + \int_{\hat{y}}^{\infty} u'[B_2(s,\hat{y})]f(s)\ ds\}$$

$$+ \{(\beta-\gamma) \int_{-\infty}^{\hat{y}} u''[B_1(s,\hat{y})](\hat{y}-\bar{y})f(s)\ ds$$

$$+ (\beta-\alpha) \int_{\hat{y}}^{\infty} u''[B_2(s,\hat{y})](y-\hat{y})f(s)\ ds\}\ d\gamma.$$

Making the obvious notation definitions, therefore,

$$\frac{d\hat{y}}{d\beta} \equiv \frac{N_3 + (\beta-\gamma)\ N_4 + (\beta-\gamma)N_5}{\Delta}\ . \tag{5}$$

The parameters N_4 and N_5 always have the same sign, and are

zero unless the manager is averse to risk. In fact,

$$\frac{d\hat{y}}{d\alpha}\bigg|_{u''(\dots)\ =\ 0} = \frac{N_3}{\Delta} > 0$$

because $N_3 > 0$. Increases in β simply increase the

desirability of higher targets for risk neutral managers.

PROBLEM 15

Risk averse managers consider bonus variance as well as mean, though, and they are willing to sacrifice a little mean for a little less variation. Higher values for β automatically increase the mean bonus for any target, so that the desired sacrifice can actually cause the manager to lower the target to a level that can met more easily (more variance in the bonus is caused for a given deviation from $\hat{y}$ by shortfalls rather than surpluses because $\alpha < \gamma$).

Snowberger went on to consider this bonus scheme in a dynamic setting, but the point of the problem has been made (and survives much longer than the Soviet system which inspired the work). Risk aversion may (or may not) alter results that seem quite natural under risk neutrality. Risk neutrality is a workable assumption if the risks are small or spread over a large number of agents so the total risk is small. It is, otherwise, worthwhile to consider the effect of risk aversion on qualitative and quantitative results.

References

(1) Fan, L.S., "On the Reward System," *American Economic Review*, 65:226-229, 1975.

(2) Snowberger, V., "The New Soviet Incentive Market: A Comment," *Bell Journal of Economics*, 8:591-600, 1977.

(3) Weitzman, M., "The New Soviet Incentive Model," *Journal of Economics*, 7:251-257, 1976.

16. **Optimal Commodity Taxation from Consumer Surplus**[1]

This problem serves to reinforce the notion that consumer surplus can be used as a rigorous measure of social welfare; optimal commodity tax results derived in Problem 8 directly from a utility function structure will be reproduced using nothing but consumer surplus. It will become clear, however, that theoretical applications of consumer surplus must be based on its true definition; (Hicksian) compensated demand curves must be the starting point.

Suppose, to add a bit more detail to the structure described in Problem 8, that production of all goods were described by constant returns to scale functions in only one factor, labor. Suppose further that u(**x**) supported compensated demand schedules for each good that varied only with respect to income and its own price.

Questions:

(a) Recall from Problem 8 that the government should arrange to tax commodities so that the compensated demand for each good is reduced by the same proportion if it is

---

[1] Material developed in Chapter 10 and Section 3 of Chapter 22 is applicable here. Specific results from Chapters 1, 5, 6 and 8 are also employed. The results derived directly from utility functions in Problem 8 are replicated directly from consumer surplus correctly defined.

PROBLEM 16

to generate a prescribed amount of tax revenue with the best set of nonwage taxes. Show that this result implies that

$$\frac{t_i^*}{p_i} = \frac{\theta}{\varepsilon_i}, \tag{1}$$

where θ is a constant and ε_i is the price elasticity of Hicksian demand.

(b) There is a deadweight loss associated with any consumption tax [a detailed definition of deadweight loss can be found on page 229, but it is a concept drawn from first principles]. In this case, let deadweight loss be equal to the loss in consumer surplus over and above any tax revenue that might collected. Replicate condition (1) by minimizing the total deadweight loss across <u>all</u> goods of generating a total tax revenue R from a set of commodity taxes.

(c) Show that using Marshallian demand to define consumer surplus would have produced an important error: the characterization of the taxes computed in part (b) would have missed income effects (effects captured in terms of income elasticities).

PROBLEM 16

Suggested Solutions:

(a) Problem 8 ended with the statement that an optimal set of commodity taxes designed to raise a specific amount of revenue R from the consumption of n different goods can be characterized by a set of n equations:

$$\sum_{k=0}^{n} \frac{t_k^*}{x_i} \left(\frac{\partial x_i}{\partial p_k} \right) \Bigg|_{\bar{u}} \equiv \theta \qquad (2)$$

for all i = 0, 1, ..., n. If the Hicksian demand for each good were to depend only on its own price, however, equation (2) would collapses immediately to

$$\frac{t_i^*}{x_i} \left(\frac{\partial x_i}{\partial p_i} \right) \Bigg|_{\bar{u}} = \theta \qquad (3)$$

because all of the other partial derivatives recorded there would vanish. Equation (1) follows immediately from multiplying the left-hand side of (3) by 1 = (p_i/p_i) and recalling the definition of the price elasticity of demand.

(b) Compensated demand can be written

$$x_i^c = h_i(p_i, y)$$

for this problem, so that the relationship of t_i and any

148

PROBLEM 16

change in consumer surplus is simply [consult only the definition of consumer surplus found on page 163]:

$$S_i(t_i) = \int_{p_i}^{p_i + t_i} h_i(z,y) \, dz. \tag{4}$$

Revenues generated by t_i are, meanwhile, simply given by

$$R_i(t_i) = t_i h_i(p_i^0 + t_i, y). \tag{5}$$

The deadweight loss associated with good x_i is then

$$D_i(t) = S_i(t) - R_i(t), \tag{6}$$

because constant returns to scale production using only labor and a fixed wage paid to labor means that the supply curve for x_i is horizontal.

The appropriate problem for the government to pose is thus

$$\min \quad \sum_{i=1}^{n} D_i(t_i)$$

$$\text{s.t.} \quad \sum_{i=1}^{n} R_i(t_i) > R;$$

the resulting first-order conditions require that

$$\frac{dD_i(t_i)}{dt_i} \; \{ \frac{dR_i(t_i)}{dt_i} \}^{-1} = -\lambda, \; i = 1, \; \ldots, \; n. \qquad (7)$$

The parameter λ is the shadow price, in terms of deadweight loss, of each dollar of tax revenue. Equation (7) therefore has the natural interpretation of requiring that the last dollar raised cost the same, in welfare terms, regardless of which good is taxed to provide it.

In light of equations (4), (5), and (6), it can be seen that (7) expands to the form

$$\frac{t_i^* \frac{\partial \bar{x}_i^c}{\partial p_i} + h_i(p_i^0 + t_i^*, \; y)}{t_i^* \frac{\partial x_i^c}{\partial p_i}} = \frac{1}{\lambda}, \; i = 1, \; \ldots, \; n, \qquad (7')$$

because

$$\frac{dS_i(t_i)}{dt_i} = h_i[(p_i^0 + t_i), y].$$

Equation (7') ultimately reduces to

PROBLEM 16

$$\frac{x_i^c}{t_i^*} \frac{dp_i}{dx_i^c} = \frac{1}{\lambda} - 1 \equiv \theta, \quad i = 1, \ldots, n. \tag{8}$$

Equation (8) reproduces (3), and the result is proven.

(c) From the Slutsky equation [pages 119-122], it is clear that

$$\varepsilon_i = \xi_i + S_i \eta_i, \tag{9}$$

where ξ_i represents the price elasticity of Marshallian demand for x_i, $S_i \equiv p_i x_i / y$ is the share of pretax expenditure devoted to x_i, and η_i is the income elasticity of Marshallian demand for x_i. Equation (9) follows from multiplying both sides of the Slutsky equations by (p_i/x_i). Imposing taxes that solve

$$\frac{\tilde{t}_i}{p_i} = \frac{\theta}{\xi_i}$$

[taxes that would emerge from part (b) if Marshallian demand were used in lieu of Hicksian demand as instructed by equation (1)] would omit the weighted effect of η_i. Goods with high (low) income elasticities would suffer higher (enjoy lower) taxes.

The points of this problem are several. First of all,

consumer surplus, properly defined, can be the tool of the theorist as well as the empiricist. The Willig piece (2) and its presentation in Section 10.5 aside, however, this problem illustrates the necessity of using Hicksian compensated demand schedules whenever a theoretical question is being investigated. The approximate measures derived from Marshallian schedules may provide useful numbers for cost-benefit studies, but they are only approximations. They may systematically omit some economic influences that are significant in other than computational contexts.

The example provided here characterizes optimal commodity taxes. The use of Marshallian measures in this process would cause the routine omission of income elasticities from the tax structure. Relying on the formulae that would emerge, a researcher would miss the dramatic display of the equity-efficiency trade-off that is evident in the expanded version of equation (1):

$$\frac{t_i^*}{p_i} = \frac{\theta}{\xi_i + s_i \eta^i} . \tag{10}$$

Necessities, usually displaying low income elasticities, would face, on the whole, higher taxes for a given revenue constraint than would luxury items that typically exhibit high income elasticities. This effect, coupled with the weaker, but paralleling influence of the price elasticities,

clearly shows necessities bearing the bulk of the tax
burden.

This is reasonable, though, since efficient taxes are
constructed to impact the various markets as little as
possible. It is far easier to raise tax revenue by taxing a
good whose consumption will fall only very little (through
both the substitution and income effects) than it is to
raise the same revenue by taxing a good whose consumption
might fall precipitously. Equation (10) captures both, and
reflects the qualitative results reported in Atkinson and
Stiglitz (1). The reader is referred to Problem 8 for a
related bibliography.

References

(1) Atkinson, A.G., and J.E. Stiglitz, "The Structure of
Indirect Taxation and Economic Efficiency," *Journal of
Public Economics*, 1:97-120, 1972.

(2) Willig, R., "Consumer Surplus without Apology,"
American Economic Review, 66:589-597, 1976.

17. Consumer Surplus with Multiple Goods[1]

Computing consumer surplus involves integrating beneath a demand schedule between specified price extremes. The difficulty here lies, of course, with the specification of the appropriate demand schedule. Problem 16 shows that the Hicksian compensated demand curve must be used, but Hicksian schedules are generally unobservable.

Section 10.5 in the text records a short discussion of how to circumvent that problem by computing upper and lower bounds for consumer surplus from Marshallian schedules. When the income elasticity of Marshallian demand is constant, these boundaries are exact. When income elasticities are not constant (at least locally), though, second-order approximations must be employed. In either case, welfare comparisons are possible.

An additional complication arises when more than one good is involved, because a variety of paths can be taken between the specified price extremes. Which of these paths is correct? Suppose, for example, that price changes in two goods, x_1 and x_2, were to be considered simultaneously. If consumer surplus were computed between

---

[1] Material from Chapters 7 and 10 is clearly applicable here. Roy's Identity [page 106] and the distinction between Marshallian and Hicksian demand curves [see page 105] are both employed repeatedly.

$$(p_1^o, \ p_2^o, \ \vec{q}, \ y_0)$$

and

$$(p_1', \ p_2', \ \vec{q}, \ y_0),$$

where $\vec{q}$ is a fixed vector of other prices and demand for x_i given income y_0 is given by $x_i(p_1, \ p_2, \ \vec{q}, \ y_0)$, how is one to choose between

(i)   integrating $x_1(p_1, \ p_2, \ \vec{q}, \ y_0)$ over the region between p_2^o and p_1' and then $x_2(p_1, \ p_2, \ \vec{q}, \ y_0)$ between p_2^o and p_2' with $p_1 = p_1'$ and

(ii) integrating $x_1(p_1, \ p_2, \ \vec{q}, \ y_0)$ over the region between p_2^o and p_2' with p_1 fixed at p_1^o and then $x_1(p_1, \ p_2, \ \vec{q}, \ y_0)$ between p_1^o and p_1' with $p_2 = p_2'$.

Economically, it should make no difference; only an index number differentiates x_1 and x_2. The mathematical story can be quite different, though, because the value of the integral can easily depend on the choice of paths between two boundaries of integration.

Constant income elasticities are again the keys. Assume, as will be shown in a later problem, that x_1 and x_2 both display constant income elasticities if and only if

155

$$\frac{\partial x_1}{\partial p_2} = \frac{\partial x_2}{\partial p_1} . \tag{1}$$

From Stokes' theorem, meanwhile, it can be shown that the integral

$$\int f(x, y, \vec{Z}) \, dx + \int g(x, y, \vec{z}) \, dy$$

is path independent if and only if

$$\frac{\partial g}{\partial x} = \frac{\partial f}{\partial y}$$

within a simply connected domain (roughly put, a domain with no "holes"). Equation (1) therefore guarantees that the path chosen in computing consumer surplus is not important, but only when demand displays constant income elasticity.

Your work here will extend this observation toward specifying an underlying indirect utility function from which a multidimensional welfare criteria can be developed. It elaborates on the latter parts of Varian (3). Constant income elasticities of demand for x_1 and x_2 are assumed throughout.

Questions:

(a)   Show that an indirect utility function of the form

PROBLEM 17

$$v(p_1, p_2, \vec{q}, y) = G[(A(p_1, p_2) + \frac{y_0^\eta y^{1-\eta}}{1-\eta}), \vec{q}], \quad \eta \neq 1 \quad (2a)$$

$$= G[(A(p_1, p_2) + y_0 \ln y), \vec{q}], \quad \eta = 1 \quad (2b)$$

produces demand schedules of the form

$$x_i(p_1, p_2, \vec{q}, y) = x_i(p_1, p_2, \vec{q}, y_0)(y^\eta/y_0^\eta) \quad (3)$$

where

$$A(p_1, p_2) = \int_{p_1}^{\bar{p}_1} x_1(s, p_2, q, y_0) \, ds + \int_{p_2}^{\bar{p}_2} x_2(\bar{p}_1, s, q, y_0) \, ds \quad (4)$$

is two-dimensional consumer surplus along path (i) and G
is monotonic. The demand schedules listed in (3) are the
most general formulations of demand characterized by
constant income elasticity.

(b) Use (a) to show that

$$(p^o, p^o, \vec{q}, y^o) \text{ is preferred to } (p', p', \vec{q}, y')$$

if and only if

157

$$\int_{p_1^o}^{p_1'} x_1(s,p_2^o, \vec{q},y_0) \, ds + \int_{p_2^o}^{p_2'} x_2(p_1',s,\vec{q},y_0) \, ds$$

$$> \frac{[(y')^{1-\eta} - (y_0)^{1-\eta}]y_0^{\eta}}{1 - \eta} \qquad \text{if } \eta \neq 1 \text{ and} \qquad (5a)$$

$$> [\ln y' - \ln y_0]y_0 \qquad\qquad \text{if } \eta = 1. \qquad (5b)$$

Suggested Solutions:

(a) From Roy's identity [page 106], Marshallian demand from (2a) is

$$- \{\frac{\partial v(p_1,p_2,\vec{q},y)}{\partial p_1}\} \ / \ \{\frac{\partial v(p_1,p_2,\vec{q},y)}{\partial y}\}$$

$$= - \{\frac{\partial A(p_1,p_2)}{\partial p_1}\} \ / \ (y/y_0)^{-\eta}$$

$$= x_1(p_1,p_2,\vec{q},y_0) \ (y/y_0)^{\eta}, \qquad \eta \neq 1.$$

The same expression results when $\eta = 1$ and equation (2b) is used as the point of departure.

(b) A circumstance $(\vec{p}^o,\vec{q},y_0)$ is preferred to $(\vec{p}',\vec{q},y')$ if and only if

$$v(\vec{p}^{\,o},\vec{q},y_0) > v(\vec{p}^{\,\prime},\vec{q},y^{\prime}). \tag{6}$$

Since G is monotonic, equation (6) is equivalent to

$$A(p_1^o,p_2^o) - A(p_1^{\prime},p_2^{\prime}) > (y_0^{1-\eta} - (y^{\prime})^{1-\eta})/(1-\eta) \tag{7}$$

for any $\vec{q}$ when $\eta \neq 1$. From equation (4), then, the left-hand side of (7) is really two line integrals; the paths are indicated in Figure 17.1. Schedule

$$A(p_1^o,p_2^o),$$

for example, integrates along the path where $p_2 = p_2^{\,o}$ until $p_1 = p_1"$ and then up until $p_2 = p_2"$. Schedule

$$A(p_1^{\prime},p_2^{\prime})$$

meanwhile integrates along the $p_2 = p_2^{\prime}$ path until $p_1 = p_1"$ and again turns up until $p_2 = p_2"$.

The minus sign in equation (7) can be handled by reversing the second path, so that the entire left-hand side of (7) is really an integral depicted in Figure 17.2 which moves along a path traced by

(i) segment (a) until $p_1 = p_1"$,

Figure 17.1

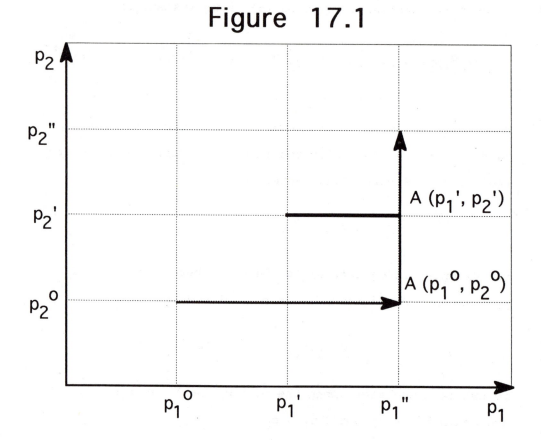

(ii) segment (b) until $p_2 = p_2''$,

(iii) back down segment (c) until $p_2 = p_2'$, and
finally

(iv) back segment (d) until $p_1 = p_1'$.

From Figure 17.2, therefore, this entire path simply moves from (p_1^0, p_2^0) to (p_1', p_2'). Since the path taken has no effect on the integral because

$$\frac{\partial x_1}{\partial p_1} = \frac{\partial x_2}{\partial p_2},$$

one can write

$$A(p_1^0, p_2^0) - A(p_1', p_2') = \int_{p_1^0}^{p_1'} x_1(s, p_2^0, \vec{q}, y_0)\ ds$$

$$+ \int_{p_2^0}^{p_2'} x_2(p_1', s, \vec{q}, y_0)\ ds. \qquad (8)$$

The desired result follows by plugging equation (8) into equation (7). The same reasoning also handles the case in which $\eta = 1$; only the right-hand side is changed. In either case, utility increases if and only if the indicated function of income increases.

A comparison of equation (5) and the standard consumer

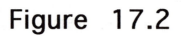

Figure 17.2

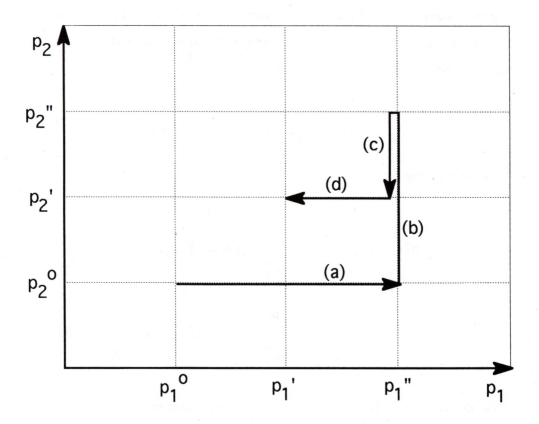

surplus computation is now appropriate. Hicksian
compensated demand schedules coincide exactly with the
Marshallian schedules when the income elasticities are zero;
in that case, equation (5) is the traditional consumer
surplus comparison. When the elasticities are constant but
not zero, (5) again provides a precise criterion that can be
applied directly. In every other circumstance, however, the
path independence property collapses and the limiting
results reported by Willig (3) must be applied. Part (a) is
an equivalence result [see Willig (2)]; some empirical
application in subsequent problems will lead to a definite
expression representing indirect utility.

References

(1) Varian, H., "A Note on Locally Constant Income
Elasticities," *Economic Letters*, 1:9-13, 1978.

(2) Willig, R., "Integrability Implications for Locally
Constant Demand Elasticities," *Journal of Economic Theory*,
12:391-401, 1976.

(3) _____, "Consumer's Surplus without Apology,"
American Economic Review, 66:589-597, 1976.

18. Estimating Two Factor, Constant Elasticity of Substitution Production Functions[1]

Production functions characterized by constant elasticities of substitution are often found to be too restrictive for effective empirical studies of complicated production processes. Duality approach [Chapter 6] can then be used to produce estimates of cost and/or profit schedules from which more general production relationships can be inferred. At times, however, CES specifications fit very well. This problem will suggest both the standard procedure for estimating a two factor CES function, with an eye toward computing the elasticity, and a word of caution. One reason to suspect that some of the resulting estimates might be biased will, more specifically, be explored.

Questions:

(a) Use the usual profit-maximizing condition for the employment of inputs to obtain a linear equation that will yield an estimate for the elasticity of substitution $\sigma = 1/(\rho-1)$ in

$$y = [a(E_L L)^\rho + (1-a)(E_K K)^\rho]^{1/\rho};$$

---

[1] Material found in Chapters 1 and 6 is applicable here. The problem underscores some of the basic coverage of Chapter 12.

L and K represent labor and capital, respectively, and E_L and E_K reflect efficiency units as in Problem 2.

(b) Suppose that an estimate $\hat{\sigma} > - 1$ were obtained from time series data which showed the general trend that higher (K/L) ratios generally accompanied gradually increasing wage rates. Use the results in part (a) of Problem 2 to suggest that $\hat{\sigma} > - 1$ might be biased away from zero and thereby overstate the possibilities of substitution.

Suggested Solutions:

(a) For the indicated production function

$$\frac{\partial y}{\partial L} = [a(E_L L)^\rho + (1-a)(E_K K)^\rho]^{(1-\rho)/\rho}[aE_L^\rho L^{\rho-1}]$$

$$= a[y/L]^{1-\rho}E_L^\rho .$$

Profit-maximizing conditions therefore require that

$$w_L = a[y/L]^{1-\rho}E_L^{\rho}$$

so that

$$(y/L) = w_1^{\frac{1}{1-\rho}} a^{\frac{1}{\rho-1}} E_L^{\frac{\rho}{\rho-1}} . \qquad (1)$$

PROBLEM 18

Expressing equation (1) in logarithmic terms, then,

$$\ln (y/L) = \{ \frac{1}{\rho-1} \ln a + \frac{\rho}{\rho-1} \ln E_L \} - \sigma \ln (w_L)$$

since $\sigma = (1/\rho-1)$ [see page 20]. Regressing

$$\ln (y/L)_t = \beta_0 + \beta_1 \ln (w_L)_t + e_t \qquad (2)$$

must therefore offer an estimate for σ; i.e., $\hat{\sigma} = -\hat{\beta}_1$.

(b) If the marginal product of L were increasing over time because (K/L) tended to climb, then $\sigma > -1$ would imply that the share of L should also rise [see Problem 2(b)]. An incentive for labor-saving technological change would thereby be created, and E_L could easily increase, as well. Since the error term e_t in equation (2) includes $(E_L)_t$, positive serial correlation would then exist and $\hat{\beta}_1$ would be an overestimate. The slope coefficient would simply pick up not only the effect of $(W_L)_t$, but also the amplifying effect of (E_L), and so it would overstate the impact of $(w_L)_t$. The resulting bias for $\sigma > -1$ would suggest that larger than actual possibility for substitution might be available.

Beyond exhibiting a procedure with which general CES production functions can be estimated, this problem illustrates that theory can be used to evaluate statistical problems as well as specify the model. An empirical study should therefore never carelessly discard the theoretical framework after the regression has been specified; it can also provide some useful implications against which the veracity of the estimates can be tested. The interested reader is referred to Binswanger (1) and Weitzman (2) for examples of the procedure suggested by part (a). Weitzman, in fact, used time series data and faces the caveat of (b); Binswanger used cross-sectional data and does not.

References

(1) Binswanger, H.P., "The Measurement of Technical Change Biases with Many Factors of Production," *American Economic Review*, 64:964-976, December 1974.

(2) Weitzman, M., "Soviet Postwar Economic Growth and Capital-Labor Substitution," *American Economic Review*, 60:676-692, 1970.

19. Estimating Constant Elasticity of Substitution
Production Functions with More than Two Factors[1]

Recall from Problem 5 that constant elasticities of
substitution within a production function of more than two
factors imposes one of two restrictions on the structure of
the production function:

(i)   the elasticities between all pairs of factors are
      equal, or

(ii) the elasticities between factors differ, but the
      elasticity between at least one pair is -1.

It is often argued that these conditions place unreasonable
restrictions on empirical studies of production processes.
Investigations of the dual cost schedules are therefore
frequently undertaken to accommodate more complex
structures. Diewert and translog functions are, in
particular, attractive alternatives within which the
correspondence between estimated parameters and elasticities
of substitution can be observed [see Section 12.10].

This problem will not bring these alternative
structures to the table; subsequent problems will do that.
You will be asked here, instead, to concentrate first on the
fundamental source of concern: exactly how restrictive are
the CES representations listed above?

----

[1] Material found in Chapter 12 is directly related to this
problem, with roots back in Chapters 1, 4, and 5.

PROBLEM 19

Questions:

(a) Consider a general production schedule

$$y - f(x_1, x_2, x_3, x_4).\qquad\qquad(1)$$

List the three possible formulations allowed by assuming constant (Allen-Uzawa) elasticities between all factors and suggest a production structure consistent with each.

(b) Show that even blocking the underlying structure as in part (a) does not satisfy the CES restrictions by demonstrating that the structure exhibited in equation (1') cannot be represented by a constant elasticity (Allen-Uzawa) schedule of the type given in equation (1).

$$y = (az_1^\tau + (1-a)z_2^\tau)^{1/\tau}\qquad\qquad(1')$$

where

$$z_1 = (b_1 x_1^\rho + (1-b_1)x_2^\rho)^{1/\rho}\quad\text{and}$$

$$z_2 = (b_2 x_3^r + (1-b_2)x_4^r)^{1/r}.$$

Suggested Solutions:

(a) The first possibility is that the elasticities between all of the factors are equal:

169

PROBLEM 19

$$y = [a_1 x_1^\rho + a_2 x_2^\rho + a_3 x_3^\rho + (1-a_1-a_2-a_3) x_4^\rho]^{1/\rho} \tag{2}$$

so that $\sigma_{ij} = (1/\rho - 1)$.

Different elasticities can be achieved in two ways. One factor could be employed in conjunction with a product of the other three in a specialized manner. The appropriate functional representation would then be

$$y = [x_1^\alpha [a_1 x_2^\rho + a_2 x_3^\rho + (1-a_1-a_2) x_4^\rho]^{(1-\alpha)/\rho}], \tag{3}$$

for which

$$\sigma_{23} = \sigma_{24} = \sigma_{34} = 1/(\rho-1) \text{ and}$$

$$\sigma_{12} = \sigma_{13} = \sigma_{14} = -1.$$

Finally, it is possible for the production of y to divide in "Cobb-Douglas" form into two subprocesses. Equation (4) will illustrate this case, a structure which clearly corresponds to equation (3) of Problem 5:

$$y = [a x_1^\rho + (1-a) x_2^\rho]^{\alpha/\rho} (b x_3^r + (1-b) x_4^r)^{(1-\alpha)/r}. \tag{4}$$

It was shown there that

$$\sigma_{12} = 1/\rho-1, \quad \sigma_{34} = 1/r-1, \text{ and}$$

170

PROBLEM 19

$$\sigma_{13} = \sigma_{14} = \sigma_{23} = \sigma_{24} = -1.$$

The elasticities quoted are applications of equation (17) in Problem 5(b), but they can be computed directly by deriving the unit cost schedules for equations (2), (3), and (4) and applying equation (7) from that same problem.

(b) The production schedule corresponding to equation (1') is the first step in a logical extension of the examples listed in part (a): z_1 and z_2 are employed to produce y through a general, two factor CES schedule. Algebraically,

$$y = [a(b_1 x_1^\rho + (1-b_1) x_2^\rho)^{\tau/\rho} + (1-a)(b_2 x_3^r + (1-b_2) x_4^r)^{\tau/r}]^{1/\tau}. \quad (5)$$

One would expect to find

$$\sigma_{12} = 1/\rho - 1 \equiv \sigma_1, \quad (6a)$$

$$\sigma_{34} = 1/r - 1 \equiv \sigma_2, \text{ and} \quad (6b)$$

$$\sigma_{13} = \sigma_{14} = \sigma_{23} = \sigma_{24} = 1/\tau - 1 \equiv \sigma. \quad (6c)$$

This is, however, not the case. Following the process outlined in Problem 5, the unit cost schedule in terms of z_i corresponding to the production structure of equation (5) is

$$c(w_1, w_2, 1) = [a^{-\sigma}w_1^{1+\sigma} + (1-a)^{-\sigma}w_2^{1+\sigma}]^{1/1+\sigma} \tag{7}$$

where w_i is the marginal cost of producing z_i; i.e.,

$$w_1 = \{ b_1^{-\sigma_1} w_1^{\sigma_1+1} + (1-b_1)^{-\sigma_1} w_2^{\sigma_1+1} \}^{\frac{1}{\sigma_1+1}}, \text{ and}$$

$$w_2 = \{ b_2^{-\sigma_2} w_3^{\sigma_2+1} + (1-b_2)^{-\sigma_2} w_4^{\sigma_2+1} \}^{\frac{1}{\sigma_2+1}}.$$

The logarithmic form of (7), when expanded, is

$$\Lambda(\vec{w}) = \frac{1}{1+\sigma} \log \{ a^{-\sigma}(b_1^{-\sigma_1} w_1^{\sigma_1+1} + (1-b_1)w_2^{\sigma_1+1})^{(\sigma+1)/(\sigma_1+1)}$$

$$+ (1-a)^{-\sigma}(b_2^{-\sigma_2} w_3^{\sigma_2+1} + (1-b_2)w_4^{\sigma_2+1})^{(\sigma+1)/(\sigma_2+1)} \}. \tag{8}$$

While the tedious arithmetic will not be recorded here, it will be quickly obvious that equations (6) will not satisfy the Uzawa [3] relationship when (8) defines $\Lambda(\vec{w})$. That relationship,

$$\frac{\partial^2 \Lambda}{\partial w_i \partial w_j} = (\sigma_{ij} - 1) \frac{\partial \Lambda}{\partial w_i} \frac{\partial \Lambda}{\partial w_j}, \quad i \neq j,$$

will, in fact, immediately reveal that the cross terms

disallow constant elasticities of substitution between any pair of factors.

The results of this problem were, of course, known after Problem 5 was completed. It was included here primarily to illustrate exactly how restrictive the assumption of constant elasticities of substitution is when production involves more than two factors. While a theorist may be able to use a restricted schedule in which the natural division of a production process is Cobb-Douglas through judicious selection of factor indexes, the same restrictions severely hamper any empirical study.

What a priori information can ever be advanced to support fixing one set of elasticities equal to -1? Looking at the generalizations allowed by more complex cost structures can provide some insight, but they are not without restrictive implications of their own. Problem 20 will explore one example, the translog cost schedule.

References

(1) Allen, R.G.D., *Mathematical Analysis for Economists,* London, Macmillan & Co., 1938 (pages 503-509).

(2) McFadden, D., "Constant Elasticity of Substitution Production Functions," *Review of Economic Studies*, 30:73-83, February 1963.

(3) Uzawa, H., "Production Functions with Constant

PROBLEM 19

Elasticities of Substitution," *Review of Economic Studies*,
29:291-299, October 1962.

20. Some Properties of the Translog Cost Function[1]

This problem will explore some of the properties of the translog cost function [see page 210]. The four variable case considered in Berndt and Wood (2) will be explored:

$$\ln \{c(\vec{w},y)\} = \ln a_0 + \ln y + \sum_{j=1}^{4} a_j \ln w$$

$$+ \frac{1}{2} \sum_{i=1}^{4} \sum_{j=1}^{4} b_{ij} \ln w_i \ln w_j. \tag{1}$$

In recording equation (1), y is the output of the production process to be considered, $\vec{w} \equiv (w_1, w_2, w_3, w_4)$ is the price vector for the production factors denoted $\vec{x} = (x_1, x_2, x_3, x_4)$, $b_{ij} = b_{ji}$,

$$\sum_{j=1}^{4} a_j = 1, \text{ and } \sum_{j=1}^{4} b_{ij} = 0$$

for all i and j. Note, in passing, that equation (1) is the dual of $y = f(\vec{x})$ [see Chapter 6 for details]. While translog schedules like this release empirical research from the restrictions of the CES functions, it will be shown here that the cross-elasticities of imputed factor demand are not

---

[1] Material found in Chapter 12, as well as some fundamentals recorded in Chapters 4, 5, and 6, will be applied here.

PROBLEM 20

necessarily symmetric. The final section will nonetheless extend the relevance of the functional form exhibited in equation (1) by outlining a procedure which can be used to test the validity of applying value-added analysis to investment and substitutability studies of $f(\vec{x})$.

Questions:

(a) Show that the parameter restrictions

$$(\sum_{j=1}^{4} a_j = 1, \quad b_{ij} = b_{ji}, \quad \text{and} \quad \sum_{j=1}^{4} b_{ij} = 0)$$

are necessary to guarantee that $c(\vec{w}, y)$ is linearly homogeneous [property (2), page 72].

(b) Derive expressions for the shares of cost devoted to each x_i under profit-maximizing conditions; i.e., compute $s_i = x_i w_i / c(\vec{w}, y)$.

(c) Use the Uzawa (3) result [Problem 5, equation (5)] to derive expressions for the (Allen-Uzawa) elasticities of substitution in terms of the shares [i.e., the s_i from part (b)] and the parameters of equation (1).

(d) Show that the cross-elasticities of input demand are not symmetric; i.e., demonstrate that $\eta_{ij} \neq \eta_{ji}$ where

176

PROBLEM 20

$$\eta_{ij} \equiv \frac{\partial x_i}{\partial w_j} \cdot \frac{w_k}{x_i} \; .$$

(e) The value added of (x_1,x_2) produced through $y = f(\vec{x})$ can be defined

$$p_v v \equiv w_1 x_1 + w_2 x_2 \qquad\qquad (2)$$

where v is real value added and p_v is some sort of deflation that might be necessary. Studying investment in x_1 or x_2 or substitution between x_1 and x_2 through equation (2) where equation (1) summarizes the real production relationship $y = f(x_1,x_2,x_3,x_4)$ requires that changes in x_3 or x_4 neither induce nor reflect any change in x_1 or x_2. One of three assumptions are typically made to support this requirement:

(i) x_3 and x_4 are perfectly correlated with y (either because of coincidental demand and supply shifts or because x_3 and x_4 enter $f(x_1,x_2,x_3,x_4)$ in a Leontief (sub)technology);

(ii) w_3 and w_4 are perfectly correlated with the price of y (either because of coincidental demand and supply shifts or because x_3 and x_4 are perfect substitutes and nonzero); or

(iii) x_1 and x_2 are (weakly) separable from x_3 <u>and</u> x_4 so that $f(x_1,x_2,x_3,x_4)$ can be written $g(h(x_1,x_2),x_3,x_4))$.

This section will explore the last possibility; the first two are, in practice, more easily checked. Weak separability requires (by definition) that the technical rates of substitution between any two factors in the separated partition be invariant with respect to changes in any and all factors outside the partition.

(i) Show that (x_1,x_2) are weakly separable from x_3 and x_4 if and only if $\sigma_{13} = \sigma_{23}$ and $\sigma_{14} = \sigma_{24}$.

(ii) Show then that weak separability requires that

$$b_{23}s_1 - b_{13}s_2 = 0 \text{ and} \tag{3a}$$

$$b_{24}s_1 - b_{14}s_2 = 0. \tag{3b}$$

(iii) What restrictions do (3a) and (3b) place on the parameters of (1) that can be tested by regressing the s_i schedules derived in (b)?

Suggested Solutions:

(a) Consider multiplying the factor price vector $\vec{w}$ by an arbitrary constant α.

$$\ln \{c(\alpha \vec{w}, y)\} = \ln a_0 + \ln y + \sum_{j=1}^{4} a_i \ln (\alpha w_i)$$

$$+ \frac{1}{2} \sum_{i=1}^{4} \sum_{j=1}^{4} b_{ij} \ln (\alpha w_i) \ln (\alpha w_j)$$

$$= \ln a_0 + \ln y + \ln \alpha \sum_{j=1}^{4} a_i + \sum_{j=1}^{4} a_i \ln w_i$$

$$+ \frac{1}{2} \{(\ln \alpha)^2 \sum_{i=1}^{4} \sum_{j=1}^{4} b_{ij} + \ln \alpha \sum_{i=1}^{4} \ln w_i \sum_{j=1}^{4} b_j$$

$$+ \ln \alpha \sum_{j=1}^{4} \ln w_j \sum_{i=1}^{4} b_{ij} + \sum_{i=1}^{4} \sum_{j=1}^{4} b_{ij} \ln w_i \ln w_j\}. \quad (4)$$

Under the restrictions listed, however, equation (4) becomes

$$\ln a_0 + \ln y + \ln \alpha + \sum_{i=1}^{4} a_i \ln w_i + \frac{1}{2} \sum_{i=1}^{4} \sum_{j=1}^{4} \ln w_i \ln w_j$$

$$= \ln c(\vec{w}, y) + \ln \alpha.$$

Slight manipulation then reveals that

$$\ln \{c(\vec{w}, y)\} = \ln \{c(\alpha \vec{w}, y)\} - \ln \alpha = \ln \{c(\alpha \vec{w}, y)/\alpha \},$$

so that applying the antilog transformation yields the desired result:

$$\alpha c(\vec{w}, y) = c(\alpha \vec{w}, y).$$

(b) Logarithmically differentiate equation (1) to observe that

$$\frac{\partial (\ln c(w, y))}{\partial \ln w_i} = a_i + \sum_{j=1}^{4} b_{ij} \ln w_j = \frac{\partial c(\vec{w}, y)}{\partial w_i} \cdot \frac{w_i}{c(\vec{w}, y)} \cdot \quad (5)$$

Since Shephard's lemma [see page 74 in Chapter 5] states that $\{\partial c(\vec{w}, y)/\partial w_i\} = x_i$, the share of costs devoted to x_i, denoted s_i, can be simply characterized by manipulating equation (5):

$$s_i = a_i + \sum_{j=1}^{4} b_{ij} \ln w_j. \quad (5')$$

(c)   Recall from Problem 5 that Uzawa (3) has shown that

$$\sigma_{ik} = - \frac{c(\vec{w}, 1)}{\dfrac{\partial c(\vec{w}, 1)}{\partial w_i}} \frac{\dfrac{\partial^2 (c(\vec{w}, 1))}{\partial w_i \partial w_k}}{\dfrac{\partial c(\vec{w}, 1)}{\partial w_k}} \cdot$$

PROBLEM 20

This relation may be adapted to accommodate any output y by simply keeping that output fixed. It is necessary, therefore, only to employ (5') to compute the indicated partials for an arbitrary $\bar{y}$. To that end, note that

$$\frac{\partial c(\vec{w},\bar{y})}{\partial w_i} = \frac{a_i c(\vec{w},\bar{y})}{w_i} + \frac{c(\vec{w},\bar{y})}{w_i} \sum_{j=1}^{4} b_{ij} \ln w_j = \frac{c(\vec{w},\bar{y})}{w_i} s_i,$$

$$\frac{\partial c(\vec{w},\bar{y})}{\partial w_k} = \frac{a_k c(\vec{w},\bar{y})}{w_k} + \frac{c(\vec{w},\bar{y})}{w_k} \sum_{j=1}^{4} b_{kj} \ln w_j = \frac{c(\vec{w},\bar{y})}{w_k} s_k,$$

$$\frac{\partial^2 c(\vec{w},\bar{y})}{\partial w_i \partial w_k} = \frac{c(\vec{w},\bar{y})}{w_i} \frac{b_{ik}}{w_k} + \frac{1}{w_i} (a_i + \sum_{j=1}^{4} b_{ij} \ln w_j) \frac{c(\vec{w},\bar{y})}{\partial w_k}.$$

As a result, applying equation (5) from Problem 5, again,

$$\sigma_{ik} = - \frac{c(\vec{w},\bar{y}) \{ \dfrac{c(\vec{w},\bar{y}) b_{ik}}{w_i w_k} + \dfrac{c(\vec{w},\bar{y})}{w_i w_k} s_i s_k \}}{\dfrac{c(\vec{w},\bar{y})}{w_i} \dfrac{c(\vec{w},\bar{y})}{w_k} s_i s_k} = - \frac{b_{ik} + s_i s_k}{s_i s_k}.$$

(6)

Observe that these elasticities are well defined, but are not constant unless the shares of both factors are invariant to changes in $\vec{w}$. This observation is consistent with the pattern established in Problem 19 for functional forms that allow constant (Allen) elasticities of substitution.

181

(d) Beginning with

$$\sigma_{ik} = - \frac{c(\vec{w}, \bar{y}) \; \partial x_i / \partial w_k}{x_i x_k},$$

it is a simple matter to show that

$$\eta_{ik} = \frac{\partial x_i}{\partial w_k} \cdot \frac{w_k}{x_i}$$

$$= \frac{\partial x_i}{\partial w_k} \cdot \frac{w_k}{x_i} \left\{ \frac{c(\vec{w}, \bar{y})}{w_k x_k} \; s_k \right\}$$

$$= \sigma_{ik} \, s_k$$

because $s_k \equiv w_k x_k / c(\vec{w}, \bar{y})$. Since s_i is not likely to equal s_k very often, the cross-elasticities of derived demand for factors are not necessarily well defined even though, from equation (6), $\sigma_{ik} = \sigma_{ki}$.

(e) Weak separability requires that the technical rate of substitution between x_1 and x_2 be invariant to changes in x_3 and x_4. Looking at the first-order conditions of

$$\min \; c(\vec{w}, y)$$

$$\text{s.t.} \quad y = f(x_1, x_2, x_3, x_4)$$

shows that one version of that technical rate is

$$\frac{\partial c(\vec{w}, y)}{\partial w_1} \Big/ \frac{\partial c(\vec{w}, y)}{\partial w_2} .$$

The other, more standard version involves the partials of $f(x)$ with respect to x_1 and x_2. Invariance with respect to x_3 and x_4 therefore requires either that

$$\frac{\partial \left(\frac{\partial f}{\partial x_1} \Big/ \frac{\partial f}{\partial x_2}\right)}{\partial x_3} = \frac{\partial \left(\frac{\partial f}{\partial x_1} \Big/ \frac{\partial f}{\partial x_2}\right)}{\partial x_4} = 0$$

or that

$$\frac{\partial \left(\frac{\partial c}{\partial w_1} \Big/ \frac{\partial c}{\partial w_2}\right)}{\partial w_3} = \frac{\partial \left(\frac{\partial c}{\partial w_1} \Big/ \frac{\partial c}{\partial w_2}\right)}{\partial w_4} = 0. \tag{7}$$

Using equation (7), then, one can observe two crucial relationships:

$$\frac{\partial c}{\partial w_2} \left(\frac{\partial^2 c}{\partial w_1 \partial w_3}\right) - \frac{\partial c}{\partial w_1} \left(\frac{\partial^2 c}{\partial w_2 \partial w_3}\right) = 0 \text{ and} \tag{8a}$$

$$\frac{\partial c}{\partial w_2} \left(\frac{\partial^2 c}{\partial w_1 \partial w_4}\right) - \frac{\partial c}{\partial w_1} \left(\frac{\partial^2 c}{\partial w_2 \partial w_4}\right) = 0. \tag{8b}$$

Equation (8a) can be manipulated to look like

$$\frac{\dfrac{\partial^2 c}{\partial w_1 \partial w_3}}{\dfrac{\partial c}{\partial w_1}} = \frac{\dfrac{\partial^2 c}{\partial w_2 \partial w_3}}{\dfrac{\partial c}{\partial w_1}} \;; \quad \text{i.e.,}$$

$$\frac{c \dfrac{\partial^2 c}{\partial w_1 \partial w_3}}{\dfrac{\partial c}{\partial w_3} \dfrac{\partial c}{\partial w_1}} = \frac{c \dfrac{\partial^2 c}{\partial w_2 \partial w_3}}{\dfrac{\partial c}{\partial w_3} \dfrac{\partial c}{\partial w_2}} \; . \tag{9}$$

Applying equation (5) from Problem 5, this time to equation (9), $\sigma_{13} = \sigma_{23}$.

Similar manipulation of (8b) yields $\sigma_{14} = \partial_{24}$, and part (i) is completed. To see why (ii) is true, notice from (i) and equation (6) that

$$\sigma_{13} = - \frac{b_{13} + s_1 s_3}{s_1 s_3} = - \frac{b_{23} + s_2 s_3}{s_2 s_3} = \sigma_{23} \text{ and}$$

$$\sigma_{14} = - \frac{b_{14} + s_1 s_4}{s_1 s_4} = - \frac{b_{24} + s_2 s_4}{s_2 s_4} = \sigma_{24} \; .$$

Cancellation of like terms and cross multiplication in these equations completes (ii):

$$b_{23}s_1 - b_{13}s_2 = 0 \text{ and} \tag{10a}$$

$$b_{24}s_1 - b_{14}s_2 = 0 . \tag{10b}$$

Equations (10a) and (10b) can be satisfied under two

conditions:

condition (I): $b_{23} = b_{13} = b_{24} = b_{14} = 0$ and $\qquad$ (11)

condition (II): $s_1/s_2 = b_{13}/b_{23} = b_{14}/b_{24}.$

Condition (II) is, furthermore, fulfilled if and only if

$$a_1/a_2 = b_{11}/b_{21} = b_{12}/b_{22} = b_{13}/b_{23} = b_{14}/b_{24} . \tag{12}$$

Equation (11) therefore gives one set of conditions that can

be tested in running regressions on the s_i; it corresponds

to the (partial) Cobb-Douglas case where $\sigma_{13} = \sigma_{23} = \sigma_{14} = \sigma_{24}$

$= -1$. Equation (12) gives a second set of restrictions that

can also be tested in running the s_i regressions. If both

of these conditions can be rejected, then $f(\vec{x})$ cannot be

presumed separable and (e.g.) using the concept of value

added is invalid (unless otherwise justified as indicated

before). Notice finally that condition (I) implies that

(s_1+s_2), the total share of x_1 and x_2, is constant; this is a

property of the underlying Cobb-Douglas technology.

Condition II meanwhile implies a fixed ratio of shares

(s_1/s_2).

This problem has, for the most part, reproduced and filled in the theoretical background to Berndt and Wood (2). Their analysis is important for at least two reasons. First of all, they found that capital and energy are complementary while labor and energy are mild substitutes. Rapid increases in the price of energy would thus favor labor (in the long run) while an investment tax credit (as well as other policies designed to induce investment) would generate an energy intensive economy.

Perhaps more importantly, working through the Berndt and Wood analysis makes it clear that imposing the restrictions consistent with weak separability derived in part (e) on the regressions indicated by equation (5') allowed them to construct chi-square tests that strongly rejected applicability of value-added techniques at the 99% level (the first two possible justifications were easily dismissed). Serious doubt was thereby placed over the published conclusions of many who had projected energy demand on the basis of ratios of energy use to real value added.

It should be noted, finally, that the separability conditions cited in (e) are easily generalizable to partitions of more than two members. The reader is refered to Berndt and Christensen (1) for details.

PROBLEM 20

References

(1) Berndt, E.R. and L.R. Christensen, "The Internal Structure of Functional Relationships: Separability, Substitution and Aggregation," *Review of Economic Studies*, 40:403-410, July 1973.

(2) _____, and D.O. Wood, "Technology, Prices and the Derived Demand for Energy," *Review of Economics and Statistics*, 57:259-268, August 1975.

(3) Binswanger, H.P., "The Measurement of Technical Change Biases with Many Factors of Production," *American Economic Review*, 64:964-976, December 1974.

(4) Uzawa, H., "Production Functions with Constant Elasticities of Substitution," *Review of Economic Studies*, 29:291-299, October 1962.

21. Flexible Functional Representations of Production Technology and Consumer Preferences[1]

The applied econometric literature has always been interested in developing flexible function forms with which to represent production technologies and consumer preferences. The notion behind this interest is familiar, by now; flexible CES structures of more conventional function forms build systematic errors into the analysis where the true underlying structure is not homothetic, displays variable returns to scale, and so on. It is thought that using more general representations might add power to the estimation of elasticities of substitution, shares, demand elasticities, scale economies, and other important behavioral parameters.

This problem will introduce one flexible form that has emerged from this literature in the context of production, explore a few of its properties, note how it collapses to more familiar forms under special assumptions, and investigate the translog approximation of its dual that is used in estimation procedures.

Define a production schedule

$$y = \phi(x_1, \ldots, x_n) = g^{-1}[f(x_1, \ldots, x_n)] \qquad (1)$$

---

[1] Material drawn from Chapters 1, 4, 5, and 6 provides more detail than the discussions found in Chapter 12.

PROBLEM 21

where

$$g(y) = ye^{\theta y} \quad \text{and} \tag{2}$$

$$f(x_i, \ldots, x_n) = [\sum_{i=1}^{n} \delta_i x_i^{\rho_i}]^{1/\rho} . \tag{3}$$

Output is represented here by y, while inputs are indexed by the x_i. Assume that each input is available at unit cost w_i. Collecting terms, then, production is to be summarized by

$$ye^{\theta y} = [\sum_{i=1}^{n} \delta_i x_i^{\rho_i}]^{1/\rho}. \tag{4}$$

Several parametric restrictions are required to guarantee that equation (4) appropriately represents usual behavior. They include, for all $(x_1, \ldots, x_n)$,

[1] $\theta > - 1/y$;

[2] $\delta_i > 0$ with $\sum \delta_i = 1$; and

[3]   either

(i) $\rho < 0$ and $\rho_i < 0$,

(ii) $\rho > 0$ and $1 > \rho_i > 0$, or

(iii) $\rho = \rho_i = 0$.

PROBLEM 21

Notice that equation (4) is simply a standard CES schedule with the elasticity of substitution between any x_i and x_n equalling $[1/(1-\rho)]$ if $\theta = 0$ and $\rho_i = \rho$. Equation (4) is even simpler when $\theta = \rho = \rho_i = 0$; it collapses to the Cobb-Douglas form.

Questions:

(a) An expansion path is said to be radial if it is a ray from the origin of input/factor space [see the graphs on page 18]. Show that expansion paths for the Cobb-Douglas technology are <u>all</u> radial. Show, as well, why they are not radial for the technology represented in equation (4) unless $\rho_i = \rho_j$ for all i and $j = 1, \ldots, n$.

(b) Show that the "returns to scale elasticity" [i.e., from page 17, $[d \ln y / d \ln \lambda]$ for $y = f(\lambda x_1, \ldots, \lambda x_n)$] is unity for the Cobb-Douglas technology and variable for the technology of equation (4).

(c) Let equation (4) be approximated in its dual representation [consult Chapter 6] by a translog representation:

$$\ln c(y,\bar{w}) = a_0 + a_y \ln y + \frac{1}{2}a_{yy} (\ln y)^2 + \sum_{i=1}^{n} a_i \ln w_i$$

190

PROBLEM 21

$$+ \frac{1}{2} \sum_{i=1}^{n} \sum_{j=1}^{n} a_{ij} \ln w_i \ln w_j + \sum_{i=1}^{n} a_{iy} \ln w_i \ln y \qquad (5)$$

[see the example on page 210]. Express the share devoted to x_i, denoted S_i, in terms of the parameters implicitly defined in equation (5).

(d) Express the Allen-Uzawa elasticities of substitution [see Problem 5] in terms of the parameters in equation (5) and the shares devoted to the various inputs.

Suggested Solutions:

(a) Expansion paths are radial if any (w_1/w_2) ratio leads a cost-minimizing firm to the same (x_1/x_2) ratio regardless of the absolute level of employment; i.e., $(\lambda \bar{x}_1/\lambda \bar{x}_2)$ must be associated with $(\bar{w}_1/\bar{w}_2)$ for any $\lambda > 0$ for all $(\bar{w}_1/\bar{w}_2)$ and $(\bar{x}_1/\bar{x}_2)$ picked from the unit isoquant. For the simple Cobb-Douglas case [see equation 4.1 on page 50],

$$\frac{w_1}{w_2} = \frac{a}{1-a} \frac{\lambda x_1}{\lambda x_2} = \frac{a}{1-a} \frac{x_1}{x_2}$$

and the expansion paths are radial.

For the formulation expressed in equation (4), however,

$$\frac{w_1}{w_2} = \frac{\partial y/\partial x_1}{\partial y/\partial x_2} = \frac{\rho_i \delta_i (\lambda x_i)^{-\rho_i-1}}{\rho_j \delta_j (\lambda x_j)^{-\rho_j-1}}$$

$$= \frac{\rho_i \delta_i (\lambda x_i)^{-\rho_i-1}}{\rho_j \delta_j (\lambda x_j)^{-\rho_j-1}} \quad \frac{\lambda^{-\rho_i-1}}{\lambda^{-\rho_j-1}}$$

$$\neq \frac{\rho_i \delta_i (x_i)^{-\rho_i-1}}{\rho_j \delta_j (x_j)^{-\rho_j-1}} \tag{6}$$

unless $\rho_i = \rho_j$.

(b)   For the simple Cobb-Douglas case, again,

$$\frac{\partial y}{\partial \lambda} = ax_1(\lambda x_1)^{-1}y + (1-a)x_2(\lambda x_2)^{-1}y = \lambda^{-1}y$$

so that

$$\frac{\partial \ln y}{\partial \ln \lambda} = \frac{\lambda}{y} \lambda y^{-1} = 1 .$$

For (4), meanwhile,

$$\frac{\partial y}{\partial \lambda} = \frac{(1/\rho) \Sigma \delta_i \rho_i x_i (\lambda x_i)^{-\rho_i}}{e^{\theta y}(1+\theta y)}$$

192

PROBLEM 21

and

$$\frac{\partial \ln y}{\partial \ln \lambda} = \frac{\lambda}{\rho} \frac{\Sigma \delta_i \rho_i x_i (\lambda x_i)^{-\rho_i}}{y e^{\theta y}(1+\theta y)} \neq 1. \tag{7}$$

(c) Given the translog approximation recorded above in equation (5),

$$\frac{\partial \ln c}{\partial \ln w_i} = a_i + \sum_{j=1}^{n} a_{ij} \ln w_j + a_{iu} \ln u$$

$$= \frac{\partial c}{\partial w_i} [w_i/c]. \tag{8}$$

Shepard's lemma [page 74] again comes into play, and yields

$$\frac{\partial c}{\partial w_i} = x_i \; ,$$

and so

$$a_i = \sum_{j=1}^{n} a_{ij} \ln w_j + a_{iu} \ln u = \frac{w_i x_i}{c} = S_i$$

(d) Recall the Uzawa result that

$$\sigma_{ik} = - \frac{c(\vec{w},1) \dfrac{\partial^2 c(\vec{w},1)}{\partial w_i \partial w_k}}{\dfrac{\partial c(\vec{w},1)}{\partial w_i} \dfrac{\partial c(\vec{w},1)}{\partial w_k}} . \tag{9}$$

We know from equation (8) that

$$\frac{\partial c(\vec{w},1)}{\partial w_i} = \frac{c(\vec{w},1)}{w_i} \{a_i + \sum_{j=1}^{n} a_{ij} \ln w_j + a_{iu} \ln u\} = S_i$$

and

$$\frac{\partial c(\vec{w},1)}{\partial w_k} = \frac{c(\vec{w},1)}{w_k} \{a_k + \sum_{j=1}^{n} a_{kj} \ln w_j + a_{ku} \ln u\} = S_k .$$

Furthermore,

$$\frac{\partial^2 c(\vec{w},1)}{\partial w_i \partial w_j} = \frac{1}{w_i}\{c(\vec{w},1)\frac{a_{ik}}{w_k}(a_i + \sum_{j=1}^{n} a_{ij} \ln w_j + a_{iu} \ln u)\frac{\partial c(\vec{w},1)}{\partial w_k}\}$$

$$= c(\vec{w},1)\{ \frac{a_{ik}}{w_i w_k} + [a_k + \sum_j a_{ij} \ln w_j + a_{iu} \ln u]$$

$$\cdot [a_{k_j} + \sum_j a_{kj} \ln w_j + a_{ku} \ln u]\}$$

$$= \frac{c(\vec{w},1)}{w_i w_k} \{a_{ik} + S_i S_k\} .$$

From equation (9) therefore, it is now clear that

$$\sigma_{ik} = - \frac{\dfrac{[c(\vec{w},1)]^2}{w_i w_k}}{\dfrac{c(\vec{w},1)}{w_i} S_i} \cdot \frac{a_{ik} + S_i S_k}{\dfrac{c(\vec{w},1)}{w_k} S_k} = - \frac{a_{ik} + S_i S_k}{S_i S_k} .$$

There are costs to approximating flexible function forms with translog representations. Thursby and Lovell (4) and Wales (5) worry about the deterioration of approximations as the range of observation expands. Guilkey and Lovell (3) worry about the range of complexity that the approximations can handle accurately. The reader is referred to these papers and others recorded in their references in the event that the procedures outlined here might appear to be useful.

References

(1) Berndt, E.R., and M.S. Khaled, "Parametric Productivity Measurement and Choice Among Flexible Functional Forms," *Journal of Political Economy*, 87:1220-1245, 1939.

(2) Berndt, E.R., and D.O. Wood, "Technology, Prices, and the Derived Demand for Energy," *Review of Economics and Statistics*, 57:259-268, 1975.

(3) Guilkey, C.K., and C.A. Knox Lovell, "On the Flexibility

of the Translog Approximation," *International Economic Review*, 21:137-143, 1980.

(4) Thursby, J., and C.A.K. Lovell, "An Investigation of the Kmenta Approximation to the CES function," *International Economic Review*, 19:363-397, 1938.

(5) Wales, T.J., "On the Flexibility of Flexible Functional Forms," *Journal of Econometrics*, 5:183-193, 1978.

22. **Some Implications of the Independence of Price and Income on the Structure of Demand**[1]

It is a fairly simple matter to test for statistical correlation between price and income in any set of demand data. If the hypothesis that such correlation exists can be rejected at a reasonable level, a long string of very strong conclusions can be drawn. The demand schedules must, for example, display (locally) constant income elasticities. For multiple goods, these elasticities must either equal unity or coincide with all of the other income elasticities. A resulting property of the cross-price derivative allows an explicit representation of the underlying indirect utility function, and exact consumer surplus comparisons are therefore possible.

Willig first expressed some of these results in (1), a work that preceded his more familiar *American Economic Review* piece (2). Varian (3) put them all more succinctly. This problem begins what will be a two part exercise to reproduce much of their work.

Questions.

(a) Suppose that the demand for x_i exhibits no

---

[1] Material found in Chapter 8 is be employed here to explore some of the consequences of empirical insights which might result from application of various parts of Chapter 12.

correlation between income and price. Show that the demand schedule must be of the form

$$x_i(\vec{p}, y) = \chi_i(\vec{p}) y^{e_i} \tag{1}$$

where $\vec{p}$ is a price vector, y is income, and e_i is the income elasticity of demand.

(b) Suppose that the demand schedules for x_1 and x_2 look like (1); i.e., suppose that

$$x_i(\vec{p}, y) = \chi_i(\vec{p}) (y/y_0)^{e_i}$$

in a neighborhood of some point $(\vec{p}, y_0)$. Show that

$$(i) \quad e_1 = e_2 \text{ with } \partial x_1/\partial p_2 = \partial x_2/\partial p_1,$$

$$(ii) \quad e_1 = 1 \text{ with } \partial x_1/\partial p_2 = 0, \text{ or}$$

$$(iii) \quad e_2 = 1 \text{ with } \partial x_2/\partial p_1 = 0.$$

It will be convenient to set units so that $y_0 = 1$.

Suggested Solutions.

Part (a) follows directly from Euler's law; it is a straightforward result. Part (b) follows after some manipulation from the Slutsky symmetry condition [property 4 on page 123] that

$$\frac{\partial h_i(\vec{p},\bar{u})}{\partial p_j} = \frac{\partial h_j(\vec{p},\bar{u})}{\partial p_i} \quad .$$

You will recall [from Section 8.5 beginning on page 125] that this symmetry condition is the key to the integrability problem.

(a)   Let the demand for a good x_i be represented

$$x_i(\vec{p},y) = \chi_i(\vec{p})g_i(y). \qquad (2)$$

Demand schedules are homogeneous of degree zero in prices and income [to see why, note that doubling (e.g.) income and prices does nothing to the first-order conditions which characterized utility maximization subject to a budget constraint - see page 100].   As a result,

$$x_i(t\vec{p},ty) = t^0 x_i(\vec{p},y) = x_i(\vec{p},y). \qquad (3)$$

Differentiating (3) with respect to t and using (2),

$$g_i(y) \sum_{j=1}^{n} p_j \frac{\partial \chi_i}{\partial p_j} + \chi_i(\vec{p})y \frac{\partial g_i}{\partial y} = 0.$$

Rearranging some terms, then,

$$\left\{ \sum_{j=1}^{n} \frac{p_j}{x_i} \frac{\partial x_i}{\partial p_j} \right\} = - \frac{y}{g_i(y)} \frac{\partial g_i}{\partial y} = - e_i, \tag{4}$$

where e_i is the income elasticity of demand:

$$e_i \equiv \frac{y}{x_i(\vec{p},y)} \frac{\partial x_i}{\partial y}.$$

The right- and left-hand sides of (4) depend exclusively on income and prices, respectively, so they must both be constant. Solving the differential equation

$$\frac{y}{g_i(y)} \frac{\partial g_i}{\partial y} = e_i$$

therefore produces the result:

$$g_i(y) = y^{e_i};$$

it is unique up to a constant.

(b) The Varian proof of this result comes from the observation that the Slutsky symmetry conditions are sufficient to guarantee that a set of demand schedules can be integrated "up" to the underlying utility schedule. Building constant elasticities of income into the Slutsky restrictions [Sections 8.2 and 8.3 beginning on page 119] is sufficient. Given (1),

$$\frac{\partial h_i(\vec{p},\bar{u})}{\partial p_j} = \frac{\partial h_j(\vec{p},\bar{u})}{\partial p_i}$$

[property 4 on page 123] can be written

$$\frac{\partial x_1}{\partial p_2} y^{e_1} + e_1 x_1 y^{e_1-1} x_2 y^{e_2} = \frac{\partial x_2}{\partial p_1} y^{e_2} + e_2 x_2 y^{e_2-1} x_1 y^{e_1} \qquad (5)$$

where units have been defined so that $y_0 = 1$. Rearranging equation (5),

$$\frac{\partial x_1}{\partial p_2} = \frac{\partial x_2}{\partial p_1} y^{e_2-e_1} + x_1 x_2 y^{e_2-1} (e_2-e_1). \qquad (6)$$

Differentiating (6) twice with respect to y will complete the construction of the requisite apparatus:

$$0 = \frac{\partial x_2}{\partial p_1}(e_2-e_1)^2 y^{e_2-e_1-1} + x_1 x_2(e_2-e_1)(e_2-1)y^{e_2-2} \qquad (7a)$$

$$0 = \frac{\partial x_2}{\partial p_1} (e_2-e_1)(e_2-e_1-1)y^{e_2-e_1-1} + x_1 x_2 (e_2-e_1)(e_2-2)y^{e_2-3}.$$

$$(7b)$$

Now let $e_1 = e_2$. Immediately, equation (6) shows that

$$\frac{\partial x_1}{\partial p_2} = y^{e_1} \frac{\partial x_1}{\partial p_2} = \frac{\partial x_2}{\partial p_1} y^{e_2} = \frac{\partial x_2}{\partial p_1}. \qquad (8)$$

When $e_1 \neq e_2$, however, equation (7a) shows that

$$\frac{\partial x_2}{\partial p_1} = - x_1 x_2 y^{e_1-1} (e_2-1) \qquad (9)$$

so that equation (7b) reduces to

$$- (e_2-1)(e_2-e_1-1) + (e_2-1)(e_2-2) = 0. \qquad (10)$$

If $e_2 \neq 1$, then e_1 must be unity to satisfy (10). From equations (6) and (9), therefore,

$$\frac{\partial x_1}{\partial p_2} = - x_1 x_2 y^{e_1-1} (e_2-1)y^{e_2-e_1} + x_1 x_2 y^{e_2-1} (e_2-e_1)$$

$$= - x_1 x_2 (e_2-1)y^{e_2-1} + x_1 x_2 y^{e_2-1} (e_2-1) = 0$$

and

$$\frac{\partial x_1}{\partial p_2} = Y_1^{e_1} \frac{\partial x_1}{\partial p_2} = 0.$$

What might be termed "indexing symmetry" can now be employed to handle the final case; simply substitute x_1 for x_2 everywhere above.

The results produced here make it clear that fairly simple econometric testing could lead to a great deal of information about the structure of demand. If price and income were found to be unrelated for a variety of goods, more specifically, then

(1) demand for each would reflect constant income elasticity and

(2) all of these income elasticities that were not equal to unity would be equal to each other.

A later problem will show how this information can be employed to write an explicit representation of the underlying indirect utility function and subsequently justify (or qualify) consumer surplus computations. The key there will be that equation (8) guarantees that the necessary integrals are independent of the chosen path of integration.

PROBLEM 22

The underlying point of departure in all of this work
is the Slutsky symmetry restriction on demand schedules: the
cross-derivative of the corresponding Hicksian compensated
demand schedules must be symmetric. Old property 4 from
page 123 is remarkably powerful.

References

(1) Willig, R., "Integrability Implications for Locally
Constant Demand Elasticities," *Journal of Economic Theory*,
12:391-401, 1976.

(2) _____, "Consumer's Surplus without Apology,"
American Economic Review, 66:589-597, 1976.

(3) Varian, H.R., "A Note on Constant Income Elasticities,"
Economic Letters, 1:9-13, 1978.

23. On the Structure of Consumer Demand[1]

Empirical studies of consumer demand have long been
conducted under a variety of assumptions. Pioneering
studies by Schultz (7), Wold (12), and Stone (8) employed
logarithmic demand schedules consistent only with log linear
utility. Similar restrictions in the work by Barten (1 and
2) and Theil (10 and 11) also require log linear utility.
Log linear utility is, in turn, both homothetic and
additive. Subsequent studies have relaxed the homotheticity
restriction [see Houthakker (4), Stone (9), and Sato (6)],
but the additivity assumption has persisted. It is
important, therefore, to devise statistical tests designed
to determine when homotheticity and/or additivity are
admissible assumptions. This problem will explore the
genesis of early results in this area produced by Jorgenson
and Lau (5).

Consider a reciprocal indirect utility function

$$\ln h = \ln h(\vec{q})$$

where $\vec{q} \equiv (q_1, \ldots, q_n)$, $q_i = p_i/y$ for all i, $\vec{p} = (p_1, \ldots, p_n)$
is the vector of prices for $\vec{x} = (x_1, \ldots, x_n)$, and y is
income. The budget constraint for the consumers whose

---

[1] Material from Chapter 12 is applicable here; results drawn
from Chapters 7, 8, and 9 will be employed.

tastes are summarized here is given by

$$\vec{p} \cdot \vec{x} \leq y.$$

Questions:

(a) Use the conditions which characterize utility maximization subject to a budget constrain [page 100] to construct an expression for the share of income devoted to any x_j in terms of $\ln q_i$ when $\ln h$ conforms to a second-order logarithmic expansion (the translog reciprocal indirect utility function):

$$\ln h(\vec{q}) = a_0 + \sum_{i=1}^{n} a_i q_i + \frac{1}{2} \sum_{i=1}^{n} \sum_{j=1}^{n} b_{ij} \ln q_j. \qquad (1)$$

Homogeneity requires that $\sum a_i = 1$ in equation (1). The expressions derived here for the shares are the regression equations through which the tests are run; the tests are constructed on the parameter estimates.

(b) Utility is additive if it can be expressed

$$\ln h = F\{ \sum_{i=1}^{n} \ln h^i(q_i)\}. \qquad (2)$$

PROBLEM 23

Note that the h^i functions in equation (2) depend only on the associated q_i; that is the essence of additivity in this context. Show b_{ij} must match $\theta a_i a_j$ identically for all $i \neq j = 1, \ldots, n$ in any translog approximation like equation (1) if the condition recorded in equation (2) is to hold.

(c) Utility as expressed in equation (1) will reflect homothetic preferences if it can be written

$$\ln h = F[\ln g(\vec{q})] \qquad (3)$$

where $g(\vec{q})$ is linearly homogeneous of degree 1 [see Section 9.2 on page 146]. Show that utility can be homothetic only if

$$\sum_{i=1}^{n} b_{ik} = \theta' a_k, \quad k = 1, \ldots, n$$

in any translog approximation like (1).

Suggested Solutions:

The key to the last two parts of this problem lies in the manner in which the second-order logarithmic expansions approximate the arbitrary $h(q)$. At the point of approximation, in particular,

$$\frac{\partial \ln h(\vec{q})}{\partial \ln q_i} = a_i, \quad i = 1,\ldots,n, \text{ and}$$

$$\frac{\partial \ln h(\vec{q})}{\partial \ln q_i \partial \ln q_j} = b_{ij}, \quad i \neq j = 1,\ldots,n.$$

(a) Roy's identity [page 106] states that

$$x_i(\vec{p},y) = -\frac{\partial v(\vec{p},y)/\partial p_i}{\partial v(\vec{p},y)/\partial y} \quad ; \quad \text{i.e.,}$$

$$x_i(\vec{p},y) = -\frac{\partial h(\vec{q})/\partial p_i}{\partial h(\vec{q})/\partial y} \quad ; \quad \text{i.e.,} \tag{4}$$

because by definition, $h(\vec{q}) \equiv 1/v(\vec{p},y)$. Multiplying both sides of equation (4) by p_i/y and dividing both the numerator and denominator of the right hand by $h(\vec{q})$ transforms this identity:

$$\frac{p_i x_i}{y} = -\frac{\partial \ln h/\partial \ln p_i}{\partial \ln h/\partial \ln y}. \tag{5}$$

PROBLEM 23

Along any schedule of the form suggested by equation (1), then

$$\frac{\partial \ln h}{\partial \ln p_j} = \frac{\partial \ln h}{\partial \ln q_j} \frac{\partial \ln q_j}{\partial \ln p_j} = (a_j + \sum_{k=1}^{n} b_{jk} \ln q_k) \, ,$$

and

$$\frac{\partial \ln h}{\partial \ln y} = - [\sum_{j=1}^{n} \frac{\partial \ln h}{\partial \ln q_j} \frac{\partial \ln q_j}{\partial \ln y}]$$

$$= - [\sum_{j=1}^{n} (a_j + \sum_{k=1}^{n} b_{jk} \ln q_k)] \, .$$

As a result,

$$\frac{p_i x_i}{y} = \frac{a_i + \sum_{k=1}^{n} b_{ik} \ln q_k}{A + \sum_{k=1}^{n} B_k \ln q_k}, \quad i = 1, \ldots, n$$

where $A \equiv \sum_{i=1}^{n} a_i$ and $B_k \equiv \sum_{j=1}^{n} b_{jk}$. These are the regression equations.

(b) Looking at equation (2) in light of equation (1), the approximating translog schedule must satisfy

$$a_j = \frac{\partial \ln h}{\partial \ln q_j} = F' \frac{\partial \ln h^i}{\partial \ln q_j}; \quad j = 1,\ldots,n \quad \text{and} \quad (6)$$

$$b_{ij} = \frac{\partial^2 \ln h}{\partial \ln q_i \partial \ln q_j} = F'' \frac{\partial \ln h^i}{\partial \ln q_i} \frac{\partial \ln h^j}{\partial \ln q_j} \quad (7)$$

for $i \neq j = 1,\ldots,n$ because $(\partial h^i/\partial x_j) = 0$. Notationally, of course,

$$F' = \partial(\ln h/(\partial \ln h^i) \text{ and}$$

$$F'' = \partial^2(\ln h)/(\partial \ln h^j)^2.$$

Combining equations (6) and (7), it is seen, then, that additivity requires that

$$b_{ij} = \theta a_i a_j, \quad i \neq j = 1,\ldots,n.$$

(c) Given equation (3), the approximation requires that

$$\frac{\partial \ln h}{\partial \ln q_i} = a_i = \frac{\partial \ln F}{\partial \ln g} \frac{\partial \ln g}{\partial \ln q_i}; \quad i = 1,\ldots,n, \text{ and} \quad (8)$$

$$
\frac{\partial^2 \ln h}{\partial \ln q_i \partial \ln q_j} = \frac{\partial \ln F}{\partial \ln g} \frac{\partial \ln g}{\partial \ln q_i \partial \ln q_j}
$$

$$
+ \frac{\partial^2 \ln F}{\partial (\ln h)^2} \frac{\partial \ln g}{\partial \ln q_i} \frac{\partial \ln g}{\partial \ln q_j} = b_{ij} \qquad (9)
$$

for $i \neq j = 1, \ldots, n$. The homogeneity of $g(\vec{q})$ now comes into play. An alternative statement of Euler's law shows that

$$
\sum_{i=1}^{n} \frac{\partial \ln g}{\partial \ln q_i} = 1. \qquad (10)
$$

Differentiating (9), then,

$$
\sum_{i=1}^{n} \frac{\partial^2 \ln g}{\partial \ln q_i \partial \ln q_j} = 0, \quad j = 1, \ldots, n. \qquad (11)
$$

Adding (9) across all $j = 1, \ldots, n$, applying equations (8), (10), and (11) and the normalization that $1 = \sum_{k=1}^{n} a_k$ finally produces the desired result:

$$
\sum_{i=1}^{n} b_{ik} = \theta' a_k, \quad k = 1, \ldots, n.
$$

Jorgenson and Lau (5) continue to provide conditions

for utility schedules that are simultaneously additive and homothetic. They produce these results with translog approximations of the direct utility function, but the conditions are identical. They also provide conditions under which (e.g.) a homothetic approximation guarantees that the original schedule is homothetic. The interested reader is referred to their paper for further details. An application of the procedures which they developed is provided there. It is enough for this problem to have illustrated how tests for traditionally accepted assumptions can be constructed.

References

(1) Barten, A.P., "Consumer Demand Functions under Conditions of Almost Additive Preferences," *Econometrica*, 32:1-38, 1964.

(2) Barten, A.P., "Maximum Likelihood Estimation of a Complete System of Demand Equations," *European Economic Review*, 1:7-73, 1969.

(3) Christensen, L.R., D.W. Jorgenson, and L.J. Lau, "Transcendental Logarithmic Utility Functions," *American Economic Review*, 65:367-383, 1975.

(4) Houthakker, H.S., "Additive Preferences," *Econometrica*, 28:244-57., 1960.

(5) Jorgenson, D.W., and L.J. Lau, "The Structure of

Consumer Preferences," *Annals of Economic and Social Measurement*, 4:49-101, 1975.

(6) Sato, K., "Additive Utility Functions with Double-Log Consumer Demand Functions," *Journal of Political Economy*, 80:102-124, 1972.

(7) Schultz, H., *Theory and Measurement of Demand*, Chicago, Chicago University Press, 1938.

(8) Stone, J.R.N., *Measurement of Consumers' Expenditures and Behaviours in the United Kingdom*, Cambridge, Cambridge University Press, 1954.

(9) Stome, J.R.N., "Linear Expenditure Systems and Demand Analysis: An Application to the Pattern of British Demand," *Economic Journal*, 64:511-527, 1954.

(10) Theil, H., "The Information Approach to Demand Analysis," *Econometrica*, 33:67-87, 1965.

(11) _____, *Principles of Econometrics*, Amsterdam, North Holland, 1971.

(12) Wold, H., *Demand Analysis: A Study in Econometrics*, New York, Wiley, 1953.

24. **Monopoly, Uncertainty, and the International Flow of Goods**[1]

Some of the traditional trade literature has linked forms of industrial organization with international flows of goods. This problem will draw from one piece of that literature contributed by White (4) in which the effect of monopoly power on import competition is explored. His motivation in writing was practical. Many policy analysts had come before Congress asking for liberalization of the antitrust legislation in markets where import competition was keen. It had been thought that allowing the increased efficiencies that accompany domestic concentration of market power in those markets would reduce imports and help the balance of trade.

These arguments were advanced in the face of results reported by Krause (2), for example, that rising steel imports seemed to have no limiting effect on domestic steel prices. White constructed a model of uncertainty in the foreign price that shed a great deal of light on the proposed policies. His analysis forms the basis of this problem.

Consider a firm with a cost schedule c(y) and an associated U-shaped average cost curve. There is a domestic

---

[1] Material found in Chapters 13 and 14 is applicable here; fundamental results from Chapters 2, 4, and 5 are employed.

demand schedule for y, $p_d = p_d(y)$ that is known to the firm.
Imports can fill some of that demand under the small country
assumption; i.e., as much y as the market will bear is
available from importers at some world price p_w. All that
the firm knows about p_w before it makes its production
decision is that it has a cumulative probability
distribution $G(p_w)$. The firm considered here sets output,
and can sell its output $\bar{y}$ at $p_d(\bar{y})$ read from the demand
curve if $p_d(\bar{y}) \leq p_w$, but can sell at only p_w if $p_d(\bar{y}) \geq p_w$.

Questions:

(a) Show that a profit-motivated, risk neutral
monopolist in this circumstance will choose an output
characterized by the equality of marginal cost and
expected marginal revenue.

(b) Show that the monopolist's output is less than the
competitive output (specifying the competitive output
carefully). Argue from this result that the monopolist
allows higher levels of imports.

(c) Show how the result produced in part (b) depends on
the price elasticity of demand.

PROBLEM 24

Suggested Solutions:

(a) For any particular output level y, a firm can generate revenue under one of two possible situations; the revenue side of (expected) profits must reflect both. If, on the one hand, the import price (p_w) lies above the price associated with y on the domestic demand curve (p_d), then the firm can earn the full amount p_dy. Since the likelihood that $p_w \geq p_d$ is $[1-G(p_d)]$, the corresponding component of expected revenue is

$$[1-G(p_d)]p_dy.$$

Whenever $p_w < p_d$, on the other hand, the world price dominates and the firm can earn only p_wy. The expected revenue generated under this circumstance is therefore

$$\int_0^{p_d} p_wyg(p_w)\ dp_w.$$

Combining these two components of expected revenue with a cost schedule produces an expression for the firm's expected profits:

$$E\pi = [1-G(p_d)]p_dy + \int_0^{p_d} p_wyg(p_w)\ dp_w - c(y). \tag{1}$$

The profit-motivated monopolist can do no better than maximize (1) with respect to y. Since p_d depends on y, the appropriate first-order condition is

$$[1-G(\hat{p}_d)][\hat{p}_d+\hat{y}(\partial p_d/\partial y)] - \hat{p}_d\hat{y}g(\hat{p}_d)(\partial p_d/\partial y) + \hat{p}_d\hat{y}g(\hat{p}_d)(\partial p_d/\partial y)$$

$$+ \int_0^{\hat{p}_d} p_w g(p_w) \; dp_w = \frac{\partial c}{\partial y}[\hat{y}]; \tag{2}$$

$\hat{y}$ and $\hat{p}_d$ reflect the monopolist's choice of output and price, respectively.

Marginal revenue along the domestic demand schedule looks like $[p_d + y(\partial p_d/\partial y)]$; marginal revenues when the world price dominates (i.e., $p_w < \hat{p}_d$) is fixed at p_w. The left-hand side of (2) therefore reduces to

$$MR(\hat{p}_d)[1-G(\hat{p}_d)] + \int_0^{\hat{p}_d} p_w g(p_w) \; dp_w, \tag{3}$$

the weighted sum of the marginal revenue generated by $\hat{y}$ across all of the possible contingencies. The expression in (3) is, in fact, the _expected_ marginal revenue of the firm's output decision.

In maximizing (1), therefore, the monopolist chooses an output such that expected marginal revenue equals the marginal cost of production. This interpretation of (2) clearly corresponds immediately with the profit-maximizing condition reported for the certainty case [see page 24].

(b)   In long-run competitive equilibrium with U-shaped average costs, pure economic profits are zero when demand is known with certainty [see Section 13.4 on page 219].   When demand is variable, however, only _expected_ pure economic profits are zero.   From (1), therefore,

$$p^*_d \left[1-G(p^*_d)\right] + \int_0^{p^*_d} p_w g(p_w)\, dp_w = c(y^*)/y^*, \qquad (4)$$

where p^*_d indicates the competitive price and y^* indicates the competitive output.   The right-hand side of equation (4) is, of course, the average cost of producing y^*.   In equilibrium, however, $AC(y^*) = MC(y^*)$ to assure zero (expected) profits, and the long-run equilibrium condition can finally be summarized by

$$p^*_d\left[1-G(p^*_d)\right] + \int_0^{p^*_d} p_w g(p_w)\, dp_w = \frac{\partial c}{\partial y}(y^*). \qquad (5)$$

The competitive equilibrium is therefore characterized by the equality of the _expected_ price, average costs, and marginal costs.

Comparisons of equations (2) and (5) can now produce the desired conclusions.   As long as $[1-G(p^*_d)] < 1$ (i.e., as long as there is a chance that $p_w > p^*_d$), it can be argued that $\hat{y} < y^*$.   To see this point, notice that marginal revenue is always less than the price for any output along a negatively sloped demand schedule [MR(y) = p(y) + y[∂p/∂y] < p(y) because ∂p/∂y < 0]. Unless the left-hand sides of equations (2) and (5) involve only the integral term (i.e., unless $G(p^*_d)$ = 1), the left-hand side of (5) must exceed that of (2) for any given output. Since the right-hand sides of both equations are marginal cost schedules, marginal costs for the monopolist must therefore be less in equilibrium than they would be for the competitors whenever [1 - $G(p^*_d)$] < 1. It is required by the shape of c(y), as a result, that $\hat{y} < y^*$. The monopolist therefore exposes the domestic market to more frequent and larger import competition by choosing to produce a lower output and setting a higher price cutoff.

(c) Writing the marginal revenue term of (2) in terms of the price elasticity of demand pays immediate dividends. The monopolist's first-order condition becomes

$$\hat{p}_d[1+(1/\varepsilon(\hat{y}))][1+G(\hat{p}_d)] + \int_0^{\hat{p}_d} p_w g(p_w) \, dp_w = \frac{\partial c}{\partial y}(\hat{y})$$

$$= [(1+G(\hat{p}_d))/\varepsilon(\hat{y})] + \{\hat{p}_d [1+G(\hat{p}_d)] + \int_0^{\hat{p}_d} p_w g(p_w) \, dp_w\}. \quad (6)$$

Notice that equation (6) can replicate equation (5) if and only if $\varepsilon(\hat{y})$ = -∞. In words, when the domestic demand schedule is horizontal, the monopolist has no "monopoly power" and simply behaves as a perfect competitor in his or her own best interest. Otherwise, $\hat{y} < y^*$, as shown in part (b), as the monopolist exercises market power derived from the sloping demand curve. The more inelastic demand, the larger that power and the smaller is $\hat{y}$ relative to y^*.

White also found similar results for models in which the world price was known but domestic demand was uncertain. Unless there are mitigating covariances, then, it is unlikely that allowing both to be uncertain would change the result.

Further analysis of the potential (marginal) cost efficiencies of monopolies showed that these efficiencies must be large enough to outweigh the increase in market power (reflected by $\varepsilon(y)$) if they are to have a favorable impact on the balance of trade. The liberalization of antitrust laws in these markets could therefore have easily been counterproductive. This is but one of many cases in which care must be taken in weighing the effect of market power - power frequently measured in terms of elasticity.

References

(1)   Esposito, L., and F.F. Esposito, "Foreign Competition and Domestic Industry Profitability," *Review of Economics and Statistics*, 53: 343-353, 1971.

(2)   Krause, L.B., "The Import Discipline: The Case of the United States Steel Industry," *Journal of Industrial Economics*, 11: 33-47, 1962.

(3)   Leland, H.E., "Theory of the Firm Under Uncertainty," *American Economic Review*, 62: 278-291, 1972.

(4)   White, L.J., "Industrial Organization and International Trade," *American Economic Review*, 64: 1013-1020, 1974.

(5)   Williamson, O.E., "Economics as an Antitrust Defense: The Welfare Tradeoffs," *American Economic Review*, 58: 18-36, 1968.

PROBLEM 25

25. **Excess Capacity as a Barrier to Entry**[1]

It should be clear that the ability of existing firms to restrict entry can have a significant effect on their long-run equilibrium position [see Section 13.5 on page 220]. Strategies that firms can exercise to preclude the entry of potential competitors are thus of more than passing interest. Several authors [see Gaskins (1) and Kamien and Schwartz (2)] have studied a "limit pricing" approach [see Section 16.13 on page 308]. This strategy observes that if output is maintained at a sufficiently high level (with a correspondingly low price), then new firms will not enter because the residual demand cannot profitably support any more firms. Limit prices tend to be very close to competitive prices.

Spence (3) proposed a second strategy that involved maintaining _excess_ capacity that could be employed to ward off threatening entrants. He envisioned, more specifically, excess capacity which would allow existing firms to expand output quickly if entry were threatened, and thereby reduce prospective profits; this capacity would be idle, at least to some degree, otherwise. This problem will explore the Spence model.

Material found in Chapters 13, 14, and 16 is applicable here; the analysis will draw heavily on the fundamental concepts of costs described in Chapters 4 and 5.

PROBLEM 25

Suppose that a firm operated along a cost schedule $c(y,k)$, where y is output, k is capacity, $(\partial c/\partial y) > 0$, $(\partial^2 c/\partial y^2) > 0$, and $(\partial^2 c/\partial y \partial k) < 0$. Let the sale of y generate revenue $R(y)$ along a demand curve $p(y)$, and assume that capacity costs r per unit (interest on debt or opportunity cost).

Questions:

(a) Characterize the efficient, cost-minimizing capacity for any y.

(b) Characterize a capacity k* for which the existing firms can always preclude entry by driving the price so low that no new firm could make a nonnegative profit.

(c) Show that providing k* increases output and reduces the price if k* is larger than the capacity that would be chosen if entry were not a concern.

(d) Show that providing k* effectively puts a lid on the possible return to capacity (capital) that is below what it could be.

Suggested Solutions:

(a) Total costs are $c(y,k) + rk$, so efficient capacity is characterized for each level of output by the solution to

$$\min \{c(y,k) + rk\}.$$

The first-order condition requires, simply, that

$$\frac{\partial c(y,k)}{\partial k} + r = 0. \tag{1}$$

(b)   Suppose that someone were to enter the market with a capacity k'.   Equilibrium would occur at a new, lower price, and everyone would set the outputs to equate their marginal cost with that price.   Notationally,

$$p' = p(y'+y) = \frac{\partial c}{\partial y}(y,k) = \frac{\partial c}{\partial y}(y',k'), \tag{2}$$

where {y,k} correspond to the output and capacity of the existing firms, {y',k'} correspond to the output and capacity of the entrant, and p(--) is the demand schedule. The entrant will proceed only if his average cost of producing y' exceeds the price p'.   Plans for entry will be canceled, therefore, if

$$p'(k,k') < \frac{c(y'(k,k'),k')}{y'(k,k')} + \frac{rk'}{y'(k,k')}. \tag{3}$$

To block all threat of entry, then, existing firms need only set k equal to the minimum value (k*) for which (3) holds

PROBLEM 25

for all k'.

(c) Existing firms simply solve the problem

$$\max R(y) - c(y,k) - rk$$

$$\text{s.t.} \quad k \geq k^*.$$

(4)

The appropriate Lagrangian is then

$$L(y,k) \equiv (R(y) - c(y,k) - rk) + t(k-k^*).$$

Since corner solutions are an interesting possibility, complete Kuhn-Tucker conditions for solutions to (4) are recorded:

$$\frac{\partial R(y)}{\partial y} - \frac{\partial c}{\partial y}(y,k) = 0$$

(5)

$$\frac{\partial c}{\partial k}(y,k) + t = 0$$

(6)

$$t(k,k^*) = 0$$

(7)

$$t \geq 0.$$

(8)

The last two constraints accomodate the boundary possibilities. If t = 0, then unconstrained maximization would yield the same result. The constraint k > k* is not, in other words, binding, and entry would have been blocked automatically even before Spence wrote his paper. Whenever t ≠ 0, however,

$$\frac{\partial c}{\partial k}(y,k) + r = t > 0 \tag{9}$$

does not coincide with (6). Capacity is higher than optimal and costs are not minimized for the output that is produced. Furthermore, since the second-order condition for a maximum with respect to y is

$$\frac{\partial^2 R}{\partial y^2} - \frac{\partial^2 c}{\partial y^2} < 0,$$

total differentiation of equation (5) reveals that

$$\frac{dy}{dk} = \frac{\partial^2 c/\partial y\partial k}{[(\partial^2 R/\partial y^2) - (\partial^2 c/\partial y^2)]} > 0.$$

The exaggerated capacity that discourages entry therefore increases output and decreases the price of the good being produced.

(d) The rate of return to a given amount of capacity (k) is equal to its nominal cost (rk) and whatever is left of maximum profits, given k, after that cost and production costs are met. Notationally, then, this return can be expressed, on a per unit basis, as

$$\rho(k) \equiv (1/k)\{ \max_{y} (R(y) - c(y,k) - rk)\} + r. \qquad (10)$$

Graphing (10) in Figure 25.1 shows that the return to capacity is limited when k* is binding. To see why, observe, first of all, that $\rho(k) \geq r$ for the existing firm to be turning a nonnegative profit. This will be shown to require that k* lie to the right of k_{max} that maximizes $\rho(k)$. Since the constraint requires $k' \geq k*$, the claim will be proven. The slope of $\rho(k)$ with respect to k is, to that end, easily computed:

$$\frac{\partial p}{\partial k} = \frac{k(\partial/\partial k) - \max (R(y) - c(y,k) - rk) - rk}{k^2}. \qquad (11)$$

By manipulating equation (11) in light of (10), it can be observed that $\partial\rho/\partial k > 0$ would require that $-\{\partial c/\partial k\} > \rho(k)$. Solutions to equation (6) satisfy

$$-\{\partial c/\partial k\} = r - t \leq \rho(k)$$

when $k \geq k*$ is binding, though, so they cannot lie on the upward-sloping region of $\rho(k)$. If the return to capacity can be thought of as a return to capital, the fear of entry is thus seen to restrict the return that capital can earn.

Spence included a probabilistic model in his paper, but its results supported qualitatively the same result:

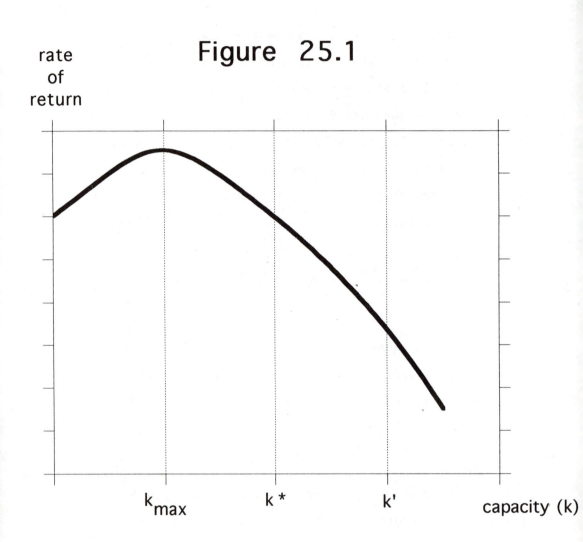

Figure 25.1

existing firms could meet the threat of entry by maintaining excess capacity and producing a bit more than they would otherwise. They may, therefore, lower the price of their output, somewhat, but not as far as predicted by the limit pricing models. In fact, Spence's probabilistic model allowed the possibility that the threat of entry could actually push the price up. There is no guarantee, therefore, that the threat of entry would cause welfare to climb, even on the consumer side of the market.

References

(1) Gaskins, D.W., "Dynamic Limit Pricing: Optimal Pricing Under the Threat of Entry," *Journal of Economic Theory*, 3: 306-322, 1971.

(2) Kamien, M.E., and N.L. Schwartz, "Limit Pricing and Uncertain Entry," *Econometrica*, 39: 441-454, 1971.

(3) Spence, A.M., "Entry, Capacity, Investment and Oligopolistic Pricing," *Bell Journal of Economics*, 8: 534-544, 1977.

26. A Locational Theory of Monopolistic Competition[1]

Harold Hotelling (3) published the first example of monopolistic competition through location in 1929. His work was the harbinger of the more sophisticated models contributed later by (e.g.) Chamberlin (2), Salop (4), and Stern (6) among others. Because modern characterizations of long-run equilibrium have simplified the Hotelling problem, it is possible to capture the essence of his work very quickly. The first two parts of this problem will, to that end, show that monopolistic competition among goods that differ only in the location of their production and sale exhibits a long-run equilibrium with too many firms. A comparison of this analysis with Salop's can then be illuminating. Before suggesting some comparisons, though, a final part of this problem points out that even this structure might be too general to allow some simple comparative statics to be determinate.

For the first two parts, consider a long road with demand for a perishable good x being equally dense along its length. Demand for x is thus proportional to the length of a road segment; without loss of generality, define units so that the constant of proportionality equals 1. Suppose further that the production of x involves a fixed cost f

---

[1] These questions are germane to the topics covered in Chapter 14; material from Chapter 13 will be applied.

and some variable cost cx. Finally, let delivery costs be a constant b per unit x per unit distance.

Questions:

(a) Show that the competitive equilibrium optimally spaces firms $\delta* = 2(f/b)^{1/2}$ units of distance apart.

(b) Monopolistic competition involves many firms selling close substitutes of the same generic good. Each firm therefore has some small degree of monopoly power over the sale of its particular "brand" of this good - a brand which can somehow be distinguished from all of the other close substitutes that are available. Long-run equilibrium is characterized by zero pure economic profit, with each firm operating along a demand curve with large, but finite price elasticity.

In this problem, good x available for sale from any one firm can be distinguished from good x available from other firms on the basis of firm location. Show that the long-run monopolistically competitive equilibrium, as described above, supports twice as many firms as the competitive solution in (a).

(c) Suppose now that demand for a good facing a firm with some market power like a monopolistic competitor is

$$p = p(x,q,a),$$

where q reflects quality and a represents advertising. Let production costs be c(x,q) and advertising costs be A(a). Use the second-order conditions for profit maximization to show that an excise tax on consumption will decrease profit-maximizing output, but has an ambiguous effect on both quality and advertising.

Suggested Solutions:

(a) Total production costs are

$$c(x) = f + cx,$$

so that the average total costs of servicing a length of road δ with a firm in the center are

$$ac(\delta) = c + (b\delta/4) + (f/\delta).$$

Notice that average delivery costs are $(b\delta/4)$ because demand is δ, costs are constant at b per unit distance, and the firm is located in the center of its market; i.e., delivery costs are

$$\int_0^{\delta/2} bs \, ds = (1/8)b\delta^2$$

for either half of the market so that _average_ delivery costs are

$$(1/2)[(1/8)(b\delta^2)]/(\delta/2) + (1/2)[(1/8)(b\delta^2)]/(\delta/2) = (b\delta/4).$$

The competitive equilibrium then consists of firms a distance $\delta*$ apart where $\delta*$ solves

$$\min \{c + (b\delta/4) + (f/\delta)\}.$$

The first-order condition requires

$$(b/4) = f(\delta*)^{-2},$$

so that

$$\delta* = 2(f/b)^{1/2}. \tag{1}$$

(b) The monopolistically competitive solution requires some knowledge of the demand side. For any price that the firm changes at its door, $\bar{p}$, the demand schedule can be written as a function of distance from the firm:

$$p(\delta) = \bar{p} - b\delta \tag{2}$$

since delivery is essentially a marketing cost. Marginal revenue for (2) is then

$$mr(\delta) = \bar{p} - 2b\delta.$$

Equilibrium requires not only that average production cost equal price [so that pure economic profits are zero], but also that marginal production cost equal marginal revenue [so that profits are maximized; see page 24]. It can be shown that tangency of the demand and average cost schedules guarantees both conditions. It is clear, then, that the new equilibrium distance δ' satisfies

$$\bar{p} - b\delta' = c + (f/\delta') \text{ and}$$

$$\bar{p} - 2b\delta' = c.$$

Combining these by purging $\bar{p}$,

$$c + (f/\delta') - b\delta' = c,$$

and so

$$\delta' = (f/b)^{1/2} = (1/2)\delta*.$$

The firms are half as far apart; there are twice as many of them.

(c) Profit maximization produces the first-order conditions that

$$\frac{\partial \pi}{\partial x} = \hat{x} \frac{\partial p}{\partial x} + p(\hat{x}, \hat{q}, \hat{a}) - \frac{\partial c}{\partial x} = 0, \tag{3}$$

$$\frac{\partial \pi}{\partial q} = \hat{x} \frac{\partial p}{\partial q} - \frac{\partial c}{\partial q} = 0, \text{ and} \qquad (4)$$

$$\frac{\partial \pi}{\partial a} = \hat{x} \frac{\partial p}{\partial a} - \frac{\partial A}{\partial a} = 0. \qquad (5)$$

The triple $(\hat{x}, \hat{q}, \hat{a})$ will be a maximum if $D^2\pi$ $(\hat{x}, \hat{q}, \hat{a})$ is negative semidefinite [see page 475]; i.e.,

$$[dx, dq, da] \begin{vmatrix} \dfrac{\partial^2 \pi}{\partial x^2} & \dfrac{\partial^2 \pi}{\partial x \partial q} & \dfrac{\partial^2 \pi}{\partial x \partial a} \\[2ex] \dfrac{\partial^2 \pi}{\partial x \partial q} & \dfrac{\partial^2 \pi}{\partial q^2} & \dfrac{\partial^2 \pi}{\partial q \partial a} \\[2ex] \dfrac{\partial^2 \pi}{\partial x \partial a} & \dfrac{\partial^2 \pi}{\partial q \partial a} & \dfrac{\partial^2 \pi}{\partial a^2} \end{vmatrix} \begin{vmatrix} \partial x \\[2ex] \partial q \\[2ex] \partial a \end{vmatrix} \le 0. \qquad (6)$$

Equation (6) will, in turn, be satisfied if the diagonal elements of $D^2\pi$ are nonpositive, $|D^2\pi| \le 0$, and all of the two by two determinants surrounding the diagonal of the form

$$\begin{vmatrix} \dfrac{\partial^2 \pi}{\partial i^2} & \dfrac{\partial^2 \pi}{\partial i \partial j} \\[2ex] \dfrac{\partial^2 \pi}{\partial i \partial j} & \dfrac{\partial^2 \pi}{\partial j^2} \end{vmatrix}$$

are nonnegative.

If an excise tax were levied against the sale of x, profits would be

PROBLEM 26

$$\pi'(\hat{x}, \hat{q}, \hat{a}) = \pi(\hat{x}, \hat{q}, \hat{a}) - t\hat{x}.$$

Only equation (3) among the first-order conditions would change. Its new form would be

$$\hat{x} \frac{\partial p}{\partial x} + p(\hat{x}, \hat{q}, \hat{a}) - \frac{\partial c}{\partial x} = t. \tag{3'}$$

The impact of the tax can now be studied by differentiating equations (3'), (4), and (5) with respect to t. The resulting linear equations summarize the results:

$$[D^2\pi(\hat{x}, \hat{q}, \hat{a})] \quad \begin{vmatrix} \partial x/\partial t \\ \partial q/\partial t \\ \partial a/\partial t \end{vmatrix} = \begin{vmatrix} 1 \\ 0 \\ 0 \end{vmatrix}.$$

Cramer's rule [see page 477] then shows that

$$\frac{\partial \hat{x}}{\partial t} = \begin{vmatrix} \dfrac{\partial^2 \pi}{\partial q^2} & \dfrac{\partial^2 \pi}{\partial q \partial a} \\ \\ \dfrac{\partial^2 \pi}{\partial q \partial a} & \dfrac{\partial^2 \pi}{\partial a^2} \end{vmatrix} \Big/ |D^2\pi| \le 0. \tag{7}$$

The sign of (7) follows from the second-order condition (6). The effect of t on $(\hat{q}, \hat{a})$ cannot be similarly determined, though. For example,

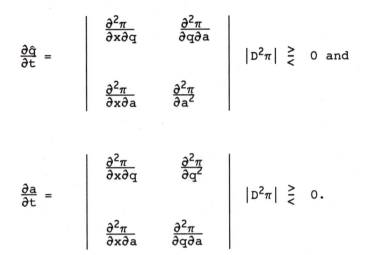

$$\frac{\partial \hat{q}}{\partial t} = \begin{vmatrix} \frac{\partial^2 \pi}{\partial x \partial q} & \frac{\partial^2 \pi}{\partial q \partial a} \\ \\ \frac{\partial^2 \pi}{\partial x \partial a} & \frac{\partial^2 \pi}{\partial a^2} \end{vmatrix} \quad |D^2 \pi| \gtreqless 0 \text{ and}$$

$$\frac{\partial a}{\partial t} = \begin{vmatrix} \frac{\partial^2 \pi}{\partial x \partial q} & \frac{\partial^2 \pi}{\partial q^2} \\ \\ \frac{\partial^2 \pi}{\partial x \partial a} & \frac{\partial^2 \pi}{\partial q \partial a} \end{vmatrix} \quad |D^2 \pi| \gtreqless 0.$$

Archibald (1) was the first to observe the qualitative implications of part (c). He provided it as an example of the Chicago criticism of Chamberlin: if the theory of monopolistic competition is to be useful, it must be provided with enough structure to allow some simple predictive analytics to be determinate. Since advertising and quality are important aspects of the nonprice competition that appears in these industries, his point here is probably well taken.

The Hotelling model presented in (a) and (b) was also introduced as the first of its type. It differs from the Salop (4) work in a fundamental way. Hotelling was able to avoid worrying terribly about how one firm affects another by characterizing equilibrium among firms that appeared simultaneously in the equilibrium position. Salop considers these interactions explicitly, though, and thereby comes up with the three potential equilibrium configurations.

References

(1) Archibald, G.C., "Chamberlin versus Chicago," *Review of Economic Studies*, 29:2-28, 1961.

(2) Chamberlin, E.H., *The Theory of Monopolistic Competition,* 5th edition, Cambridge, Mass., Harvard University Press, 1946.

(3) Hotelling, H., "Stability in Competition," *Economic Journal*, 39: 41-57, 1929.

(4) Salop, S., "Monopolistic Competition Reconstituted," Federal Reserve Board mimeo, 1977.

(5) Salop, S., and J.E. Stiglitz, "A Framework for Analyzing Monopolistically Competitive Price Determination," Federal Reserve Board mimeo, 1975.

(6) Stern, N., "The Optimal Size of Market Areas," *Journal of Economic Theory*, 4: 154-173, 1972.

27. **Product Diversity under Monopolistic Competition**[1]

Michael Spence has contributed a major portion of a literature studying the product diversity provided by monopolistic competition. The reader is referred immediately to the references cited for an introduction to this work. This problem will concentrate on Spence (4), and his observations that large fixed costs (whether production setup costs or marketing costs like advertising) on complementary goods can lead to the production of inadequate quantities of too few goods. Inelastic demand heightens the likelihood that fixed costs will influence product diversity because the firms' inability to be price discriminators is more significant. The complementarity result underscores why Chamberlin considered close substitutes in his initial model. Spence continues to argue that high (low) own and cross elasticities of demand can lead to a monopolistically competitive equilibrium with too many (few) products. The concluding remarks will suggest why the former results add at least intuitive support to the latter. The reader is referred to Problem 26 for a description of long-run equilibrium in monopolistically competitive markets.

Let there be n goods in the monopolistically

---

[1] Material found in Chapters 13, 14, and 15 is applicable here. The analysis presented will draw from prior coverage in Chapters 2, 4, and 10; a measure of welfare derived from consumer and producer surplus will also be employed.

competitive industry; index them $\vec{x} \equiv (x_1, \ldots, x_n)$. Each x_i is produced by a single firm whose costs are

$$c_i(x_i) + F_i,$$

where the $c_i = c_i(x_i)$ are variable costs and the F_i are fixed costs. Denote demand for x_i by $p_i = p_i(\vec{x})$ so that the effects of changes in x_j on the price of x_i can be reflected for all j.

Questions:

(a) Assume that the firms can discriminate fully along $p_i(\vec{x})$; i.e., assume that the ith firm can charge $p_i(x_1, \ldots, k_i, \ldots, x_n)$ for the k_i^{th} unit of x_i sold. This is surely not a realistic assumption, but it will help make a point. Revenues for the ith firm under perfect price discrimination can then be represented

$$R_i(x_i) = \int_0^{x_i} p_i(\vec{x} - x_i e_i + s e_i) \, ds, \qquad (1)$$

where e_i is a vector of (n-1) zeros and a single 1 in the ith place. Profits for the ith firm, then, are simply

$$\pi_i(x_i) = R_i(x_i) - c_i(x_i) - F_i. \qquad (2)$$

Total welfare generated by the industry can meanwhile be

PROBLEM 27

represented

$$W(\vec{x}) = \sum_{i=1}^{n} \int_{0}^{x_i} pi(\vec{x}-x_i e_i+se_i) \ ds - \sum_{i=1}^{n} (c_i(x_i)+F_i); \qquad (3)$$

W is the sum of consumer and producer surpluses [see Chapter 10 and Section 13.7 on page 222]. There is some problem in using the regular (Marshallian) demand curve, but (3) holds in approximation and can be interpreted as the amount of money above production costs consumers are willing to spend for $\vec{x}$. With this apparatus, show that there exists a Nash equilibrium (of firms maximizing $\pi_i(x_i)$ given the outputs of the others) that maximizes $W(\vec{x})$.

(b) Two goods are said to be strong complements if an increase (e.g.) in x_i not only increases p_j, but also increases the marginal revenue of the jth firm producing a given x_j. Assume now that each firm can charge only one price for all it sells.

(i) Show first that strong complementarity implies

$$\frac{\partial x_j}{\partial x_i} > 0, \ i \neq j = 1,\ldots,n, \qquad (4)$$

for a profit-maximizing producer of x_j.

(ii) Show further that monopolistic competition leads

to a suboptimally low production of too few products if they produce strong complements.

Suggested Solutions:

Solutions to both parts follow directly from the apparatus that has been constructed. Welfare-maximizing competitive solutions are first characterized and then contrasted with the monopolistically competitive equilibrium. In part (a), the characterizations are identical. They are not in (b,ii), though, and tracing the effects of moving from the competitive equilibrium to the monopolistically competitive solution produces the desired result. Part (b,i) is computational.

(a) First observe that an optimal allocation of production that maximizes $W(\vec{x})$ exists. This is because a maximum exists for any subset of possible production mixes within $\vec{x}$ if the $p_i(\vec{x})$ and $c_i(x_i)$ are appropriately shaped. Since there are a finite number of <u>distinct</u> subsets of $\vec{x}$, one of these constrained optima is the unconstrained optimum of $W(\vec{x})$. Call that optimum $\vec{x}* \equiv (x_1*,\ldots,x_n*)$. Since, from equations (1), (2), and (3)

$$W(\vec{x}) = \sum_{i=1}^{n} \pi_i(x_i),$$

though, it can be argued that each component of $\vec{x}*$ is chosen to maximize its contribution to $W(\vec{x})$; i.e., x_i* maximizes $\pi_i(x_i)$ <u>given</u> the other $\{x_j*\}_{j\neq i}$. That is precisely how monopolistic competitors would behave, so $\vec{x}*$ is a possible Nash equilibrium for a monopolistically competitive market.

(b) First notice that marginal revenue for the ith firm is

$$mr_i(\vec{x}) \equiv p_i + x_i(\partial p_i/\partial x_i).$$

If x_i and x_j are strong complements, then,

$$\frac{\partial mr_i(\vec{x})}{\partial x_j} = \frac{\partial p_i}{\partial x_j} + x_i \frac{\partial^2 p_i}{\partial x_i \partial p_j} > 0. \tag{5}$$

The profit-maximizing monopolistic competitor of x_i meanwhile produces according to the first-order condition that marginal revenue equal marginal cost; i.e., that

$$p_i + x_i(\partial p_i/\partial x_i) = (\partial c_i/\partial x_i). \tag{6}$$

Differentiating equation (6) with respect to x_j completes the process:

$$\frac{\partial p_i}{\partial x_j} + \frac{\partial p_i}{\partial x_i}\frac{\partial x_i}{\partial x_j} + \frac{\partial p_i}{\partial x_i}\frac{\partial x_i}{\partial x_j} + x_i\{\frac{\partial^2 p_i}{\partial x_i \partial x_j} + \frac{\partial^2 p_i}{\partial x_i^2}\frac{\partial x_i}{\partial x_j}\}$$

$$= \frac{\partial^2 c_i}{\partial x_i^2} \frac{\partial x_i}{\partial x_j} \quad .$$

As a result,

$$\frac{\partial x_i}{\partial x_j} = \frac{(\partial p_i/\partial x_j) + x_i(\partial^2 p_i/\partial x_i \partial x_j)}{(\partial^2 c_i/\partial x_i^2) - 2(\partial p_i/\partial x_i) - x_i(\partial^2 p_i/\partial x_i^2)} > 0. \qquad (7)$$

The sign follows because the denominator is positive from the appropriate second-order conditions.

The second part is a bit more complicated. For a given set of commodities, the competitive optimum is characterized by the equality of price and marginal cost; i.e.,

$$p_i(\vec{x}) = (\partial c_i/\partial x_i). \qquad (8)$$

The second-order condition accompanying (8) further requires that

$$(\partial^2 c_i/\partial x_i^2) > (\partial p_i/\partial x_i). \qquad (9)$$

In moving from solutions of equation (8) to solutions of equation (6), therefore, production of every x_i must fall. To see this, notice first of all that

$$x_i(\partial p_i/\partial x_i) < 0.$$

If x_i were to rise from the solution to (8), then, equation (9) says that the right-hand side would fall slower (if $\partial^2 c_i / \partial x_i^2 < 0$) than the left-hand side. Larger x_i could therefore never accommodate the negative $x_i(\partial p_i / \partial x_i)$ term added in equation (6). This effect is amplified if $(\partial^2 c_i / \partial x_i^2) > 0$.

Production must therefore fall if equation (6) is to be satisfied. From equation (7), furthermore, each reduction amplifies all the rest, and the effect can be quite dramatic, especially when demand is inelastic. To compound the problem, notice that

$$\frac{\partial \pi_i}{\partial x_j} = x_i \frac{\partial p_i}{\partial x_j} + p_i \frac{\partial x_i}{\partial x_j} > 0.$$

Reductions in x_i cause profits to fall at the other firms. The movement to equation (6) could therefore even make some of the existing firms unprofitable. Output of the remaining firms would therefore be lower under monopolistic competition, and there may even be fewer firms.

The points made by this problem are several. First of all, Spence has shown that when the goods are not strong substitutes and the firms discriminate as in part (a), consumers still receive a positive net benefit; in other words, their surplus is not totally extracted as it would be by a perfectly (first degree) discriminating monopolist [see

245

Section 14.5 on page 241]. In addition, part (a) shows that
the ability to discriminate can actually favorably influence
product selection by covering fixed costs. Since
monopolistic competition can support a welfare maximum if
the firms can discriminate, then any market failure
associated with monopolistic competition is essentially
caused by their inability to discriminate, for whatever
reason.

Part (b) meanwhile proves that monopolistic
competition is an unlikely structure across complementary
goods. Horizontal merger is, however, more likely in such
cases than the widespread shutdown predicted here.

Finally, Spence continued in his paper to argue that
circumstances characterized by high (low) own and cross
elasticities of demand were likely to spawn monopolistic
competition among too many (few) firms. The results
reproduced here are at least suggestive of these final
conclusions. Inelastic demand provides one situation in
which the differences between perfect price discrimination
and one price marketing are severe; the optimality result in
part (a) can hardly be approximated in such a circumstance.
Furthermore, low cross elasticities approach the realm of
complementarity, and part (b) would then come into play.
The Spence result just quoted thereby garners substantial
intuitive support. The interested reader is referred to
that later portion of Spence (4).

References

(1) Dixit, A.K., and J.E. Stiglitz, "Monopolistic Competition and Optimum Product Diversity," *American Economic Review*, 67: 297-308, 1977.

(2) Owen, B., and A.M. Spence, "Television Programming, Monopolistic Competition and Welfare," Institute for Mathematical Studies in the Social Sciences, Stanford University, 1975.

(3) Spence, A.M., "Monopoly, Quality and Regulation," Institute for Mathematical Studies in the Social Sciences, Stanford, University, 1975.

(4) Spence, A.M., "Product Selection, Fixed Costs, and Monopolistic Competition," *Review of Economic Studies*, 43: 271-286, 1976.

28. Resource Stock Externalities[1]

The ability of a firm to exert some market power is not the only way in which a market can fail to operate most efficiently. This problem will explore a nonpecuniary diseconomy whose basis lies at the very heart of perfect competition; the competitive market will be shown to overproduce when each firm ignores its individual negative effect on the availability of a crucial factor of production. It is patterned after the partial equilibrium analysis of resource stock externalities by Vernon Smith (3). He considers a competitive fishing industry in which the catch of each ship diminishes the fish population and makes it more difficult for the others to make a profitable catch. A second problem will compare these results with those produced by Smith (4) in general equilibrium.

Consider an industry with n firms each producing y_i in accordance with

$$y_i = f(x_i, Y), \tag{1}$$

where x_i is some factor like labor and

$$Y \equiv \sum_{i=1}^{n} y_i$$

---

[1] Material found in Chapters 1 through 4 will be employed to explore some of the ramifications of competitive markets – concepts developed most fully in Chapter 13.

is the industry's total output. Equation (1) reflects a

diseconomy of industry production if

$$\frac{\partial f}{\partial y} (x_i, Y) \equiv f_2(x_i, Y) < 0;$$

for notational ease in this problem, subscripts after the

functionals denote partial derivatives. Let p reflect the

price of output, w be the price of x, and π be the canonical

profit of a firm in the industry that keeps firms from

entering or leaving the industry. Finally, for simplicity,

assume that all the firms are identical so that

$$Y = nf(x_i, \ Y) = nf[(X/n), \ Y] \tag{1'}$$

where $X \equiv \sum_{i=1}^{n} x_i$, $x_i \equiv (X/n)$, and $y_i = (Y/n)$.

Questions:

(a) Characterize the employment of factors by a

competitive firm, and use those equations and (1') to

show that the elasticity of industry supply is positive

as long as $f(x_i, y)$ reflects a diseconomy; i.e., as long

as $f_2(x_i, Y) < 0$.

(b) Show that marginal costs exceed average costs at the

PROBLEM 28

long-run competitive equilibrium,.

(c) Characterize optimal industry output (cost-
minimizing output) and show that it is less than the
amount supplied under the competitive equilibrium. Also
show that competitive firms employ factors efficiently.

Suggested Solutions:

The method of solution for this problem simply
involves manipulating the appropriate first-order conditions
and relevant definitions. The most efficient way of
summarizing the efficient use of factors is by expressing
the ratio (w/π) in terms of competitive and optimal
solutions [denoted $(\hat{x}_i, \hat{Y})$ and (x_i^*, Y^*), respectively].

(a) In choosing a level of x_i that solves

$$\max \{pf(x_i, Y) - wx_i\},$$

each firm can earn a variety of returns by adjusting output
along the first-order condition

$$pf_1(\hat{x}_i, \hat{Y}) = w. \tag{2}$$

If the canonical return is π, though, the firm's choice must
also satisfy

$$\pi = pf(\hat{x}_i, \hat{Y}) - w\hat{x}_i. \tag{3}$$

The firms' individual behavior can thus be summarized by

$$\frac{w}{\pi} = \frac{f_1(\hat{x}_i, \hat{Y}}{f(\hat{x}_i, \hat{Y}) - f_1(\hat{x}_i, \hat{Y})} . \tag{4}$$

The competitive industry supply schedule can now be computed by differentiating equations (2), (3), and (1') with respect to p:

$$f_1(\hat{x}_i, \hat{Y}) + p\{f_{11}(\hat{x}_i, \hat{Y}) \frac{\partial \hat{x}_i}{\partial p} + f_{12}(\hat{x}_i, \hat{Y}) \frac{\partial \hat{Y}}{\partial p} \} = 0; \tag{5}$$

$$f(\hat{x}_i, \hat{Y}) + p\{f_1(\hat{x}_i, \hat{Y}) \frac{\partial \hat{x}_i}{\partial p} + f_2(\hat{x}_i, \hat{Y}) \frac{\partial \hat{Y}}{\partial p} \} - w \frac{\partial \hat{x}_i}{\partial p} = 0; \tag{6}$$

$$\frac{\partial y}{\partial p} = n\{f_1(\hat{x}_i, \hat{Y}) \frac{\partial \hat{x}_i}{\partial p} + f_2(\hat{x}_i, \hat{Y}) \frac{\partial \hat{Y}}{\partial p} \} + f(\hat{x}_i, \hat{Y}) \frac{\partial n}{\partial p} = 0. \tag{7}$$

Plugging equation (2) into equation (6), notice that the supply schedule must satisfy

$$\frac{\partial \hat{Y}}{\partial p} = - \frac{f(\hat{x}_i, \hat{Y})}{pf_2(\hat{x}_i, \hat{Y})} = - \frac{Y}{p\{nf_2(\hat{x}_i, \hat{Y})\}} .$$

PROBLEM 28

The elasticity of industry supply is then

$$\eta_Y = \frac{\partial \hat{Y}}{\partial p} \; \frac{p}{\hat{Y}} = - \frac{1}{nf_2(\hat{x}_i, \hat{Y})} > 0$$

as long as $f_2(x_i, Y) < 0$.

(b) The long-run equilibrium competitive price corresponds to average cost, so

$$p = \frac{\pi + w\hat{x}_i}{\hat{Y}_i} = \frac{n\pi + w\hat{X}}{\hat{Y}} \equiv c. \tag{8}$$

It is clear, then, that

$$\frac{\partial \hat{Y}}{\partial c} \; \frac{c}{\hat{Y}} = \eta_Y = - \frac{1}{nf_2(\hat{x}_i, \hat{Y})} \, .$$

As a result, the relationship between the average and marginal cost schedules can be formalized:

$$\partial(c\hat{Y}/\partial\hat{Y}) = c[1 + (\hat{Y}/c)(\partial c/\partial\hat{Y})] = c[1 - nf_2(\hat{x}_i, \hat{Y})]. \tag{9}$$

Since $f_2(x_i, Y) < 0$, marginal costs exceed average costs at the competitive equilibrium.

(c) To optimize industry output, it is necessary to choose

PROBLEM 28

(x,n) to minimize the cost of producing an arbitrary output.
Since the firms are identical, the problem is

$$\min \ \{wX + n\pi\}$$

$$\text{s.t. } \overline{Y} = nf(X/n,\overline{Y}).$$

By setting up the appropriate Lagrangian, the first-order
conditions are easily computed:

$$w - \lambda f_1((X^*/n),Y^*) = 0 \qquad\qquad (10)$$

$$\pi - \lambda\{f((X^*/n),Y^*) - (X^*/n)f_{1(}(X^*/n),Y^*)\} = 0. \qquad (11)$$

Combining equations (9) and (10), then, it is seen that

$$\frac{w}{\pi} = \frac{f_1((X^*/n),Y^*)}{f((X^*/n),Y^*) - (X^*/n)f_1((X^*/n),Y^*)}$$

replicates (4). The competitive solution therefore uses its
inputs optimally.

It can be shown, however, that the competitive
solution produces too much. To see this, observe that the
optimal industry output is characterized by paying each
factor its marginal revenue product; i.e., one
interpretation of equations (9) and (10) is that

$$w = \lambda \frac{\partial Y}{\partial X}[(X^*/n),Y^*] = p^* \frac{\partial Y}{\partial X}[(X^*/n),Y^*] \text{ and} \qquad (10')$$

$$\pi = \lambda \frac{\partial Y}{\partial n}[(X^*/n),Y^*] = p^* \frac{\partial Y}{\partial n}[(X^*/n),Y^*]. \tag{11'}$$

The second equalities in both (10') and (11') follow from interpreting the Lagrangian λ as the shadow price of one more unit of output - the price of output at Y^*. Since

$$Y = nf((X/n),Y),$$

differentiating equations (10') and (11') reveals that:

$$(w/p^*) = \{f_1((X^*/n),Y^*)/[1-nf_2((X^*/n),Y^*)]\} \text{ and} \tag{10''}$$

$$(\pi/p^*) = \{[f((X^*/n),Y^*) -$$

$$(X^*/n)f_1((X^*/n),Y^*)/[1-nf_2((X^*/n),Y^*)]\} \tag{11''}$$

Combining (10'') and (11'') in a way suggested by (8),

$$\frac{\pi + (X^*/n)w}{Y^*} = \frac{\{p^*[f-(X/n)f_1] + p^*(X/n)f_1\}/\{1-nf_2\}}{f}$$

$$= \frac{p^*}{1-nf_2((X^*/n),Y^*)}.$$

The optimal price is therefore

$$p^* = \{(1-nf_2[(X^*/n),Y^*])(\pi + (X^*/n)w)\}/Y^*,$$

254

the marginal cost of producing Y* [see equation (9)].
Instead of average cost pricing prescribed in part (b) for
the competitive equilibrium, the optimal price is higher
whenever $f_2(x_i, Y) < 0$.

The significance of overproduction by a competitive
market is obvious when cast in terms of renewable resources
like fish or trees. These resources reproduce at a fixed
rate, and overexploitation can cause the population to
diminish toward extinction. Competiton may also exploit a
nonreplenishable resource too intensely.

References

(1) Gordon, H.S., "The Economic Theory of a Common Property
Resource: The Fishery," *Journal of Political Economy*, 62:
124-142, 1954.

(2) Plourde, C., "Exploitation of Common Property
Replenishable Natural Resources," *Western Economic Journal*,
9: 256-266, 1971.

(3) Smith, V., "Economics of Production from Natural
Resources," *American Economic Review*, 58: 409-431, 1968.

(4) Smith, V., "General Equilibrium with a Replenishable
Natural Resource," *Review of Economic Studies, Symposium on
the Economics of Natural Resources*, 105-116, 1974.

29. The Edgeworth Geometry of General Equilibrium[1]

Graphical illustrations of Walrasian equilibrium that are remarkably robust [see Sections 17.2 and 17.3 starting on page 315]. The underlying geometry can be used to support a variety of results from a wide subset of the economic literature. This problem will support three propositions from three separate arenas.

The first treats the stability patterns of multiple equilibria; it can be viewed as an elementary introduction to the dynamic modeling of general equilibrium [see Sections 21.4 through 21.6 starting on page 398]. It will even be suggestive of the sufficiency of gross substitutability [page 395] in guaranteeing unique equilibria.

A second part will exhibit an optimal import tariff in a two-country model of international trade. The final section will apply similar techniques to futures markets. This modeling has been constructed to illustrate several of the important results reported by Foley. He and Hahn (2 and 4) independently argued that markets achieve equilibria that can be dramatically different when they are not free; in fact, equilibria may _not_ _exist_ at all if transactions are not costless. The Edgeworth geometry will show it all.

---

[1] Material found in Chapters 17 and 21 is applicable here; the nature of exchange equilibria will be explored and applied in several different contexts, including one in which the Stackelberg behavior of Chapter 16 plays a role.

PROBLEM 29

Questions:

(a) Consider Figure 29.1. Argue that I and III are stable equilibria, but that II is an unstable equilibrium if prices adjust according to the usual rule:

If $f_i(\vec{p})$ represents excess <u>demand</u> for x_i [page 315], then

$$\dot{p} \gtreqless 0 \text{ if and only if } f_i(\vec{p}) \gtreqless 0. \tag{1}$$

Condition (1) simply states that the price p_i will rise (remain constant or fall) when the demand for x_i exceeds (equals or falls short of) supply. Two goods are "gross substitutes" if any only if [see page 395 in Chapter 21]

$$\frac{\partial f_i(\vec{p})}{\partial p_i} > 0 \text{ and } \frac{\partial f_j(\vec{p})}{\partial p_i} > 0.$$

A theorem on the same page [page 395] states that:

If all goods are gross substitutes for all prices, and if $\vec{p}*$ is an equilibrium price vector, then it is <u>the</u> unique price vector.

Explain why Figure 29.1 violates the condition of gross substitutability.

Figure 29.1

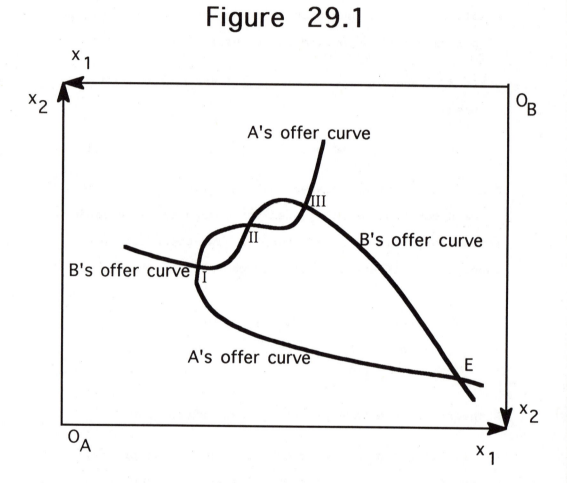

(b) The concept of an optimal import tariff is often raised in the literature of international trade. Let A and B be countries, for the moment, and assume the offer curves intersect only twice (<u>including</u> the endowment). Illustrate a tariff (<u>ad</u> <u>valorem</u> tax) that optimally restricts B's sale of x_2 from A's point of view. Use the geometry to compute this optimal tariff.

(c) It is usually assumed in standard general equilibrium theory that markets are costless. When they are not, the equilibria are certainly different; and they might not even exist. The market may, in short, simply be too costly to be worthwhile, and so it fails.

Again, let two offer curves intersect twice. Let x_i be consumption in period 1 and x_2 be consumption in period 2. Assume that the world ends after period 2. Carefully explain what has happened when A and B move from the endowment E to the equilibrium E' in a costless market. Then assume that the market is costly; suppose that a borrower must pay not only an interest premium to the lender (in period 2), but also the cost of setting up the market (in period 1). If r_b is the rate of interest paid by the borrower and r_1 the rate received by the lender, then assume, in particular, that

$$r_b = r_1 + c. \qquad (2)$$

The parameter c reflects the cost of the market.   In this context,

> (i) graphically characterize equilibrium when markets are costly according to (2);
>
> (ii) argue that $r_b > r > r_1$, where r is the interest paid and received in the costless case; and
>
> (iii) show that there exists a $\bar{c}$ such that $c \geq \bar{c}$ means that no market will form.

Suggested Solutions:

(a) Consider the price line drawn from the endowment E through the region between equilibria II and III in Figure 29.2.   At those prices, A offers to sell less x_1 than B demands, and B puts more x_2 up for sale than A is willing to buy; i.e,

$$(x_1^{EA} - x_1^{A}) < (x_1^{B} - x_1^{EB}), \text{ and}$$

$$(x_2^{A} - x_2^{EA}) < (x_2^{EB} - x_2^{B}).$$

According to equation (1), therefore, p_1 will rise, p_2 will fall, and the price line will be forced to rotate toward III.   Precisely the same reasoning can be employed to show that:

> (i) price lines above III (like p_1) will rotate toward III,

Figure 29.2

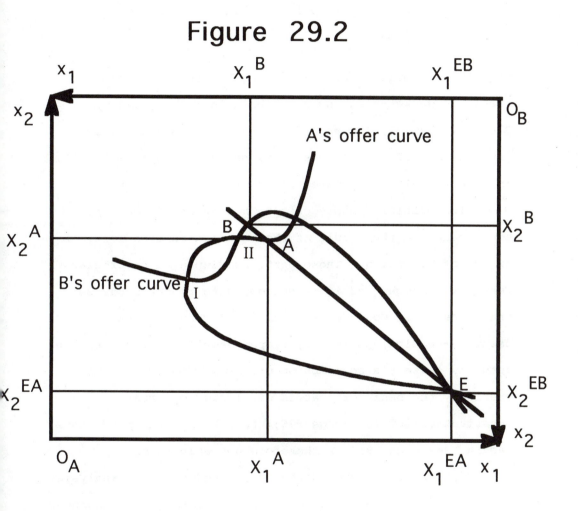

(ii) price lines between II and I (like ρ_2) will
      rotate toward I, and

(iii) price lines below I (like ρ_3) will rotate
      toward I.

Finally, the price lines connecting E with I, II, and III
result in market-clearing equilibria in both x_1 and x_2.
Clearly, then, I, II, and III are all possible equilibria
given E, but II is unstable. Any perturbation from II will,
in fact, result in a new equilibrium at either I or III.

The multiple intersections that spawn the multiple
equilibria are the result of the backward-bending portions
of the offer curves. Those portions display a particular
behavior, though, and it is enlightening to characterize
that behavior. Consider B's curve. Throughout its
backward-bending, positively sloped section, decreases in p_1
actually cause B's consumption of x_2 to increase. This is
precisely the behavior that is disallowed by gross
substitutability [see page 395]; the theorem recorded above
[again, see page 395] is therefore not surprising.

Support for a second theorem, based on index analysis,
is also found. The indexing condition stated for uniqueness
requires that [also page 395] "the income effect (not be),
large enough to 'wipe out' the substitution effect." It
speaks to the Slutsky representation of $(\partial x_2/\partial p_1)$ [see page
119], and also precludes the offending backward-bending

262

offer curves drawn in Figures 29.1 and 29.2.

(b) A must behave like a Stackelberg oligopolist [see Section 16.6 beginning on page 295] to exploit its optimal tariff; i.e., A must assume that B will move along its offer curve. Maximizing welfare subject to B's offer curve is therefore the best strategy. Point E' in Figure 29.3 represents the point that achieves that maximum. It can be supported by a domestic price ratio $(\bar{p}_1/\bar{p}_2)$ given by the slope of line (a) and a foreign price equal to the slope of line (b). A imports x_2, so an ad valorem tax t* attached to $\bar{p}_2$ must satisfy

$$\bar{p}_1/\{\bar{p}_2(1+t^*)\} = \text{slope (b)}.$$

Constructing a set of secondary axes with its original E allows that

$$\bar{p}_1/\{\bar{p}_2(1+t^*)\} = \text{slope (b)} = \frac{E'N}{EN}. \tag{3a}$$

From the same perspective,

$$\bar{p}_1/\bar{p}_2 = \text{slope (a)} = \frac{E'N}{MN}. \tag{3b}$$

Manipulating equation (3a) in light of (3b), then,

$$(1+t^*) = \frac{E'N}{MN} \frac{EN}{E'N} = \frac{EN}{MN}$$

Figure 29.3

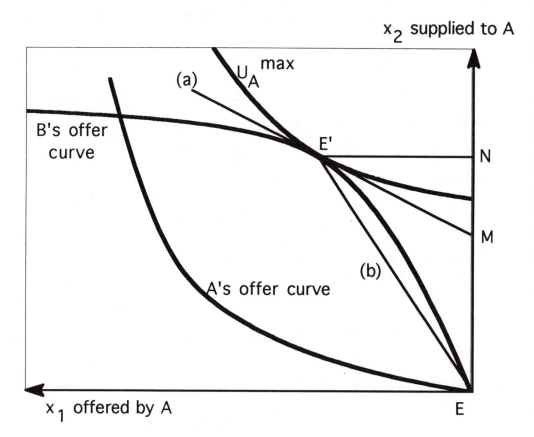

and

$$t* = \frac{EN - MN}{MN} = \frac{EM}{MN}.$$

(c) One way to model the costs of setting up futures markets is to manipulate one's interpretation of offer curves. To see how this can be done, begin by carefully delineating the costless model. In Figure 29.4 for example, individual A wants to finance increased period 2 consumption by lending some period 1 endowment. B wants to borrow in period 1, though, so equilibrium is achieved at E'. The slope of line (a) is the ratio of the prices of period 1 and period 2 consumption; it equals $\{-1/(1+r)\}$, where r is the interest rate paid by B <u>and</u> received by A.

Now suppose that setting up this market were costly. Suppose, in particular, that it cost a fixed markup over the lender's return and that this markup must be paid by the borrower as the loan is processed. If c represents the cost, then,

$$r_b = r_1 + c, \tag{2}$$

where r_b represents the interest paid by the borrower and r_1 the interest collected by the lender.

Figure 29.4

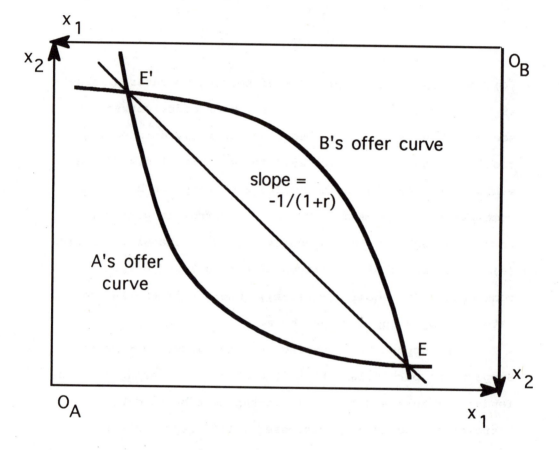

Geometrically, then, one is looking for a level of $\hat{x}_2$ such that the horizontal distance between the two offer curves (within the core) precisely equals the horizontal distance between price lines emanating from E and characterized by slopes $\{-1/(1+r_b)\}$ and $\{-1/(1+r_1)\}$, respectively. In such a circumstance, the amount of period 1 consumption foregone by A would be divided between B and the cost of setting up the market in accordance with equation (2). The full payment in period 2 consumption would also be transferred from B to A.

Figure 29.5 displays such an equilibrium. Notice that A is receiving a lower return than before ($r_1 < r$), but B is paying a higher rate than before ($r_b > r$). Both participants therefore bear some of the cost. It is also entirely possible that the market has become too costly for any transaction to be undertaken. The final graph, Figure 29.6, shows a core reflecting a disparity between r_b and r_1 that is so large that the core lies entirely inside. No market will appear because it can make neither A nor B better off. There exists, in fact, a $\bar{c}$ such that $c > \bar{c}$ precludes the appearance of a futures market.

To see this, let $M_k(e)$ be the slope of k's offer curve at E (k = A, B) and assume that x_1 and x_2 are gross substitutes. The offer curves are thus nicely shaped, and a core with a wider angle than the area between the curves can never intersect both sides. Clearly, then

267

Figure 29.5

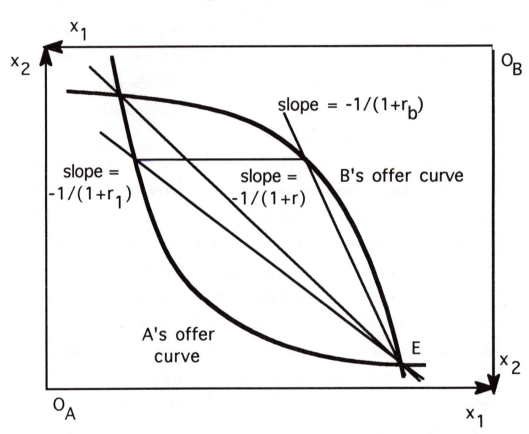

Figure 29.6

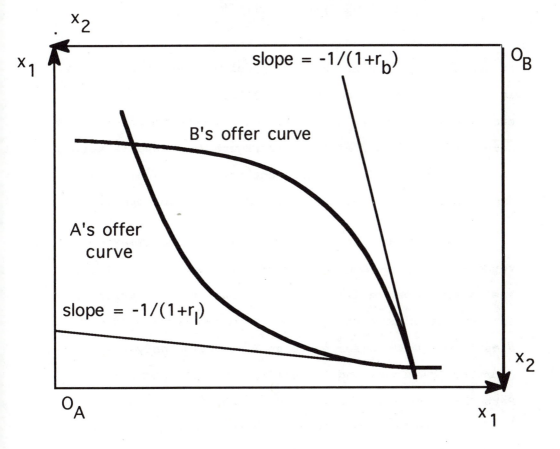

PROBLEM 29

$$M_A(E) - M_B(E) \leq \frac{1}{1 + r_1} - \frac{1}{1 + r_1 + \bar{c}}$$

defines the prospect $\bar{c}$; i.e.,

$$[M_A(E) - M_B(E)](1 + r_1)(1 + r_b) = \bar{c}.$$

It would seem, though, that the problem is one of thinness in a special sense: the scope of Pareto improving transactions is small. If the area between the offer curves were larger (the dotted lines in Figure 29.6) and fatter, then the likelihood of nonexistent equilibria would be diminished (though certainly not entirely eradicated).

This problem was designed to exhibit the immense versatility of the Edgeworth geometry. Parts (a) and (b) are fairly standard illustrations. The optimal tariff has, in fact, been shown to equal $(\varepsilon*-1)^{-1}$, where $\varepsilon*$ is the elasticity of B's offer curve at E' by using only this geometry [see Caves and Jones (1), page 239, Figure 12.7]. Part (b) is the first step of that proof.

The last part of the problem is, however, less traditional. It was inspired by the work of Foley (2) and Hahn (4). Both had observed that the Arrow-Debreu general equilibrium model had predicted the existence of many more markets than were actually observed. These markets were, in fact, to be so extensive that rational beings could plan their entire lifetimes in one sitting. When pressed about this contradiction, economists had always pointed to uncertainty and risk. They had asserted that the future was simply too uncertain for there to be enough people to support all of the predicted futures markets. Foley and Hahn found another culprit, though, and the Edgeworth geometry supports their analysis. The interested reader may also consult Green and Sheshinski (3) for more recent extensions of the initial work.

References

(1) Caves, R.E., and R.W. Jones, *World Trade and Payments*, Boston, Little, Brown, 1973.

(2) Foley, D., "Economic Equilibria with Costly Markets," *Journal of Economic Theory*, 2: 276-291, 1970.

(3) Green, J., and E. Sheshinski, "Competitive Inefficiencies in the Presence of Constrained Transactions," *Journal of Economic Theory*, 10: 343-357, 1975.

(4) Hahn, F., "Equilibrium with Transactions Cost," *Econometrica*, 39: 417-439, 1971.

30. The Rybczynski and Stolper-Samuelson Theorems[1]

The Rybczynski and Stolper-Samuelson theorems, two results most usually thought to pertain to the international trade literature, are actually elementary propositions drawn from the fundamental theory of general equilibrium. This problem will present both in that context.

Suppose that two goods (y_1 and y_2) were produced in accordance with homogeneous production functions of degree 1 [see page 15] in two factors (x_1 and x_2); i.e., let

$$y_i = f_i(x_{1i}, x_{2i}), \quad i = 1, 2.$$

Let x_1 and x_2 be available in fixed supply, so that

$$x_{j1} + x_{j2} \leq \bar{x}_j, \quad j = 1, 2.$$

It is convenient to represent production in terms of employment ratios, so let

$$y_i = x_{2i}f_i([x_{1i}/x_{2i}], 1) \equiv \phi_i(\chi_i), \quad i = 1, 2,$$

where $\chi_i \equiv [x_{1i}/x_{2i}]$. Recall, then, from Problem 3 that

$$w_i = p_i(d\phi_i/d\chi_i), \quad i = 1, 2, \text{ and} \tag{1}$$

---

[1] Material found in Chapters 1, 3, and 4 is applicable here in the general equilibrium structure described in Chapters 17 and 18; results from Problem 3 are also employed.

$$w_2 = p_i[\phi_i(\chi_i) - \chi_i(d\phi_i/d\chi_i)], \quad i = 1, 2. \tag{2}$$

These relationships are enough to prove two of the most important theorems in applied microtheory.

Questions:

(a) Show that χ_1 and χ_2 both move in the same direction in response to a change in the relative factor prices $\omega \equiv w_2/w_1$.

(b) [Stolper-Samuelson] Show that an increase (decrease) in the relative price of y_2 vis a vis y_1 (denoted $\rho \equiv p_2/p_1$) causes the real wage of the factor used intensively in y_2 (in y_1) to rise. The production of y_i is said to be intensive in x_j if and only if $(x_{ji}/x_{ki}) > (x_{j1}/x_{kl})$ for $i \neq 1$ and $k = j$. In particular, y_i is intensive in x_1 if and only if $\chi_i > \chi_j$ for $i \neq j$; otherwise, y_i is intensive in x_2.

(c) [Rybczynski] Holding $\rho \equiv p_2/p_1$ fixed, show graphically that increasing the availability of one factor causes the industry using that factor intensively to expand and the other industry to contract.

(d) Consider production possibility frontiers before and after the supply increase noted in (c). If neither y_1

nor y_2 is inferior, indicate the region on the new production frontier where the new equilibrium must lie if ρ is allowed to move. Argue that the price of the expanding good must fall.

Suggested Solutions:

The first two parts follow entirely from manipulating equations (1) and (2). Parts (c) and (d) can be proven that way, too, but it reinforces the value of the Edgeworth geometry to proceed without calculus for at least one-half of this problem.

(a) From Problem 3,

$$w_1 = p_1(d\phi_i/d\chi_i) \text{ and} \tag{1}$$

$$w_2 = p_i[\phi_i(\chi_i) - \chi_i(d\phi_i/d\chi_i)], \quad i = 1, 2. \tag{2}$$

It follows from standard cost-minimizing conditions [see page 50] that

$$\omega \equiv \frac{w_2}{w_1} = [\phi_i(\chi_i)/(d\phi_i/d\chi_i)] - \chi_i, \quad i = 1, 2. \tag{3}$$

Employment ratios therefore depend only on the ratio of factor prices.

Equation (3) also reveals that

$$\frac{d\omega}{d\chi_i} = \frac{\{[d\phi_i/d\chi_i^2] - \phi_i(\chi_i)[d^2\phi_i/d\chi_i^2]\}}{[d\phi_i/d\chi_i]^2} - 1$$

$$= - \frac{\phi_i(\chi_i)[d^2\phi_i/d\chi_i^2]}{[d\phi_i/d\chi_i]^2} > 0; \quad i = 1, 2. \tag{4}$$

The employment ratios in both industries therefore respond in the same direction to changes in ω.

(b) It is clear, from equation (1), that

$$w_1 = p_1(d\phi_1/d\chi_1) = p_2(d\phi_2/d\chi_2).$$

As a result,

$$\frac{p_1}{p_2} \equiv \rho = \frac{[d\phi_1/d\chi_1]}{[d\phi_2/d\chi_2]}. \tag{5}$$

Differentiating equation (5) and applying (4) will now pay dividends, but adopting the standard convention that

$$d\phi_i/d\chi_i \equiv \phi_i'(\chi_i) \quad \text{and} \quad d^2\phi_i/dx^2_i \equiv \phi_i''(\chi_i)$$

greatly simplifies the notation. Performing the appropriate differentiation, then:

$$\frac{d\rho}{d\omega} = \frac{\phi_1''(\chi_1)}{\phi_2'(\chi_2)} \frac{d\chi_1}{d\omega} - \frac{\phi_1'(\chi_1)\phi_2''(\chi_2)}{[\phi_2'(\chi_2)]^2} \frac{d\chi_2}{d\omega}$$

$$= - \frac{\phi_1''(\chi_1)}{\phi_2'(\chi_2)} \quad \frac{[\phi_1'(\chi_1)]^2}{\phi_1(\chi_1)\phi_1''(\chi_1)}$$

$$+ \frac{\phi_1'(\chi_1)\phi_2''(\chi_2)}{[\phi_2'(\chi_2)]^2} \quad \frac{[\phi_2'(\chi_2)]^2}{\phi_2(\chi_2)\phi_2''(\chi_2)}$$

$$= \quad \frac{\phi_1'(\chi_1)}{\phi_2(\chi_2)} \quad - \frac{[\phi_1'(\chi_1)]^2}{\phi_2'(\chi)\phi_1(\chi_1)} \tag{6}$$

Dividing equation (6) by ρ and recalling from equation (5) that

$$\rho = [d\phi_1/d\chi_1]/[d\phi_2/d\chi_2],$$

one can observe that

$$\frac{1}{\rho} \frac{d\rho}{d\omega} = \frac{\phi_2'(\chi_2)}{\phi_2(\chi_2)} - \frac{\phi_1'(\chi_1)}{\phi_1(\chi_1)} . \tag{7}$$

Notice, however, that equation (2) translates into

$$\phi_i(\chi_i) = (w_2/p_i) + \chi_i\phi_i{}'(\chi_i)$$

$$= \phi_i{}'(\chi_i)[\chi_i + (w_2/p_i\phi_i(\chi_i)]$$

$$= \phi_i{}'(x_i)[x_i + (w_2/w_1)].$$

As a result,

$$\frac{1}{\rho} \frac{d\rho}{d\omega} = \frac{1}{x_2 + \omega} - \frac{1}{x_1 + \omega} .$$

Clearly, therefore

$$\frac{d\rho}{d\omega} \gtreqless 0 \text{ as } x_2 \lesseqgtr x_1. \tag{8}$$

When the relative price of y_2 rises (falls), therefore, the real return of the factor used intensively in the production of y_2 must rise (fall), as well. If (x_{11}/x_{12}) $= x_1 < x_2 = (x_{21}/x_{22})$, for example, then the production of y_2 would be using x_1 intensively, and equation (8) would predict that $\omega = w_2/w_1$ would increase (decrease) as ρ fell (rose).

(c) Part (a) revealed that the factor employment ratios depend on ρ. To see this, simply recall equation (5):

$$\rho = \phi_1{}'(x_1)/\phi_2{}'(x_2) \tag{5}$$

and notice from equation (2) that

$$\rho = [\phi_1{}'(\chi_1) - \chi_1\phi_1{}'(\chi_1)]/[\phi_2{}'(\chi_2) - \chi_2\phi_2{}'(\chi_2)], \qquad (9)$$

as well. These are two equations in χ_1 and χ_2 that are
fixed by ρ. When an increase in $\bar{x}_1$ is graphed, therefore,
χ_1 and χ_2 must be fixed if χ does not change. These ratios,
are, of course, exhibited by the slopes of lines connecting
the equilibrium with the y_1 and y_2 origins.

Figure 30.1 illustrates the situation. The origin for
the y_1 isoquants moves to the left from O_1 to $O_1{}'$ when $\bar{x}_1$
increases. Point E is the initial equilibrium, and

$$(\text{slope } O_1E) = \chi_1 > \chi_2 = (\text{slope } O_2E)$$

shows that y_1 uses x_1 intensively. Holding ρ fixed, then,
the new equilibrium must lie along a line from $O_1{}'$ with the
same slope as O_1E if χ_1 is to be held constant. That line
is drawn and labeled $O_1{}'E'$. If χ_2 is to be constant,
though, the new equilibrium must lie along O_2E'. Line O_2E,
in fact, intersects line $O_1{}'E'$ at E', the new equilibrium.
It is clear from the geometry that E' is closer to the O_2
origin than E. The increase in $\bar{x}_1$ has therefore caused the
production of y_2, the industry not using x_1 intensively, to
contract. The resources released by y_2 plus the additional
units of x_1 now go into producing y_1, so y_1 must have
expanded.

Figure 30.1

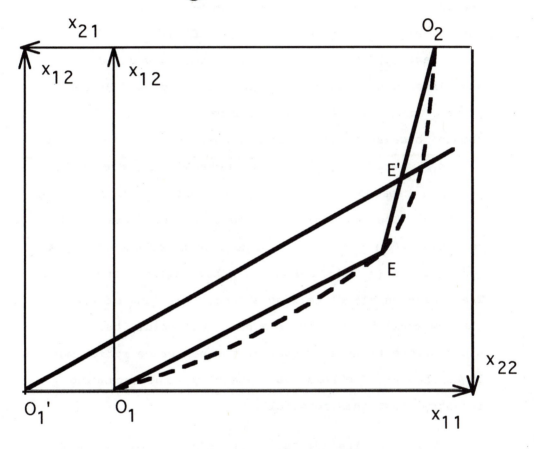

(d) Figure 30.2 shows two production possibility frontiers
for the two cases shown in Figure 30.1; line AEB is the
original ppf along which point E reflects initial
equilibrium. When $\bar{x}_1$ increases, y_1 can expand under total
specialization further than y_2 because y_1 uses x_1
intensively. As a result, [A'-A] > [B'-B].

Part (c), the Rybczynski theorem, showed that E'
associated with $\bar{\rho}$ must lie below point C on A'E'B' because
y_2 must contract. A new equilibrium cannot lie below E',
though, because of the normality assumption. To get below
E', (p_1/p_2) would have to be increased above $\bar{\rho}$ even while
(x_1/x_2) increased; in words, x_1 would have had to have been
inferior. The new equilibrium could not be above D, either,
because $(p_1/p_2) < \bar{\rho}$ would then have been accompanied by a
reduction in (x_1/x_2); and x_1 would have again been inferior.
The region on A'E'B' between E' and D must therefore contain
the new equilibrium. At this new equilibrium, though, the
slope of the frontier, equal to the new price ratio, must be
lower than $\bar{\rho}$. The relative price of y_1, the expanding
industry, must therefore fall.

These results are "old standards." They can be found
in any trade text, and are used extensively throughout the
trade and tax incidence literatures. Kemp's text (2) is an
excellent source for discussions and applications of both.
Both are extended there to accommodate intermediate goods

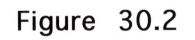

Figure 30.2

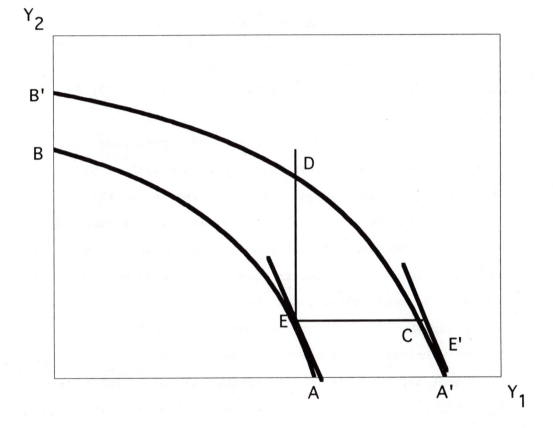

and variable returns to scale. A later problem here will produce similar results in an incidence question. The interested reader is, nonetheless, referred to the original papers and recent extensions cited below.

References

(1) Jones, R.W., "The Structure of Simple General Equilibrium Models," *Journal of Political Economy*, 73: 557-572, 1965.

(2) Kemp, M., *The Price Theory of International Trade and Investment,* Englewood Cliffs, N.J., Prentice-Hall, 1969.

(3) Minabe, N., "The Stolper-Samuelson, The Rybczynski Effect, and the Heckscher-Ohlin Theory of Trade Pattern and Factor Price Equalization: The Case of Money-Commodity, Many-Factor Country," *Canadian Journal of Economics and Political Science,* 33: 401-419, 1967.

(4) Rybczynski, T.N., "Factor Endowments and Relative Commodity Prices," *Economica*, 22: 336-341, 1955.

(5) Samuelson, P.A., "Prices of Factors and Goods in General Equilibrium," *Review of Economic Studies*, 21: 1-20, 1953.

(6) Uekawa, Y., "On the Generalization of the Stolper-Samuelson Theorem," *Econometrica*, 39: 197-218, 1971.

31. The Optimal Tariff in General Equilibrium[1]

Problem 29 contained a brief section on optimal
tariffs in a very limited general equilibrium model (two
goods available in fixed amounts). This problem extends
that discussion to include many goods available in amounts
limited only by a convex production boundary. The problem
will follow the introductory analysis of Chapter 12 in Kemp
(1), and will maintain the emphasis of that discussion.
Computation will not be nearly as important as the
construction of a framework with which a variety of
circumstances can be analyzed.

The initial exercise will set up that framework, and
the subsequent sections will exploit it. Both the Kemp text
and the trade literature go well beyond these results, and
the interested reader will find Kemp's list of references
exhaustive.

Let there be n traded commodities, $x_1, \ldots, x_n$, and let
excess foreign demand for each be represented by

$$z_i = z_i(\vec{p}*), \quad i = 1, \ldots, n,$$

where $\vec{p}* = (p_1*, \ldots, p_n*)$ are the prices facing those foreign

---

[1] Material found in Chapters 17 and 18 is applicable here;
additional definitions are provided as required. Some of
the fundamental concepts of utility and monopoly are also
drawn from Chapter 7 and Chapter 14, respectively.

PROBLEM 31

participants in the market. The balance of international payments requires that

$$\sum_{i=1}^{n} p \cdot z(\vec{p}^*) = 0. \tag{1}$$

Denote the frontier of domestic production [see page 351] by

$$T(\vec{x}) \equiv T(x_1, \ldots, x_n) = 0$$

and domestic welfare by $u(\vec{x})$. Assume that foreign prices and domestic prices are distorted only by tariffs; i.e., assume that

$$p_i = \pi_i p_i^*, \quad i = 1, \ldots, n, \tag{2}$$

where $\vec{p} \equiv (p_1, \ldots, p_n)$ is the domestic price vector and

$$\pi_i = \begin{cases} (1 + \tau_i) & x_i \text{ imported so } z_i(\vec{p}^*) < 0 \\ (1 + \tau_i)^{-1} & x_i \text{ imported so } z_i(\vec{p}^*) > 0. \end{cases} \tag{2'}$$

Questions:

(a) Show that the optimal set of tariffs $(\hat{\tau}_1, \ldots, \hat{\tau}_n)$ must satisfy

PROBLEM 31

$$\sum_{i=1}^{n} \hat{\pi}_i p_i^* \frac{\partial z_i}{\partial p_j^*} = 0, \quad j = 1, \ldots, n, \qquad (3)$$

where $\hat{\pi}_i$ is defined by (1) at $\tau_i = \hat{\tau}_i$.

(b) Show that it is always possible to set at least one tariff optimally at zero.

(c) Suppose that some intermediate goods were traded that appear only in the production frontier [and not in $u(-)$]. Show that equation (2) would still hold.

(d) Suppose there were only two traded goods. Show that setting an optimal import tariff $\hat{\tau}_1$ would be equivalent to setting an optimal export tariff $\hat{\tau}_2$ and that $\hat{\tau}_1 = \hat{\tau}_2$.

(e) Characterize the optimal tariff on x_i if x_i were produced and sold both at home and abroad by a monopolist [the answer to this first appeared in Pollak (2)].

Suggested Solutions:

(a) Given the specification of the problem, the appropriate Lagrangian is

PROBLEM 31

$$L(\vec{x}, \vec{p}^*, \lambda_1, \lambda_2) = u\{[x_1 - z_1(\vec{p}^*)], \ldots, [x_n - z_n(\vec{p}^*)]\}$$

$$+ \lambda_1 \sum_{i=1}^{n} p_i^* z_i(\vec{p}^*) + \lambda_2 T(\vec{x}). \tag{4}$$

The first-order conditions pertaining to the p_j^* are most useful. Differentiating (4) with respect to those p_j^*, one finds that

$$- \sum_{i=1}^{n} \frac{\partial u}{\partial x_i} \frac{\partial z_i}{\partial p_j^*} + \lambda_1 \left(\sum_{i=1}^{n} p_i^* \frac{\partial z_i}{\partial p_j^*} + z_j(\vec{p}^*) \right) = 0 \tag{5}$$

for $j = 1, \ldots, n$. It is clear from (1), however, that

$$\sum_{i=1}^{n} p_i^* \frac{\partial z_i}{\partial p_j} + z_j(\vec{p}^*) = 0$$

so that equation (5) reduces immediately to

$$\sum_{i=1}^{n} \frac{\partial u}{\partial x_i} \frac{\partial z_i}{\partial p_j^*} = 0, \quad j = 1, \ldots, n. \tag{5'}$$

In equilibrium, though,

$$\frac{\partial u}{\partial x_i} = k p_i$$

286

PROBLEM 31

for some k and all i = 1,...,n [see page 100 in Section 7.1]. Furthermore, equation (2) shows that

$$\pi_i p_i{}^* = p_i, \quad i = 1,\ldots,n.$$

As a result, equation (5') can finally be written

$$\sum_{i=1}^{n} \hat{\pi}_i p_i{}^* \frac{\partial z_i}{\partial p_j{}^*} = 0, \quad j = 1,\ldots,n. \tag{5"}$$

(b) Excess demand schedules are homogeneous of degree zero [see page 317]. If $\hat{\pi}_0$ is a solution to (5"), therefore, $a\hat{\pi}_0$ is a solution, as well. One is thereby set free to select some $\hat{\pi}_j$ arbitrarily and to solve for the remaining n−1 rates; and setting $\hat{\pi}_j = 1$ sets the corresponding tariff equal to zero.

(c) Order the goods so that the first m goods are final goods that enter utility and the last (n−m) goods are purely intermediate. The production frontier is thus

$$T(x_1,\ldots,x_m,\ldots,x_n) = 0,$$

but

$$x_i = z_i(\vec{p}{}^*) \text{ for } i = m + 1,\ldots,n.$$

Optimal tariffs therefore solve a maximization problem with

two constraints:

$$\max u[x_1 - z_1(\vec{p}^*), \ldots, x_m - z_m(\vec{p}^*)]$$

$$\text{s.t.} \quad T\{x_1, \ldots, x_m, z_{m+1}^*(\vec{p}), \ldots, z_n^*(\vec{p})\} = 0, \quad \text{and}$$

$$\sum_{i=1}^{n} p_i^* z_i(\vec{p}^*) = 0.$$

Setting up the Lagrangian as above, one produces first-order conditions for $x_i (i = 1, \ldots, m)$ and $p_j^* (j = 1, \ldots, n)$:

$$\frac{\partial u}{\partial x_i} = \lambda_2 \frac{\partial T}{\partial x_i} \qquad \text{and} \tag{6}$$

$$- \sum_{i=1}^{m} \frac{\partial u}{\partial x_i} \frac{\partial z_i}{\partial p_j^*} + \lambda_1 \left(\sum_{i=1}^{n} p_i^* \frac{\partial z_i}{\partial p_j^*} + z_j(\vec{p}^*) \right)$$

$$= - \lambda_2 \sum_{i=m+1}^{n} \frac{\partial T}{\partial x_i} \frac{\partial z_i}{\partial p_j^*} \tag{7}$$

for $i = 1, \ldots, m$ and $j = 1, \ldots, n$. The middle term is still zero, so plugging equation (6) into equation (7) reveals that

PROBLEM 31

$$\lambda_2 \sum_{i=1}^{n} \frac{\partial T}{\partial x_i} \frac{\partial z_i}{\partial p_j^*} = 0; \quad j = 1, \ldots, n. \tag{8}$$

In equilibrium, though,

$$\frac{\partial T}{\partial x_i} = k'p_i$$

for some k' and $i = 1, \ldots, n$ with $\pi_i p_i^* = p_i$. Equation (8) therefore replicates equation (5"):

$$\sum_{i=1}^{n} \hat{\pi}_i p_i^* \frac{\partial z_i}{\partial p_j^*} = 0, \quad j = 1, \ldots, n.$$

(d) The simplest way to demonstrate this proposition is to write (5") in matrix form. Since one tariff can always be zero, the case in which y faces an optimal import tariff can be represented for the two good examples by

$$\left| (1+\hat{\tau}_1)p_1^* \quad p_2^* \right| \left| \begin{array}{cc} \dfrac{\partial z_1}{\partial p_1^*} & \dfrac{\partial z_1}{\partial p_2^*} \\ \\ \dfrac{\partial z}{\partial p_1^*} & \dfrac{\partial z}{\partial p_1^*} \end{array} \right| = \left| \begin{array}{c} 0 \\ 0 \end{array} \right| ;$$

289

PROBLEM 31

i.e.,

$$\left| \begin{array}{cc} \{(1+\hat{\tau}_1)p_1*/p_2*\} & 1 \end{array} \right| \left| D\vec{z}(\vec{p}*) \right| = \left| \begin{array}{c} 0 \\ 0 \end{array} \right| .$$

The opposite case supposes that y_2 faces an optimal export tariff and solves

$$\left| \begin{array}{cc} p_1* & \{p_2*/(1+\hat{\tau}_2)\} \end{array} \right| \left| D\vec{z}(\vec{p}*) \right| = \left| \begin{array}{c} 0 \\ 0 \end{array} \right| . \qquad (9)$$

Manipulating equation (9) only slightly,

$$\left| \begin{array}{cc} \{p_1*(1+\hat{\tau}_2)/p_2*\} & 1 \end{array} \right| \left| D\vec{z}(\vec{p}*) \right| = \left| \begin{array}{c} 0 \\ 0 \end{array} \right| .$$

Clearly, then, $\hat{\tau}_1$ and $\hat{\tau}_2$ are solutions to the same equation and $\hat{\tau}_1 = \hat{\tau}_2$.

(e) The domestic country can charge the optimal tariff only by exploiting its monopoly power over its own goods (if other countries produced identical goods, the optimal tariffs would all be zero because the foreign excess demand schedules would be perfectly elastic). If the export sector were controlled by a monopoly, to begin with, that monopoly power would already be exploited privately, and the optimal tariff would be zero. Domestic welfare would be lower, of

290

course, because domestic prices would already include the optimal tariff.

These exercises are only the beginning of a thorough discussion of optimal tariffs. The reader is referred to Chapter 13 in Kemp (1) for an exhaustive presentation. Kemp spends a good deal of effort delineating the circumstances under which the best tariffs are all nonnegative, all nonpositive, and sometimes mixed in sign. Additional time is spent there deducing the impact of domestic distortions on the optimal tariff. The references cited there are also a fine source of supplementary material.

References

(1) Kemp, M., *The Pure Theory of International Trade and Investment*, Englewood Cliffs, N.J., Prentice-Hall, 1969.

(2) Pollak, J.J., "'The Optimal Tariff' and the Cost of Imports," *Review of Economic Studies*, 19: 36-41, 1951-52.

32. Incidence of the Corporate Profits Tax[1]

Questions of tax incidence are among the fundamental problems of public finance: "Who is really paying this particular tax?" is frequently a question of no small significance. Almost as frequently, the answer to such a question requires a full investigation of the general equilibrium feedbacks involved. An excellent example of how this need arises can be provided by the tax on corporate profits. Is that tax passed forward onto customers or backward onto labor or is it borne by corporate capital?

Harberger (1) presented a general equilibrium model to answer those questions in 1962, and this problem is based on but a small part of that work. It is, nonetheless, a typical general equilibrium treatment in the Heckscher-Ohlin tradition of international trade.

To set the context for the problem, let

$$y_1 = f_1(x_{11}, x_{21}) \text{ and } y_2 = f_2(x_{12}, x_{22})$$

be linearly homogeneous production schedules representing the corporate and noncorporate sectors of a full employment economy so that

$$x_{11} + x_{12} = \bar{x}_1 \text{ and } x_{21} + x_{22} = \bar{x}_2.$$

---

[1] Material found in Chapters 17 and 18, building on concepts covered in Chapters 1, 9, 13, and 14, is applicable here.

PROBLEM 32

Assume that both sectors are perfectly competitive in both the product and the factor markets. Define units so that

$$p_1 = p_2 = w_1 = w_2 = 1$$

before a tax of t is placed on the return of x_{11} - the specific factor designed here to be corporate capital.

Let the demand side of the economy be defined by a demand schedule for y_i designated

$$y_i = \xi_i(p_1/p_2)$$

and let ε_i be the price elasticity of demand in terms of relative prices. Finally, make x_2 the numéraire, so that w_2 = 1 even after t is imposed.

Questions:

(a) Use the properties of competitive equilibria [see Chapter 13] to show that

$$\frac{dy_1}{y} = \varepsilon_1[dp_1 - dp_2],$$

$$\frac{dy_1}{y_1} = s_1^1 \frac{dx_{11}}{x_{11}} + s_1^2 \frac{dx_{21}}{x_{21}},$$

$$\frac{dx_{12}}{x_{12}} - \frac{dx_{22}}{x_{22}} = \sigma_2 [dw_1 - dw_2], \text{ and}$$

$$\frac{dx_{11}}{x_{11}} - \frac{dx_{21}}{x_{21}} = \sigma_2 [(dw_1 + t) - dw_2],$$

where σ_j is the elasticity of substitution in sector j = 1, 2 and s_1^k is the share paid to factor k = 1, 2 in sector 1.

(b) Show that

$$dx_{11} = - dx_{12},$$

$$dx_{22} = - dx_{21},$$

$$dw_2 = 0,$$

$$dp_1 = s_1^1 (dw_1 + t), \text{ and}$$

$$dp_2 = s_2^1 dw_1.$$

Of course, s_2^1 is the share paid to factor x_1 in sector 2.

(c) Construct a linear system in terms of dw_1, (dx_{11}/x_{11}), and (dx_{21}/x_{21}), alone.

(d) Show that imposing t on x_1 can only cause w_1 to rise if sector 1 employs x_2 intensively.

(e) How would the qualitative solution to part (d) change if the corporate sector [sector 1] were to have enough monopoly power to charge a markup (m) for every unit of y_1 that it sold?

Suggested Solutions:

The solutions to these parts are typical of the manipulation required to transform a simple general equilibrium model into a tractable state. The appropriate steps which are usually followed are outlined by the very organization of the problem.

(a) From the definition of the price elasticity of demand [page 235] and the normalization of prices, it is clear that

$$\frac{dy_1}{y_1} = \varepsilon_1 \frac{d(p_1/p_1)}{p_1/p_2} = \varepsilon_1 [dp_1 - dp_2]. \tag{1}$$

Total derivatives are appropriate here because there are only two goods; the demand side is therefore fully characterized by a single demand schedule that relates y_1 to the relative price (p_1/p_2). Euler's law [see page 481] meanwhile states that

PROBLEM 32

$$Y_1 = \frac{\partial f_1}{\partial x_1} x_{11} + \frac{\partial f_2}{\partial x_2} x_{21}.$$

As a result,

$$dy_1 = \frac{\partial f_1}{\partial x_1} dx_{11} + \frac{\partial f_1}{\partial x_2} dx_{21},$$

so that

$$\frac{dy_1}{y_1} = \{\frac{\partial f_1}{\partial x_1} \frac{x_{11}}{y_1}\} \{\frac{dx_{11}}{x_{11}}\} + \{\frac{\partial f_2}{\partial x_2} \frac{x_{21}}{y_1}\} \{\frac{dx_{21}}{x_{21}}\}$$

$$\equiv s_1^1 \frac{dx_{11}}{x_{11}} + s_1^2 \frac{dx_{21}}{x_{21}} \tag{2}$$

where s_i^j is the share paid to factor x_i in the jth sector.

Finally, the production of y_1 and y_2 can be summarized in terms of their elasticities of substitution [see page 13]:

$$\frac{d(x_{1j}/x_{2j})}{x_{1j}/x_{2j}} \equiv \sigma_j \frac{d(w_1/w_2)}{(w_1/w_2)}, \quad j = 1, 2.$$

For the noncorporate sector, therefore,

$$\frac{dx_{12}}{x_{12}} - \frac{dx_{22}}{x_{22}} = \sigma_2[dw_1 - dw_2]. \tag{3a}$$

296

PROBLEM 32

For the corporate sector, however, the change in w_1 must include the tax. As a result,

$$\frac{dx_{11}}{x_{11}} - \frac{dx_{21}}{x_{21}} = \sigma_1[(dw_1+t) - dw_2].\qquad (3b)$$

(b)   Full employment leads to the conclusion that

$$dx_{11} = - dx_{12} \text{ and } dx_{21} = - dx_{22}.\qquad (4)$$

Choosing x_2 as the numéraire, one also sees that $dw_2 = 0$. Finally, since payments to factors exhaust revenues entirely under perfect competition, one sees that (e.g.)

$$p_2 dy_2 + y_2 dp_2 = w_1 dx_{12} + x_{12} dw_1 + w_2 dx_{22} + x_{22} dw_2$$

$$= w_1 dx_{12} + x_{12} dw_1 + w_2 dx_{22}.\qquad (5)$$

But

$$dy_2 = \frac{\partial f_2}{\partial x_1} dx_{12} + \frac{\partial f_2}{\partial x_2} dx_{22}$$

$$= (w_1/p_2) dx_{12} + (w_2/p_2) dx_{22}\qquad (6)$$

297

PROBLEM 32

from profit-maximizing first-order conditions for competitive firms. Plugging equation (6) into (5) and recalling that $w_1 = 1$, it is now clear that

$$dp_2 = (x_{12}/y_2)\, dw_1$$

$$= (w_1 x_{12}/y_2)\,[dw_1/w_1]$$

$$= s_2^1\, \frac{dw_1}{w_1} = s_2^1\, dw_1 \tag{7}$$

Similarly,

$$dp = s_1^1\, [dw_1 + t_1]. \tag{8}$$

(c) Inserting equations (7) and (8) into equation (1), one finds that

$$\frac{dy_1}{y_1} = \varepsilon_1 [s_1^1 (dw_1 + t) - s_2^1\, dw_1].$$

This relation combines with equation (2) to reveal that

$$\varepsilon_1 [s_2^1 - s_1^1]\, dw_1 + s_1^1 (dx_{11}/x_{11}) + s_1^2 (dx_{21}/x_{21}) = \varepsilon_1 s_1^1 t. \tag{9a}$$

In addition, equations (3a) and (3b) combine with equation (4) to show that

$$\sigma_2 \, dw_1 - \frac{x_{21}}{x_{22}} \frac{dx_{21}}{x_{21}} + \frac{x_{11}}{x_{12}} \frac{dx_{11}}{x_{11}} = 0 \text{ and} \qquad (9b)$$

$$-\sigma_1 \, dw_1 - \frac{dx_{21}}{x_{21}} + \frac{dx_{11}}{x_{11}} = \sigma_1 t. \qquad (9c)$$

In matrix notation, then

$$\begin{vmatrix} \varepsilon_1[s_2^1 - s_1^1] & s_1^1 & s_1^1 \\ \sigma_2 & -\frac{x_{21}}{x_{22}} & \frac{x_{11}}{x_{12}} \\ \sigma_1 & -1 & 1 \end{vmatrix} \begin{vmatrix} dw_1 \\ dx_{21}/x_{21} \\ dx_{11}/x_{11} \end{vmatrix} = \begin{vmatrix} \varepsilon_1 s_1^1 t \\ 0 \\ \sigma_1 t \end{vmatrix}.$$

(d) Cramer's Rule applies, so

$$dw_1 = \begin{vmatrix} \varepsilon_1 s_1^1 t & s_1^1 & s_2^1 \\ 0 & -\frac{x_{21}}{x_{22}} & \frac{x_{11}}{x_{12}} \\ \sigma_1 t & -1 & 1 \end{vmatrix} D^{-1} \qquad (10)$$

where

$$\{\varepsilon_1[S_2^1-S_1^1] \ [\frac{x_{11}}{x_{12}} - \frac{x_{21}}{x_{22}}] - \sigma_2 - \sigma_1[\frac{S_2^1 x_{21}}{x_{22}} + \frac{S_1^1 x_{11}}{x_{12}}]\} \equiv D > 0$$

is the determinant of the matrix in (9). The sign of D comes from observing that:

(i) $\sigma_1 < 0$ and $\sigma_2 < 0$ make the last two terms negative and

(ii) $\varepsilon_1 < 0$ plus the fact that $S_2^1 > S_1^1$ if and only if y_1 employs x_2 intensively (i.e., if and only if $\frac{x_{21}}{x_{11}} > \frac{x_{22}}{x_{12}}$).

Every term in D is therefore positive. From equation (10), then

$$dw_1 = \{\varepsilon_1 S_1^1 t \ [\frac{x_{11}}{x_{12}} - \frac{x_{21}}{x_{22}}] + \sigma_1 t \ [\frac{S_1^1 x_{11}}{x_{12}} + \frac{S_2^1 x_{21}}{x_{22}}]\} \ D^{-1}. \quad (11)$$

It is clear, now, that dw_1 can be positive only if the first term in equation (11) is positive; the second term is necessarily negative because $\sigma_1 < 0$. Since $\varepsilon_1 < 0$, dw_1 can be positive only if $(x_{11}/x_{12}) < (x_{21}/x_{22})$; $dw_1 > 0$ only if sector 2 uses x_1 relatively more intensively and sector 1 uses x_2 relatively more intensively.

(e) Only equation (8) would change among the critical equations. It would become

$$dp_1 = S_1^1[dw_1 + t] \, [1 + m].\tag{8'}$$

Equation (9a) would then become

$$\varepsilon_1[S_2^1 + S_1^1(1+m)]dw_1 + S_1^1 \frac{dx_{11}}{x_{11}} + S_1^2 \frac{dx_{21}}{x_{21}} = \varepsilon_1 S_1^1(1+m)t.\tag{9a'}$$

Plowing this change through the matrix algebra, one would find that

$$dw_1 = \frac{\varepsilon_1 S_1^1 t(1+m)[\frac{x_{11}}{x_{12}} - \frac{x_{21}}{x_{22}}] + \sigma_1 t[\frac{S_1^1 x_{11}}{x_{12}} + \frac{S_2^1 x_{21}}{x_{22}}]}{\varepsilon_1[S_2^1 - S_1^1(1+m)][\frac{x_{11}}{x_{12}} - \frac{x_{21}}{x_{22}}] - \sigma_2 - \sigma_1[\frac{S_2^1 x_{21}}{x_{22}} + \frac{S_1^1 x_{11}}{x_{12}}]}.$$

The qualitative results emerging from the perfectly competitive case are thus quite likely to remain intact for all but the largest values of m.

Harberger applied his results to empirical evidence

from the United States economy and concluded that corporate capital did, in fact, bear a significant portion of the corporate profits tax. It should be emphasized, however, that his results were based on linear approximation. Reliance on equations like (1) that involve total derivatives is, in fact, reliance on first-order Taylor series approximation. The results are, therefore, reliable only for small changes in the tax rate. Since the corporate tax rate has been set as high as 50% for larger corporations, the reliability of the Harberger results had been questioned.

Shoven investigated that reliability in two papers [(4) and with Whalley (5)] employing a fixed point computational algorithm devised by Scarf (3) [it was based on Brouwer's Theorem - see page 320]. While their computational technique was limited by its reliance on specific parametric values, it easily accommodated large differentials in the tax rate; and the Shoven and Whalley results ultimately supported Harberger's conclusion.

References

(1) Harberger, A.C., "The Incidence of the Corporate Income Tax," *Journal of Political Economy*, 70: 215-240, 1962.

(2) Mieszkowski, P.M., "On the Theory of Tax Incidence," *Journal of Political Economy*, 75: 250-262, 1967.

(3) Scarf, H., *The Computation of Economic Equilibria,* New Haven, Conn., Yale University Press, 1975.

(4) Shoven, J., "The Incidence and Efficiency Effects of Taxes on Income from Capital," *Journal of Political Economy,* 84: 1261-1283, 1976.

(5) Whalley, J. and J. Shoven, "A General Equilibrium Calculation of the Effects of Differential Taxation of Income from Capital in the United States," *Journal of Public Economics,* 1: 281-321, 1972.

33. **Uniqueness of Equilibria with Production**[1]

The concept of a fixed point index [pages 319-320] has been used extensively in researching the uniqueness of general equilibria. Works by Dierker (1 and 2), Mas-Colell (4), and Varian (9) are examples of this research. Except for the works of Mas-Colell (4) and Small (7), however, most of this research has been confined to exchange economies with no production.

One problem with extending the analysis to include production has been the absence of a natural function whose fixed points could be interpreted as economic equilibria. Kehoe (3) solved that problem for Leontief technologies, though, and this problem will present his suggestion. Inspired initially by some earlier work by Todd (8), he employs a specialized projection relationship to construct a mapping from the simplex to itself whose fixed points are equilibria. His subsequent discussion, not covered here, develops an index uniqueness rule for this mapping.

Let the consumption side of the model be formalized by a vector of n excess demand schedules in n prices for n goods according to:

---

[1] Material found in Chapters 17 and 18 is applicable here. Some fairly nonconventional mathematics is employed, but it all boils down to manipulation of fixed point theorems and Walras's law [see Section 17.4 beginning on page 317 for coverage in the exchange case.

$$\vec{\xi}(\vec{\pi}) \equiv \{\xi_1(\pi_1, \ldots, \pi_n), \ldots, \xi_n(\pi_1, \ldots, \pi_n)\}. \tag{1}$$

Assume that

(A.1) each $\xi_i(\vec{\pi})$ is continuously differentiable over $R^n - \{0\}$,

(A.2) each $\xi_i(\vec{\pi})$ is homogeneous of degree zero, and

(A.3) $\sum\limits_{i=1}^{n} \pi_i \xi_i(\vec{\pi}) = 0$ [Walras's law; page 317].

Production is formalized by an m x n activity matrix A [a Leontief technology - see page 20]. Aggregate production is therefore given by $A\vec{y}$ where $\vec{y} \equiv (y_1, \ldots, y_m)$ is a vector of activity levels. Further assume that

(A.4) A includes n free disposal activities (i.e., $-I_n$ is a submatrix of A) and

(A.5) there can be no production without inputs.

Define an equilibrium for the economy described by $(\vec{\xi}(\vec{\pi}), A)$ as a price vector $\vec{\pi}^*$ such that

(i) $(\vec{\pi}^*)'A \leq 0$,

(ii) there exists some $\vec{y}^* \geq 0$ such that $A\vec{y}^* = \vec{\xi}(\vec{\pi}^*)$, and

(iii) $\sum\limits_{i=1}^{n} \pi_i^* = 1$.

PROBLEM 33

Questions:

(a) Interpret each of the equilibrium conditions.

(b) Another way of defining continuity for $f:R^n \rightarrow R^m$ is to require that for $\vec{x}$ in its domain and any $\varepsilon > 0$, there exists a $\delta > 0$ such that every point within δ of $\vec{x}$ (in Euclidean terms) is mapped to within ε of $f(\vec{x})$ [the definition on page 478 deals with sequences converging to $\vec{x}$, but this is equivalent].

Define $p^N: R^n \rightarrow N$ by the rule that sends any q contained in R^n to the closest point in N. Show that p^N is continuous if N is convex (for those readers not concerned with the technicalities of this proof, at least show a counterexample that points to the necessity of N's being convex).

(c)   Define g: $s^n \rightarrow s^n$ by

$$g(\vec{\pi}) = p^{S_A}(\vec{\pi} + \vec{\xi}(\vec{\pi})),$$

where

$$S_A \equiv \{\vec{\pi}\epsilon R^n | \vec{\pi}' \; A \leq 0 \text{ and } \sum_{i=1}^{n} \pi_i = 1\}$$

is a simplex [see page 319].   Show, using part (b), that

306

PROBLEM 33

$g(\vec{\pi})$ is continuous.

(d) Show that fixed points of $g(\vec{\pi})$ are equilibria for the economy $(\vec{\xi}(\vec{\pi}), A)$.

Suggested Solutions:

(a) Condition (i), that $(\vec{\pi}^*)'A \leq 0$, implies that no excess profits can be made by running any activity; the best any activity can do is break even. Condition (ii) requires that supply equal demand in all markets, and combines with Walras' law (A.3) to show that every activity operated at a nonzero level makes zero profit:

$$(\vec{\pi}^*)'Ay^* = (\vec{\pi}^*)' \; \vec{\xi}(\vec{\pi}^*) = 0.$$

This is a competitive equilibrium [recall Chapter 13]. Condition (iii) simply calls upon (A.2) to place $\vec{\pi}^*$ on the n-dimensional simplex S^n.

(b) Consider the three possible cases. First of all, if q were to lie within the interior of N, then there would exist an $\varepsilon > 0$ such that $p^N(q)$ would be the identity mapping within $S(q, \varepsilon)$, the sphere of radius ε around q. The function p^N would certainly be continuous under this circumstance.

Now suppose, as a second possibility, that q were to

Figure 33.1

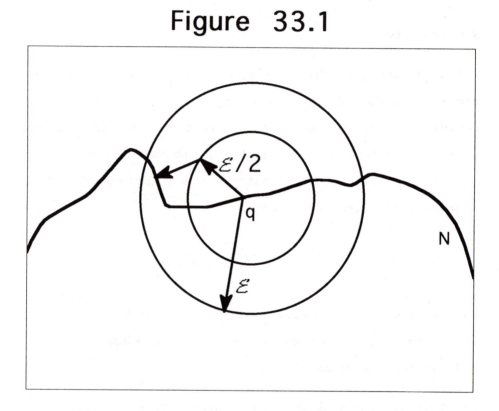

lie on the boundary of N. Then every $S(q,\varepsilon)$ would contain some points for which p^N would <u>not</u> be the identity mapping. For any $\varepsilon > 0$, however, $S(q,\varepsilon/2)$ would be mapped entirely into $S(q,\varepsilon)$ regardless of the convexity of N. This is because any $x\epsilon S(q,\varepsilon/2)$ could be no further than $\varepsilon/2$ from <u>both</u> its image $p^N(x)$ <u>and</u> q. The radius ε must therefore bound the distance between q and $p^N(x)$. The definition of continuity is once again satisfied, this time by setting $\delta = \varepsilon/2$. Figure 33.1 illustrates this second possibility in R^2.

The convexity of N has thus far not been required. That story changes, though, when q does not lie inside N. Figure 33.2 illustrates a counterexample for this case. Designating $q_0 \equiv p^N(q)$, it is clear that any neighborhood of q would contain points (the shaded area) that would be mapped to z and not q_0; and so there would exist no δ satisfying the definition of continuity.

If N were convex, though, continuity could be demonstrated. Figure 33.3 displays the limiting case in which the boundary of N shows a linear segment surrounding q_0; the line connecting q and q_0 must be orthogonal to that segment if $p^N(q) = \bar{q}$. For any $S(q_0,\varepsilon)$ contained within that segment, $\delta = \varepsilon$ would surely satisfy the requirement for continuity. To see this, simply note that any $x\varepsilon S(q,\varepsilon)$ would be orthogonally mapped into such an $S(q_0,\varepsilon)$.

If N were strictly concave, moreover, the image of $S(q,\varepsilon)$ would match, and $\delta = \varepsilon$ would still work. Figure 33.4

309

Figure 33.2

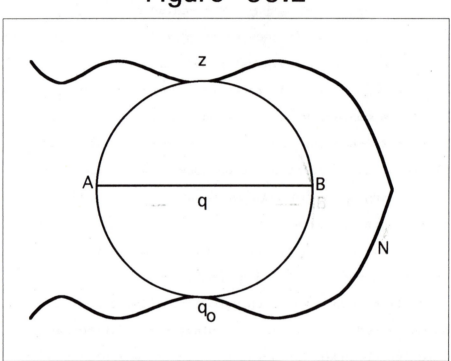

Figure   33.3

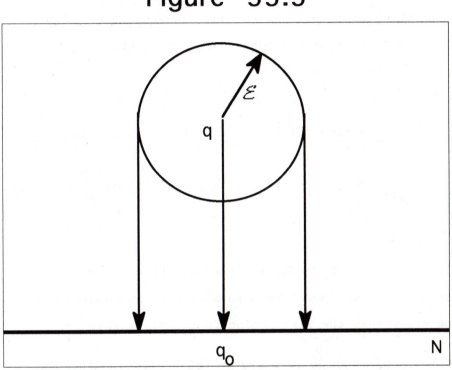

PROBLEM 33

illustrates this final case. Continuity is thus assured in each of the possible cases.

(c) The excess demand schedules given in equation (1) are continuous by assumption. If S_A were convex, therefore, then the g mapping would be continuous because it would be the composition of two continuous schedules. S_A <u>is</u> convex, though, because

$$[\alpha\vec{\pi}_1 + (1-\alpha)\vec{\pi}_2]'A = \alpha\vec{\pi}_1'A + (1-\alpha)\vec{\pi}_2'A \le 0 \text{ and}$$

$$\sum_{i=1}^{n} (\alpha\vec{\pi}_{i1} + (-\alpha)\vec{\pi}_{i2}) = \alpha \sum_{i=1}^{n} \vec{\pi}_{i1} + (1-\alpha) \sum_{i=1}^{n} \vec{\pi}_{i2} = 1$$

for any $\vec{\pi}_1$ and $\vec{\pi}_2$ in S_A, a subset of the simplex, so Brouwer's fixed point theorem applies. It remains only to be shown that the fixed point is in equilibria.

(d) The p_A^S mapping is based on the Euclidean distance between a point and its image. A fixed point minimizes that distance. The problem of finding a fixed point is therefore to solve:

$$\min_{\vec{p}} F(\vec{p}, \vec{\pi}^*)$$

s.t. $\vec{p}'A \le 0$ and $\langle \vec{p}', \vec{e} \rangle = 1$,

Figure   33.4

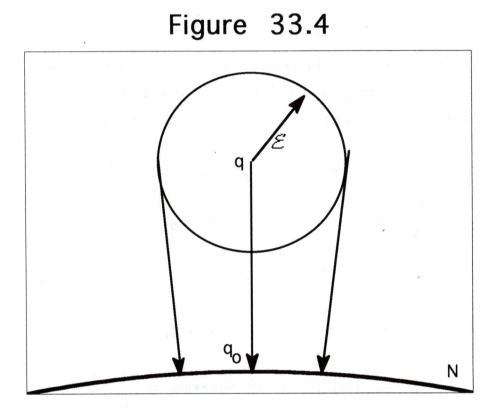

where $\vec{e} \equiv (1,\dots,1)$ is the unit vector and

$$F(\vec{p},\vec{\pi}^*) \equiv \frac{1}{2} \sum_{i=1}^{n} [p_i - \pi_i^* - \xi_i(\vec{\pi}^*)].\qquad (2)$$

For interior solutions (nonzero prices), the Kuhn-Tucker conditions [see page 503] guarantee the existence of Lagrange multipliers $\vec{y} = (y_1,\dots,y_m)$ and λ such that

$$DF(\vec{p}^*,\vec{\pi}^*) + A\vec{y} + \lambda\vec{e} = 0,\qquad (3)$$

$$(\vec{p}^*)'A \le 0,$$

$$(\vec{p}^*)'A\vec{y} = 0, \text{ and}\qquad (4)$$

$$(\vec{p}^*)'\vec{e} = 1.$$

Given equation (2), (3) can be expressed as

$$\vec{p}^* - \vec{\pi}^* - \vec{\xi}(\vec{\pi}^*) + A\vec{y} + \lambda\vec{e} = 0.\qquad (3')$$

It can now be seen that $\vec{p}^* = \vec{\pi}^*$. To that end, notice that equation $(3')$ would collapse to

PROBLEM 33

$$\vec{\xi}(\vec{\pi}^*) = A\vec{y} + \lambda\vec{e} \qquad\qquad (3")$$

if it were true. Furthermore, Walras's law [still page 317]
and equation (4) would show that

$$0 = (\vec{\pi}^*)'\vec{\xi}(\vec{\pi}^*)$$

$$= (\vec{\pi}^*)'[A\vec{y} + \lambda\vec{e})$$

$$= 0 + \lambda(\vec{\pi}^*)'\vec{e}. \qquad\qquad (5)$$

Equation (5) could be true only if $\lambda = 0$, and that would
make equation (3") read

$$\vec{\xi}(\vec{\pi}^*) = A\vec{y}.$$

This is, however, the equilibrium condition that supply
equals demand in all goods.

Kehoe continued from this point to construct an index
number criterion for uniqueness much like the one cited in
the text. In fact, the criteria developed from his
production model include many previous results as special
cases. His criteria can, for example, be used to show that
both nonsubstitutability (implying that n - 1 activities are

315

used in equilibrium) [see Section 18.9] and the weak axiom
of reveal preference [see page 133] imply uniqueness. Both
were previously known, but it is reassuring to see them fall
out of a new model.

His is a stronger result than either, of course, and
its only possible limitation is its dependence on the
Leontief technology. The significance of that dependence
can be diminished, however, by approximating any smooth unit
isoquant by a finite number of linear segments; Figure 33.5
shows how. Including activities in A defined by the
vertices of these segments incorporates nearly the same
degree of possible substitution. The activity analysis
modeling of production also has the advantage of having
computable fixed points. The algorithm developed by Scarf
(5 and 6) actually computes fixed points for Leontief
production models, and it can be applied directly to the
model outlined here. By placing the uniqueness restrictions
demonstrated by Kehoe on A, one can therefore do general
equilibrium comparative statics by simulation and be sure
that the changes being observed are not derived from a
change in equilibria.

References

(1) Dierker, E., "Two Remarks on the Number of Equilibria of
an Economy," *Econometrica*, 40: 951-953, 1972.

Figure   33.5

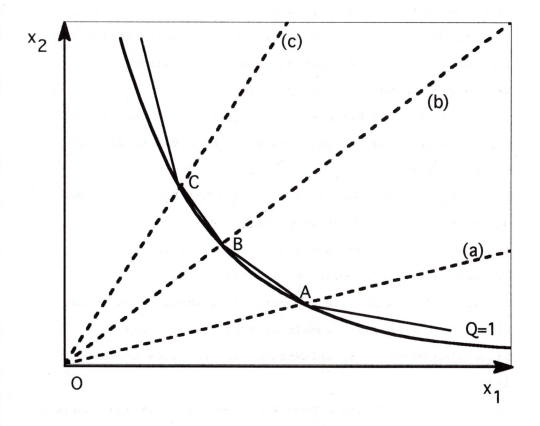

(2) Dierker, E., *Topological Methods in Walrasian Economics*, New York, Springer-Verlag, 1974.

(3) Kehoe, T., "An Index Theorem for General Equilibrium Models with Production," Cowles Foundation Paper No. 516, Yale University, 1979, and presented at the Summer Meetings of the Econometric Society in Montreal, 1979.

(4) Mas-Colell, A., "On the Continuity of Equilibrium Prices in Constant Returns Production Economies," *Journal of Mathematic Economics*, 2: 21-33, 1975.

(5) Scarf, H., "An Example of an Algorithm for Calculating General Equilibrium Prices," *American Economic Review* 59: 669-677, 1969.

(6) Scarf, H., *The Computation of Economic Equilibria*, New Haven, Conn., Yale University Press, 1975.

(7) Small, S., "Global Analysis and Economics, IV," *Journal of Mathematical Economics*, 1: 119-127, 1974.

(8) Todd, M., "A Note on Computing Equilibria in Economies with Activity Analysis Models of Production," CORE Discussion Paper 7736, Université Catholique de Louvain, 1977.

(9) Varian, H., "A Third Remark on the Number of Equilibria of an Economy," *Econometrica*, 43: 985-986, 1974.

34. Uncertainty and Tax Incidence in General Equilibrium[1]

The existence of uncertainty and risk aversion frequently undermines longstanding results produced under certainty and/or under the auspices of linear decision rules. This problem will explore one such circumstance within a general equilibrium context. It will not delineate the solution methodology as completely; it will, instead, concentrate on the interpretation and manipulation of the mathematical products of standard methodology. Work that stops short of this type of interpretation "endgame" is bad economics, so it is as important to become skilled in interpretation as it is to become skilled in the application of solution techniques.

Suppose that there were perfect markets for two goods (x_1 and x_2) with well-defined world prices p_1 and p_2. Let the production of these goods in an open economy be represented by linearly homogeneous production schedules on two factors (K and L). Let the supply of both be perfectly inelastic, but let their perfect mobility guarantee full employment. In particular, let

$$x_1 = F^1(K_1, L_1) \equiv L_1 f_1(k_1) \text{ with } k_1 = K_1/L_1,$$

---

[1] Material found in Chapters 17 and 18 is applicable here, but this problem will draw heavily upon more fundamental concepts described in Chapters 1, 9, 12, and 13.

represent production in sector 1, and

$$x_2 = \alpha F^2(K_1, L_2) \equiv \alpha L_2 f_2(k_2) \text{ with } k_2 = K_2/L_2,$$

represent production in sector 2; note the use of "per capita" production functions [see Problem 3].

The parameter α reflects uncertainty in production for the second sector of the type modeled by Bardhan and Srinivasan (1), Batra (2), Ratti and Stone (5), and others. The specific results of this problem are, in fact, lifted directly from Ratti and Stone. Individual producers in sector 2 will, in particular, maximize the expected utility (given identical utility schedules) of the profits that they generate, so that their decisions can be represented as the results of a maximization procedure applied to $u_2(\pi_1)$. Part (d) will show why; certainty in the production process embodied in sector 1 is the key.

Questions:

(a) Set up the solution methodology for determining the effect of a tax on the return to K_1 on factor employment captured by changes in L_1, L_2, k_1, and k_2. That is, let

$$w = w_1 = w_2$$

represent the wage paid to L in either sector, and

PROBLEM 34

$$r = r_2 = (1 - t_1)r_1$$

characterize the relative costs of K_1 and K_2. Manipulate the model to a point where, by Cramer's Rule, you could solve for dL_1/dt_1, dL_2/dt_1, dk_1/dt_1, and dk_2/dt_1.

(b) The denominator of the three equation system that produces dL_2/dt_1, dk_1/dt_1, and dk_2/dt_1 turns out to be

$$D = p_1 p_2 f_1'' \; f_2'' \; [k_2 - k_1]^2 E\{u_2'(\pi_2)\}E\{\alpha u_2'(\pi_2)\}$$

$$+ \; [(w/r)+k_2]L_1 p_2[f_2 f_2''/f_2']E\{u_2''\{\alpha p_2 F_1^2 - r]^2\} \; E\{\alpha u_2'\}$$

$$+ \; [(w/r)+k_1]L_2 p_1[f_1 f_1''/f_1']E\{u_2''\}$$

$$+ \; p_1 p_2 f_1'' f_2''[f_2/f_2' L_2(k_2 - k_1)^2 E\{u_2''\}[\alpha p_2 F_1^2 - r]\}E\{\alpha u_2'\}.$$

Assess the sign of D.

(c) For the tax outlined in part (b),

$$\frac{dr}{dt_1} = \frac{rk_1}{k_2 - k_1} [1 - \frac{\phi(t_1)}{D}] \tag{1}$$

where

PROBLEM 34

$$\phi(t_1) = [\tfrac{w}{r}+k_2]L_2[\tfrac{w}{r}+k_2]p_1 f_1'' E\{u_2'\}E\{u_2'[\alpha p_2 F_1^2 - r]^2\}$$

$$+ \frac{k_2}{k_1} L_1 p_2 \frac{f_2 f_2''}{f_2'} [\tfrac{w}{r}+k_2]\ E\{u_2'\}E\{u_2''[\alpha p_2 F_1^2 - r]^2\}.$$

If the certainty result holds that

$$\frac{dr}{dt_1} = \frac{rk_1}{k_2 - k_1},$$

show that the certainty result holds under risk
neutrality, but that the effect of t_1 on r is diminished
under uncertainty.   Produce the same conclusions for
$[dr/dt_2]$ and $[dr/dt]$ where t_2 and t represent taxes on
labor employed in sector 1 and the product of sector 1,
respectively.   Use the following relationships:

$$\frac{dr}{dt_2} = \frac{w}{k_2 - k_1}[1 - \frac{\phi(t_2)}{D}], \qquad (2a)$$

$$\frac{dr}{dt} = \frac{w+rk_1}{k_1 - k_2}[1 - \frac{\phi(t)}{D}], \qquad (2b)$$

322

PROBLEM 34

$$\phi(t_2) = [\tfrac{w}{r}+k_1][\tfrac{w}{r}+k_2]L_2P_1f_1''E\{u_2'\}A$$

$$+ [\tfrac{w}{r}+ k_2]L_1P_2[f_2f_2''/f_2']E\{\alpha u_2'\}A \ ,$$

$$\phi(t) = \frac{w+rk_2}{w+rk_1} [\tfrac{w}{r}+k_2]L_1[f_2f_2''/f_2']E\{\alpha u_2'\}A$$

$$+ [\tfrac{w}{r}+k_1]L_2P_1[f_1f_1''/f_1']E\{u_2'\} \ , \quad \text{and}$$

$$A \equiv E\{u''[\alpha p_2F_2^2 - r]\} \ .$$

The terms outside the square brackets on the right-hand sides of (2a) and (2b) represent, as before, the certainty results. Prove that the equivalence between equal rate input taxes, on the one hand, and the identical rate commodity tax, on the other, survives the introduction of uncertainty. Finally, show that capital suffers most under t_1 among equal yield tax alternatives.

(d) Show that the certainty results are obtained even with expected utility maximizing behavior in sector 2.

Suggested Solutions:

(a) In sector 1, profit maximization given $x_1 = L_1f_1(k_1)$ produces familiar first-order conditions [see Problem 3]:

323

$$w_1 = p_1[f_1(-) - k_1 f_1'(-)] \text{ and} \tag{3a}$$

$$r = p_1 f_1'(-). \tag{3b}$$

The second sector, complicated by the maximization of the expected utility of prospective profits,

$$E\{u_2(\pi_2)\} = E\{u_2[p_2 \alpha F^2(K_2, L_2) - r_2 K_2 - w_2 L_2\}$$

produces different first-order conditions:

$$0 = E\{u_2'(\pi_2)[p_2 \alpha F_2^2 - w_2]\}$$

$$= E\{u_2'(\pi_2)[p_2 \alpha[f_2 - k_2 f_2'] - w_2]\}, \text{ and} \tag{4a}$$

$$0 = E\{u_2'(\pi_2)[p_2 \alpha F_1^2 - r_2]\}$$

$$= E\{u_2'(\pi_2)[p_2 \alpha f_2' - r_2]\}, \tag{4b}$$

given $x_2 = \alpha F^2(K_2, L_2) = L_2 f_2(k_2)$. Because $w_1 = w_2$ and $r_2 = r = (1 - t_1)r_1$, equations (3a) through (4b) combine to require that

PROBLEM 34

$$E\{u_2'[p_2\alpha f_2' - (1-t_1)p_1 f_1']\} = 0, \text{ and} \qquad (5a)$$

$$E\{u_2'[p_2\alpha(f_2' - k_2 f_2') - p_1(f_1 - k_1 f_1')]\} = 0. \qquad (5b)$$

Differentiating these two equations with respect to t_1 and combining the results with the derivatives of the input constraints,

$$dL_1 = -dL_2 \text{ and} \qquad (6a)$$

$$dL_2 = -\frac{1}{k_2 - k_1} \{L_1 dk_1 + L_2 dk_2\}, \qquad (6b)$$

generate 4 equations through which the effect of changes in t_1 on L_1, L_2, k_1, and k_2 can be deduced. The consequent adjustments in factor returns can then be determined by working with the pricing equations: equations (3a) through (4b). Note that (6a) and (6b) follow from supply constraints

$$L_1 + L_2 = \bar{L} \text{ and}$$

$$K_1 + K_2 = \bar{K} = L_1 k_1 + L_2 k_2 .$$

325

(b) Recalling that $f_j''(-) < 0$ and $u_j'' \leq 0$, it is clear that the first three terms in the recorded specification of D are necessarily nonnegative; the first, in fact, is strictly positive. The fourth term has a questionable sign, but only because the sign of

$$E\{u_2''(\pi_2)[\alpha p_2 F_1^2 - r]\}$$

is not immediate. To explore that sign under the assumption that absolute risk aversion [see page 177],

$$R_2(\pi_2) \equiv - u_2''(\pi_2) / u_2'(\pi_2) ,$$

is decreasing, consider the two possibilities in turn:

(i) In good states of nature [i.e., when
$$\alpha p_2 F_1^2(0) \geq r],$$
$\pi_2 > 0$ and $- u_2''(\pi_2) / u_2'(\pi_2) < R_2(0)$.
As a result, rearranging and multiplying by a positive number reveals that

$$- u_2''(\pi_2)[\alpha p_2 F_1^2 - r]$$

$$< u_2'(\pi_2)[\alpha p_2 F_1^2 - r]R_2(0). \qquad (7)$$

326

(ii)   In bad states of nature [i.e., when

$$\alpha p_2 F_1^2(0) \leq r],$$

$\pi_2 < 0$ and $- u_2''(\pi_2) / u_2'(\pi_2) \geq R_2(0)$.
As a result, multiplying this time
by a negative number reveals that

$$- u_2''(\pi_2)[\alpha p_2 F_1^2 - r]$$

$$< u_2'(\pi_2)[\alpha p_2 F_1^2 - r]R_2(0). \tag{8}$$

Taking expectations of the weighted sum of equations (7) and
(8), finally notice that

$$E\{u_2''(\pi_2)[\alpha p_2 F_1^2 - r]\} < R_2(0)E\{u_2'(\pi_2)[\alpha p_2 F_1^2 - r]\} = 0$$

because the first-order condition for maximizing $E\{u_2(\pi_2)\}$
requires that

$$E\{u_2'(\pi_2)[\alpha p_2 F_1^2 - r]\} = 0. \tag{9}$$

For decreasing absolute risk aversion, therefore,

$$D = (+) + (+) + (+) + (+) > 0.$$

Moreover, for $u_2'(-) = 0$,

$$D = (+) + 0 > 0 ,$$

as well.

It should also be clear, at this point, that the same mathematical argument applied to the case of increasing absolute risk aversion generates the opposite result; i.e., if $R_2'(\pi_2) > 0$, then

$$E\{u_2''(\pi_2)[\alpha p_2 F_1^2 - r]\} > 0.$$

And finally, if $R_2'(\pi_2) = 0$, then the analysis shows that

$$\{u_2'(\pi_2)[\alpha p_2 F_1^2 - r]\} = R(0)\{u_2'(\pi_2)[\alpha p_2 F_1^2 - r] = 0$$

in all cases, and so

$$E\{u_2''(\pi_2)[\alpha p_2 F_1^2 - r]\} \equiv 0.$$

(c) With the sign of D determined, it is possible to interpret the results recorded in equations (1) through (2b). Notice, first of all, that

PROBLEM 34

$$\phi(t) = \begin{cases} (+)(-)(-)+(+)(-)(-) > 0 & u_2''(-) < 0 \\ \\ 0 & u_2''(-) = 0. \end{cases}$$

Risk neutrality and equation (1) therefore produce the certainty result that

$$\left.\frac{dr}{dt_1}\right|_{u_2''=0} = \frac{rf_1}{k_2 - k_1}[1 - 0]$$

and that decreasing risk aversion reduces that sensitivity:

$$\left.\frac{dr}{dt_1}\right|_{u_2''<0} = \frac{rf_1}{k_2 - k_1}[1 - (+)] < \left.\frac{dr}{dt_1}\right|_{u_2''=0} = \frac{rf_1}{k_2 - k_1}.$$

Similarly, the effect of a tax on labor is less pronounced under increasing absolute risk aversion:

PROBLEM 34

$$\left.\frac{dr}{dt_2}\right|_{u_2''<0} = \frac{w}{k_2 - k_1}[1 - (+)] < \left.\frac{dr}{dt_2}\right|_{u_2''=0} = \frac{w}{k_2 - k_1}$$

as is the effect of a commodity tax on x_1:

$$\left.\frac{dr}{dt}\right|_{u_2''<0} = \frac{w + rf_1}{k_2 - k_1}[1 - (+)] < \left.\frac{dr}{dt}\right|_{u_2''=0} = \frac{w + rf_1}{k_2 - k_1}.$$

Setting $dt_1 = dt_2 = dt$ to study the effect of equal rate taxes, equations (1) through (2b) combine to show that

$$\frac{dr}{dt} + \frac{dr}{dt_1} = \frac{dr}{dt_2}$$

regardless of risk preference; the equivalence of these taxes thus survives the introduction of risk aversion. To study equal yield taxes, a more complicated story must be told. Equal yields require, first of all, that

$$rK_1 \, dt_1 = wL_1 \, dt_2 = p_1L_1f_1(-) \, dt;$$

i.e.,

PROBLEM 34

$$dt_1 = [p_1 L_1 f_1 / rK_1] \, dt \quad \text{and}$$

$$dt_2 = [p_1 L_1 f_1 / wL_1] \, dt \, .$$

As a result,

$$\left. dr \right|_{t_1} = \frac{p_1 f_1}{(k_2 - k_1)} \, [1 - \frac{\phi(t_1)}{D}] \, dt,$$

$$\left. dr \right|_{t_2} = \frac{p_1 f_1}{(k_2 - k_1)} \, [1 - \frac{\phi(t_2)}{D}] \, dt, \quad \text{and}$$

$$\left. dr \right|_{t} = \frac{p_1 f_1}{(k_2 - k_1)} \, [1 - \frac{\phi(t)}{D}] \, dt.$$

Since $\phi(t_1) = \phi(t_2) = \phi(t) = 0$ with risk neutrality, all of these taxes affect the price of capital in the same way. With risk aversion registered by $u_2''(-) \neq 0$, however,

$$\phi(t_1) > \phi(t) > \phi(t_2) \quad \text{if } k_2 > k_1 \text{ and}$$

$$\phi(t_1) < \phi(t) < \phi(t_2) \quad \text{if } k_2 < k_1.$$

As a result,

331

$$\left. dr \right|_{t_1} \; < \; \left. dr \right|_t \; < \; \left. dr \right|_{t_2} \; < \; 0, \qquad k_2 \; < \; k_1,$$

and

$$0 \; < \; \left. dr \right|_{t_1} \; < \; \left. dr \right|_t \; < \; \left. dr \right|_{t_2} \; , \qquad k_2 \; < \; k_1.$$

Regardless of the direction of the effect, therefore, capital is worse off.

(d) To erase the uncertainty from the modeling, let $\alpha \equiv 1$ in all states of nature. The expected value operator then disappears from all of the ϕ expressions <u>and</u> equation (4b). The latter, now reading

$$\frac{\partial u}{\partial K_2} \; = \; u_2'(\pi_2)[P_2 F_1^2 \; - \; r] \; = \; 0$$

can only be satisfied by

$$[P_2 F_1^2 \; - \; r] \; = \; 0 \qquad\qquad\qquad (10)$$

(because $u_2' > 0$). Plugging (10) into the ϕ equations therefore reveals that

PROBLEM 34

$$\phi(t_1)\Big|_{\alpha=1} = \phi(t_2)\Big|_{\alpha=1} = \phi(t)\Big|_{\alpha=1} = 0 ,$$

and equations (1) through (2b) replicate the indicated certainty results.

This problem has been a notationally arduous excursion through only part of Ratti and Stone (5). They continue to consider other tax results, and the interested reader is referred to their article for further details. The uncertainty results can be found in Batra (2), but this exercise should have provided the insight with which to glean those results from the Ratti and Stone paper by considering special cases.

References

(1) Bardhan, P.K., and T. N. Srinivasan, "Cropsharing Tenancy in Agriculture: A theoretical and empirical analysis," *American Economic Review*, 61: 48-64, 1971.

(2) Batra, R.N., "Resource Allocation in a General Equilibrium Model of Production under Uncertainty," *Journal of Economic Theory*, 8: 50-63, 1974.

(3) Batra, R.N., and A. Ullah, "Competitive Firm and the Theory of Input Demand under Price Uncertainty," *Journal of Political Economy*, 82: 537-548, 1974.

(4) Penner, R.G., "Uncertainty and the Short Run Shifting of

the Corporation Tax," *Oxford Economic Papers,* 19: 99–110, 1967.

(5) Ratti, R., and P. Stone, "The General Equilibrium Theory of Tax Incidence under Uncertainty," *Journal of Economic Theory,* 14: 68–83, 1977.

(6) Sandmo, A., "On the Theory of Competitive Firm under Price Uncertainty," *American Economic Review,* 61: 65–73, 1971.

35. Resource Stock Externalities in General Equilibrium[1]

Problem 28 concentrated your attention on a resource stock externality model presented under the assumptions of partial equilibrium by Vernon Smith (3). This problem will explore his subsequent analysis of the same problem under general equilibrium.

Let there continue to be n firms producing fish (y_1) and n firms producing some other good (y_2) in accordance with

$$y_1 = f_1(x_1, Y) \text{ and } y_2 = f_2(x_2). \tag{1}$$

Assume that $f_1(0,Y) = f_1(x_1,0) = f_2(0) = 0$. The sole factor of production common to both is assumed to be available in fixed supply:

$$x_1 + x_2 = (\bar{X}/n) \equiv \bar{x}. \tag{2}$$

The variable Y represents the biomass of fish available in the ocean. That population is perpetuated from one time period to another by a reproductive function denoted F(Y), and there exist levels $\hat{Y}$ and $\bar{Y}$ such that

---

[1] Material found in Chapters 17 and 18 is applicable here, but the analysis will draw heavily on fundamental concepts presented in earlier chapters; recall that Problem 28 made reference to Chapters 2, 4, 10, 13, 14, and 15.

$F(\bar{Y}) = F(0) = 0$ and $F'(\hat{Y}) = 0$.

The variable y_1 reflects the number of fish lost to the population per firm per time period, so steady state can be characterized by

$$F(Y) = nf_1(x_1,Y) = 0. \tag{3}$$

Let each consumer's utility schedule be given by

$$u = u(y_1,y_2)$$

and let the wage paid each unit of x be w.

Questions:

(a) Characterize the production frontier between y_1 and y_2 for a given $\bar{x}$ and Y. Graph the frontier, and show what happens to it when Y increases for a fixed $\bar{x}$.

(b) Characterize the locus of pairs (y_1,y_2) that satisfy equations (1), (2), and (3) for a particular $\bar{x}$. Graph this locus, and compute its slope. Relate its slope to the slope of the production frontier.

(c) Compare competitive equilibrium with Pareto optimality.

(d) Show that the competitive equilibrium can be moved
into line with Pareto optimality by charging fishermen

$$\hat{c} = - \{ n \frac{\partial f_1}{\partial Y} \frac{\partial f_2}{\partial x} / \frac{dF}{dY} \frac{\partial f_1}{\partial x} \}$$

for each fish caught.

Suggested Solutions:

Parts (a) and (b) follow from the total derivatives of
their defining equations. Part (c) follows directly from
the definitions of competitive equilibrium and Pareto
optimality, and the answer to part (d) will become clear in
the course of doing (c).

(a) The production frontier $P(\bar{x}, Y)$ is a locus of pairs
(Y_1, Y_2) that satisfy the market-clearing conditions recorded
in equations (1) and (2) for a given $(\bar{x}, Y)$. From those
clearing conditions, one sees that

$$dy = \frac{\partial f_1}{\partial x} dx_1,$$

$$dy_2 = \frac{\partial f_2}{\partial x} dx_2, \text{ and}$$

$$dx_1 = - dx_2$$

for any given Y. As a result,

$$\left.\frac{dy_2}{dy_1}\right|_{p(\bar{x},y)} = \frac{\partial f_2}{\partial x}\, dx_2 \,/\, \frac{\partial f_1}{\partial x}\, dx_1 = -\, \{\frac{\partial f_2}{\partial x} \,/\, \frac{\partial f_1}{\partial x}\} < 0.$$

Figure 35.1 illustrates such a frontier, as well as the effect of increasing Y on such a frontier; altering Y has no effect on the maximum amount of y_2 that can be produced (designated $\bar{y}_2$), but it does change the potential for y_1.

(b) Smith's notion of a *bionomic* equilibrium $B(\bar{x})$ is of locus of pairs (y_1, y_2) that satisfy not only equations (1) and (2) for a given $\bar{x}$, but also equation (3). It can be shown that $B(\bar{x})$ is shaped like a teardrop falling from $\bar{y}_2$.

To see this, note first of all that $Y = 0$ and $Y = \bar{Y}$ can both satisfy equations (1), (2), and (3) at $(0, \bar{y}_2)$:

$$0 = f_1(0,0), \quad \bar{y}_2 = f_2(\bar{x}), \quad 0 + \bar{x} = \bar{x}, \quad \text{and} \quad F(0) = nf_1(0,0) = 0.$$

Meanwhile,

$$0 = f_1(0,\bar{Y}), \quad \bar{y}_2 = f_2(\bar{x}), \quad 0 + \bar{x} = \bar{x}, \quad \text{and} \quad F(\bar{Y}) = nf_1(0,\bar{Y}) = 0.$$

Now consider Y' and Y'' such that $0 < Y' < Y'' < \hat{Y} < \bar{Y}$ (where $\hat{Y}$ is defined by

Figure 35.1

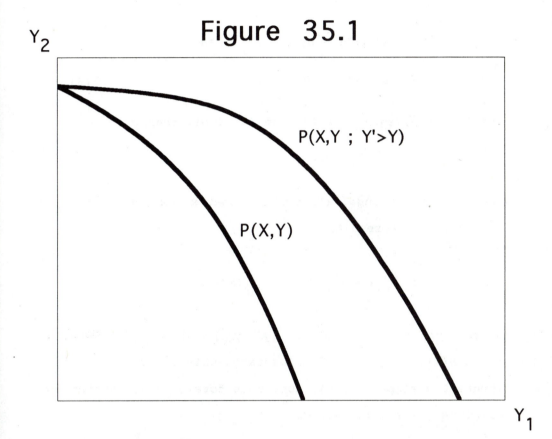

$$F'(\hat{Y}) = 0 \text{ and } F(Y') = F(Y'').$$

Let

$$nf_1(x'_1, Y') = ny'_1 = F(Y') \text{ and} \qquad (4)$$

$$nf_1(x''_1, Y'') = ny''_1 = F(Y''). \qquad (5)$$

Clearly, then, equations (4) and (5) imply that

$$y'_1 = y''_1$$

Since $Y' < Y''$, though, $x'_1 > x''_1$ so that $\bar{x} - x'_1 \equiv x'_2 < x''_2$ $\equiv \bar{x} - x''_1$. As a result,

$$f_2(x'_2) \equiv y'_2 < y''_2 \equiv f_2(x''_2).$$

For $y_1 - y'_1 = y''_1$, therefore, (y'_1, y'_2) and (y''_1, y''_2) both lie on $B(\bar{x})$. Figure 35.2 illustrates this locus. To compute the slope of $B(\bar{x})$, note that totally differentiating equations (1) and (3) yields

$$dy_1 = \frac{\partial f_1}{\partial x} dx_1 + \frac{\partial f_1}{\partial Y} dY,$$

$$dy_2 = \frac{\partial f_2}{\partial x} dx_2,$$

Figure 35.2

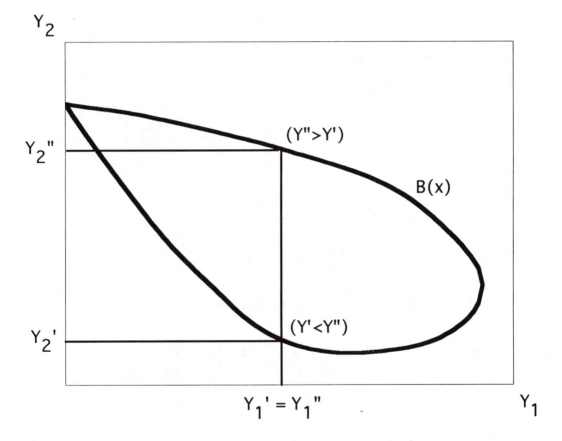

$$dx = - dx, \text{ and}$$

$$[\frac{dF}{dY} - n \frac{\partial f_1}{\partial Y}] \, dY = n \frac{\partial f_1}{\partial x} \, dx_1.$$

Combining these, one sees that

$$dy_1 = \frac{\partial f_1}{\partial x} \, dx_1 + \frac{\partial f_1}{\partial Y} \, [n \frac{\partial f_1}{\partial x} \, dx_1 / (\frac{dF}{dy} - n \frac{\partial f_1}{\partial Y})]$$

$$= \frac{- \frac{\partial f}{\partial x} (\frac{dF}{dY} - n \frac{\partial f_1}{\partial Y}) - \frac{\partial f_1}{\partial Y} \, n \frac{\partial f_1}{\partial x}}{\frac{\partial f_2}{\partial x} (\frac{dF}{dY} - n \frac{\partial f_1}{\partial Y})} \, dy_2.$$

Further manipulation finally concludes with

$$\frac{dy_2}{dy_1}\Big|_{B(\bar{x})} = - \{\frac{\partial f_2}{\partial x} / \frac{\partial f_1}{\partial x}\} + \{n \frac{\partial f_1}{\partial Y} \frac{\partial f_2}{\partial x} / \frac{\partial f_1}{\partial x} \frac{dF}{dY} \}$$

$$= \frac{\partial y_2}{\partial y_1}\Big|_{P(\bar{x},Y)} + \{n \frac{\partial f_1}{\partial Y} \frac{\partial f_2}{\partial x} / \frac{\partial f_1}{\partial x} \frac{dF}{dY}\}. \qquad (6)$$

(c) From equation (1) and the representation of consumer

utility, it is clear that competitive equilibrium is characterized by a price ratio defined by

$$\frac{P_1}{P_1} = \frac{\partial u}{\partial y_1} \Big/ \frac{\partial u}{\partial y_2} = \frac{\partial f_2}{\partial x} \Big/ \frac{\partial f_1}{\partial x} ; \qquad (7)$$

the social indifference curve must be tangent to the production frontier $P(\bar{x}, Y)$ [see page 351]. To see this, note that every firm will hire x to the point where its marginal revenue produce equals w;

$$P_2 \frac{\partial f_2}{\partial x_2} = w = P_1 \frac{\partial f_1}{\partial x_1}.$$

Pareto optimality is meanwhile characterized by the first-order conditions to the problem

$$\max_{x_1, x_2, Y} \{u[f_1(x_1, Y), f_2(x_2)]\}$$

$$\text{s.t.} \ x_1 + x_2 = \bar{x} \ \text{and}$$

$$F(Y) = nf_1(x_1, Y).$$

The appropriate first-order conditions are

$$\frac{\partial u}{\partial y_1} \frac{\partial f_1}{\partial x} - \lambda - \mu n \frac{\partial f_1}{\partial x} = 0,$$

$$\frac{\partial u}{\partial y_2} \frac{\partial f_1}{\partial x} - \lambda = 0, \text{ and}$$

$$\frac{\partial u}{\partial y_1} \frac{\partial f_1}{\partial Y} + \mu \left[\frac{dF}{dY} - n \frac{\partial f_1}{\partial Y}\right] = 0.$$

Combining these conditions to eliminate the shadow prices, one finds that

$$\frac{\partial u}{\partial y_1} \frac{\partial f_1}{\partial x} - \frac{\partial u}{\partial y_2} \frac{\partial f_2}{\partial x} + [n \frac{\partial f_1}{\partial x} \frac{\partial u}{\partial y_1} \frac{\partial f_1}{\partial Y} / (\frac{dF}{dY} - n \frac{\partial f_1}{\partial Y}) = 0.$$
(8)

After some algebra that amounts to collecting terms, equation (8) becomes

$$\{\frac{\partial u}{\partial y_1} / \frac{\partial u}{\partial y_2}\} = \{\frac{\partial f_2}{\partial x} / \frac{\partial f_1}{\partial x}\} - \{n \frac{\partial f_1}{\partial Y} \frac{\partial f_2}{\partial x} / \frac{dF}{dY} \frac{\partial f_1}{\partial x_1}\}.$$
(9)

Since the right-hand sides of (6) and (9) match, one sees that Pareto optimality is characterized by tangencies between the social indifference curves and the $B(\bar{x})$ locus.

Figure 35.3 shows a Pareto optimal point at E^*; it must always lie in the upper, negatively sloped region of $B(\bar{x})$ [see Smith (4), page 113]. Competitive equilibrium can harvest too many fish or too few fish depending on the

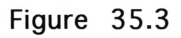

Figure 35.3

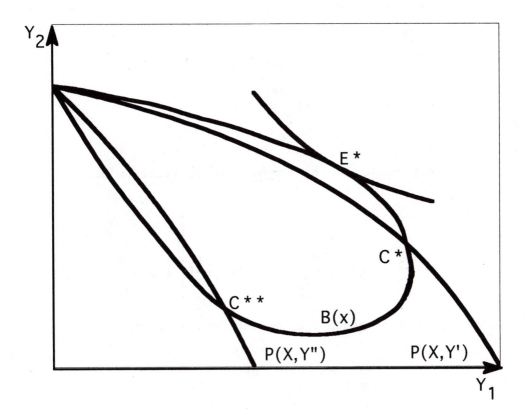

$P(\bar{x},Y)$ locus. Figure 35.3 also shows both possible cases at c^* and c^{**} respectively.

(d) If a charge of c were placed on every fish caught, then the firm would maximize $\{(p_1-c)f_1(x_1,Y) - w_1x_1\}$ with respect to x_1. The first-order condition for the hiring decision would then read

$$(p_1-c)\ \frac{\partial f_1}{\partial x} - w = 0.$$

The tangency condition for competitive equilibrium would then become

$$\frac{p_1}{p_2} = \frac{\partial u}{\partial y_1}\ /\ \frac{\partial u}{\partial y_2} = \frac{\partial f_2}{\partial x}\ /\ \frac{\partial f_1}{\partial x} + c.$$

Pareto optimality could then be achieved by setting

$$\hat{c} = -\ n\ \{\ \frac{\partial f_1}{\partial Y}\frac{\partial f_2}{\partial x}\ /\ \frac{dF}{dY}\frac{\partial f_1}{\partial x}\ \}.$$

Since $dF/dY < 0$, $\hat{c} > 0$ in the upper region of $B(\bar{x})$.

The emphasis of the Smith paper is on constructing and analyzing the production frontiers. That has been the emphasis of this problem, as well. Comparing these results with those of Problem 28 is nonetheless interesting. When general equilibrium feedbacks are allowed, the competitive industry need not overfish. If one believes that markets work well enough for these feedbacks to be registered at the fisheries, then one should now view the partial equilibrium results with some skepticism. If one does not believe that these feedbacks are noticed by the fishermen, however, one might still argue strongly that previous results are more germane.

References

(1) Gordon, H.S., "The Economic Theory of a Common-Property Resource: The Fishery," *Journal of Political Economy*, 62: 124-142, 1954.

(2) Plourde, C., "Exploitation of Common Property Replenishable Natural Resources," *Western Economic Journal*, 9: 256-266, 1971.

(3) Smith, V., "Economics of Production from Natural Resources," *American Economic Review*, 58: 409-431, 1968.

(4) Smith, V., "General Equilibrium with a Replenishable Natural Resource," *Review of Economic Studies, Symposium on the Economics of Natural Resources*, 105-116, 1974.

36. Investment Timing and the Effect of a Tax Credit[1]

Pontryagin's maximization principle is an immensely valuable tool when optimization is to be conducted over time. Roughly put in one of its simplest forms, the principle is applied to problems of the following type:

$$\max \int_0^\infty \alpha(t)u[z(t),y(t)] \, dt$$

$$\text{s.t. } \dot{z}(t) = g[z(t),y(t)].$$

$$\tag{1}$$

Dot notation signifies, as usual, rate of change. The solution procedure calls for setting up a kind of Lagrangian called a Hamiltonian defined

$$u[z(t),y(t)] - \lambda(t)g[z(t),y(t)],$$

where $\lambda(t)$ is, in economic terms, the "shadow price" of increasing $\dot{z}(t)$ in terms of utility. This is, of course, the standard interpretation of such multipliers. Throughout, $\alpha(t)$ is the discounting factor. The dynamics of any possible solution to (1) are then summarized by

---

[1] Material found in Chapters 13 and 19 is applicable here.

$$\dot{z}(t) \; = \; g[z(t),y(t)],$$

$$\lambda(t) \; = \; h[z(t),y(t)], \text{ and}$$

$$(2)$$

a boundary condition on $z(t)$,

$$z(0) \equiv z_0.$$

Optimality meanwhile requires that any path from z_0 must satisfy not only the dynamic equations recorded in (2), but also the "transversality conditions" given by equation (3):

$$\lim_{t \to \infty} \alpha(t)\lambda(t) \; = \; 0 \text{ and}$$

$$\lim_{t \to \infty} \alpha(t)\lambda(t)z(t) \; = \; 0.$$

$$(3)$$

The interested reader is referred to Arrow and Kurz (1) for a thorough presentation of the procedure [Chapter 2] and a myriad of investment examples [subsequent chapters].

The present problem will focus on a simple illustration of the procedure drawn from the foundation of the competitive firm [see Chapter 13]. It will not concentrate on the technicalities of the Pontryagin method as much as it

PROBLEM 36

on the technicalities of the Pontryagin method as much as it will on the richness of the economics it can represent. Results involving responses to various investment tax credits will be drawn from phase diagrams representing the dynamic equations (2). This exercise is thus more of an example in how some intuition can (rigorously) suggest some conclusions without the potentially overburdening mathematics tagging along.

Questions:

(a) Suppose that

$$F(x_1) \equiv \max_{x_2} \ [f(x_1, x_2) \ - \ w_2 x_2]$$

were to summarize the production process of a profit-maximizing firm with $y = f(x_1, x_2)$ as its production function. Suppose further that x_1 depreciates at a rate δ over time and that investment in any one period is costly; i.e., investment in x_1 of an amount I costs $C(I)$. Assume that $dc/dI > 0$ and $d^2c/dI^2 > 0$. Let $\rho > 0$ be the discount factor. Characterize graphically in terms of $x_1(t)$ and $\lambda(t)$ defined by the appropriate Hamiltonian the investment pattern that maximizes the firm's discounted net value:

PROBLEM 36

$$\int_0^\infty \{F[x_1(t)] - C[I(t)]\} \, e^{-pt} \, dt.$$

Notice, as you start, that the model specifies that

$$\dot{x}_1(t) = I(t) - \delta x_1(t) \; ;$$

i.e., the change in the stock of x_1 is investment net of depreciation.

(b) The apparatus constructed in part (a) can now be used to consider a proportional, temporary investment tax credit that reduces the cost of investment by $\tau I(t)$.   In particular, show that:

(i) If the credit is unanticipated and presumed permanent, then investment will peak immediately after it is imposed, fall toward a (higher) long-run equilibrium level, plummet suddenly when it is suspended, and then finally rise back to the old equilibrium level.

(ii) If the credit is fully anticipated, investment will fall prior to its imposition, peak immediately after it is imposed, begin to fall toward a new

351

equilibrium, but rise substantially just before it is suspended, plummet when it is suspended, but then finally rise back toward the old level.

The distortions created by the temporary credit can therefore extend beyond its period of duration in either circumstance.

Suggested Solutions:

The procedure employed will cast these investment decisions in terms of a dynamic optimization problem like (1). Graphing combinations of $(z(t), \lambda(t))$ such that

$$\dot{\lambda}(t) = \dot{z}(t) = 0$$

can then divide the positive orthant into four parts, and the paths allowed by the equations recorded in (2) can be then charted. The intersection of the loci can also be shown to satisfy equation (3), so any path found in the sections leading to the intersection is optimal. The remainder of the problem involves manipulating these optimal paths. It is a common procedure used frequently in a variety of dynamic contexts.

(a) Put most concisely, the initial problem is to

$$\max \int_0^\infty \{F[x_1(t)] - C[I(t)]\} e^{-\rho t} dt$$

$$s.t. \quad \dot{x}_1(t) = I(t) - \delta x_1(t).$$

The appropriate Hamiltonian,

$$H \equiv F[x_1(t)] - C[I(t)] + \lambda(t)[I(t) - \delta x_1(t)],$$

$$(4)$$

is the firm's net value in any given period: its rental
dividend $[F(x_1) - C(I)]$ plus the value of its investment
$[\lambda(I - \delta x_1)]$. The Lagrangian multiplier $\lambda(t)$ is simply the
shadow price of investment, and so it is the present value
of the rents earned by investment discounted by both the
interest rate and the rate of depreciation (both reduce the
future value of an asset in formally similar ways); i.e.,

$$\lambda(t) = \int_t^\infty \frac{\partial F(x_1)}{\partial x_1} e^{-\delta(v-t)} e^{-\rho(v-t)} dv = \int_t^\infty \frac{\partial F(x_1)}{\partial x_1} e^{-(\delta+\rho)(v-t)} dv$$

since the rent paid x_1 is the partial of $F(x_1)$ with respect
to x_1 [remember Chapter 2]. Given such a shadow price, the
firm will choose $I(t)$ to maximize its value in a period.
More succinctly the firm maximizes the Hamiltonian H given
in (4) with respect to $I(t)$ and solves the resulting first-

order condition that

$$\frac{\partial C(I)}{\partial I} = \lambda(t).$$

(5)

In application of the Pontryagin result quoted above, it becomes clear that equation (5) combines with

$$\dot{x}_1(t) = I(t) - \delta x_1(t) \quad \text{and}$$

$$\lambda(t) = [\delta + \rho]\lambda(t) - \partial f/\partial x_1$$

(6)

to describe firm behavior. Solving these dynamic equations subsequently requires a boundary condition, $x_1(0) = x_{10}$, and the existence of an investment path satisfying the transversality conditions:

$$\lim_{t \to \infty} \{\lambda(t) e^{-\rho t}\} = 0 \text{ and}$$

$$\lim_{t \to \infty} \{\lambda(t) x_1(t) e^{-\rho t}\} = 0.$$

(7)

These expressions come directly from equation (3) with

$$\alpha(t) \equiv e^{-\rho t}.$$

Also observe that the second equation recorded in (7) simply requires that the limiting value of investment be zero.

A phase diagram is now a useful tool with which to summarize this behavior <u>and</u> to characterize optimal policy. Figure 36.1 is such a diagram. Two schedules, loci of points such that

$$\dot{\lambda}(t) = 0 \text{ and } \dot{x}_1(t) = 0,$$

respectively, are drawn there. For a given $\lambda(t)$ and x_1 above locus AA, the second equation in (6) shows that

$$\dot{\lambda}(t) > 0$$

because $[\partial F/\partial x_1]$ would be smaller; arrows drawn above locus AA must, therefore, point upward. For x_1 below locus AA, meanwhile,

$$\dot{\lambda}(t) < 0,$$

and the arrows are drawn pointing down.

Concentrating now on the second locus, BB, note that increasing $\lambda(t)$ above BB increases investment [see (5)] for any given $x_1(t)$ and therefore, from (6),

$$\dot{x}_1(t) > 0.$$

Figure 36.1

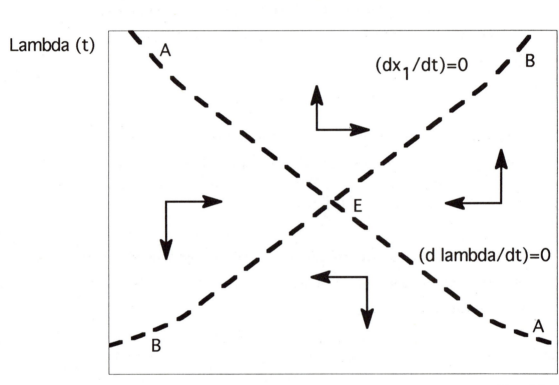

Arrows above locus BB must, as a result, point to the right.
The reverse once again is true, as well; arrows drawn below
locus BB point to the left.   These observations are the
genesis of the blocked arrows in the four quadrants of
Figure 36.1.

The arrows subsequently spawn the 4 heavily drawn paths
in Figure 36.2.   Two of these paths converge to E, and are
optimal if they satisfy equations (7) at the intersection of
the dotted loci of Figure 36.1 [see Arrow and Kurz (1), page
51].   Since $\lambda(t)$ and $x_1(t)$ both converge to finite values at
that point, though, both parts of (7) are clearly met with ρ
> 0.   The optimal policy is therefore one of finding the
point corresponding to x_{10} on the converging arrows and
setting the shadow price for investment equal to the
associated λ.   Investing as instructed by equation (5) then
completes the process.

(b)   The tax credit modeled

$$C[I(t)] \ - \ \tau I(t)$$

(8)

has the effect of lowering the

$$\dot{x}_1(t) \ = \ 0$$

Figure 36.2

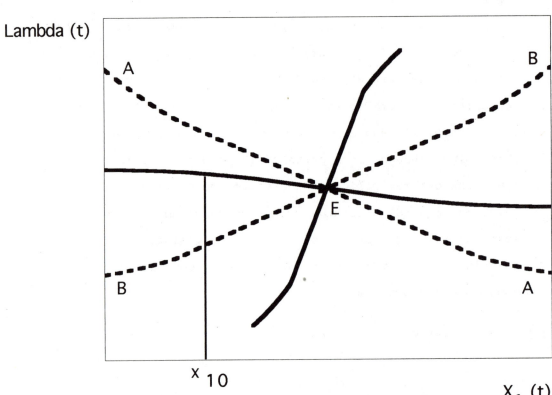

Lambda (t)

A

B

E

B

A

X$_{10}$

X$_1$ (t)

locus because lower values for $\lambda(t)$ would then be associated with arbitrary levels of investment. More precisely,

$$dC(I(t)/dI(t) - \tau = \lambda(t)$$

(9)

would relate investment to its shadow price. Even if the firm started in equilibrium at point E, the credit under condition (i) would therefore have the immediate impact of causing the firm to lower $\lambda(t)$ to get onto the optimal path toward the new equilibrium at E'. The firm would then proceed toward E' in accordance with (5). Investment would therefore jump discontinuously with the imposition of the credit, and then gradually diminish toward a new (higher) long-run equilibrium level at E'.

Sudden, unanticipated removal of the credit would have the reverse effect anywhere along the new path. The firm would immediately jump to the path back to E and cause a discontinuous increase in $\lambda(t)$ and a fall in investment below the original long-run equilibrium level (the firm would have too much capital and would allow it to depreciate). In approaching E, though, $\lambda(t)$ and investment would both rise until the old equilibrium levels were reachieved at E. Figure 36.3 illustrates the two alternative equilibria with optimal paths drawn to each.

If both the imposition and the removal of the credit were anticipated, on the other hand, an entirely different

Figure 36.3

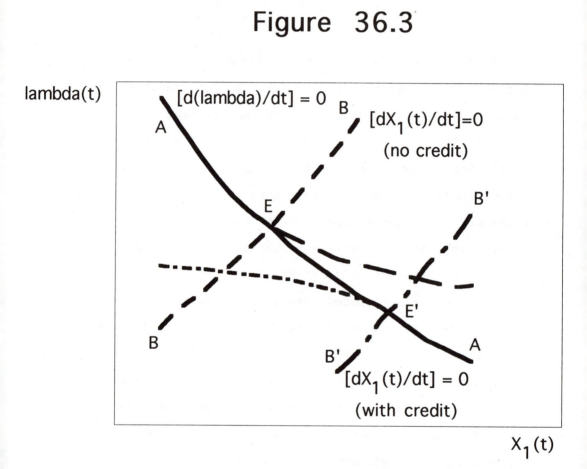

story would unfold. The firm's movement of its investment shadow price <u>would</u> then be continuous. It would adjust $\lambda(t)$ so that

(1) the firm would reach the path to E' precisely when the credit appeared, and

(2) the firm would reach the path back to E precisely when the credit was revoked.

The firm would, more precisely, move out of equilibrium <u>before</u> the credit appeared by reducing $\lambda(t)$, $x_1(t)$ through depreciation, and investment in anticipation of the credit. When the credit took effect, then, the $\lambda(t)$ being computed would suddenly be associated through (9) with a much higher level of investment - higher even than the old equilibrium level because the path to E' requires a declining investment pattern. The firm would therefore delay investment until the credit were in place, and then expand rapidly to take immediate advantage of the break.

While the credit was in effect, the firm would initially move along the path to E' (declining $\lambda(t)$ and I(t)). Eventually, though, the firm would begin to prepare for the credit's suspension by climbing up to the path back to the old E. At that moment, the credit would be suspended and the same $\lambda(t)$ would discontinuously associated with significantly lower investment - lower even than the original equilibrium level because movement back to the old

Figure 36.4

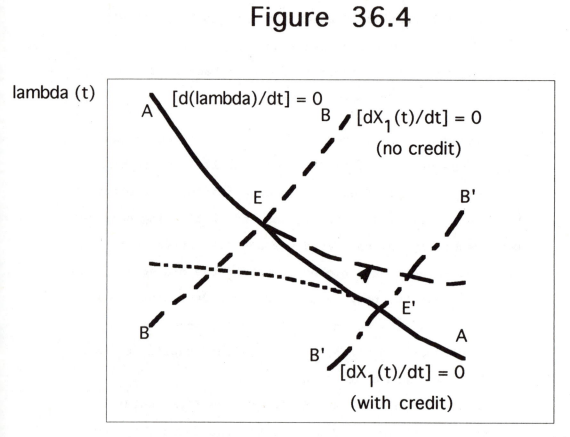

equilibrium would now require an increase in both $\lambda(t)$ and $I(t)$. Figure 36.4 illustrates this second scenario; it shows divergence from the path to E' in anticipation that the credit will disappear in the certain future.

It can be argued, now, that firms both delay investment in anticipation of a tax credit and increase investment in anticipation of its revocation. The impact of an anticipated credit is therefore felt not only during its tenure, but also before it takes effect and after it expires; unanticipated credits influence any contemporaneous and ex post facto decisions.

The case in which the credit is unanticipated, but of certain duration once it is in place, can also be handled with the phase diagrams. It should be no surprise that the path for this intermediate case lies somewhere between the two exhibited in Figures 36.3 and 36.4. Despite the importance of these and other related questions [see, e.g., Hall and Jorgenson (3), Gould (2), and Harford (4)], the major point of this problem was the introduction of the maximum principle.

This has been a simple, rather stylized example derived from the very foundation of the theory of the firm. The Arrow and Kurz (1) volume is a complete treatment of the most general results for finite and infinite time horizons. The interested reader need not go much further than that

volume for a thorough reference library. In these days when
resources and/or distinctions between types of capital can
be crucial, the two sector models of Chapter 4 are
particularly germane; Weitzman (7) has also contributed
there. Perhaps the best assessment of this entire
literature is found in Koopmans (5).

References

(1) Arrow, K. J., and M. Kurz, *Public Investment, the Rate
of Return, and Optimal Fiscal Policy*, Baltimore, Johns
Hopkins Press for Resources for the Future, Inc., 1970.

(2) Gould, F., "Adjustment Costs in the Theory of Investment
of the Firm," *Review of Economic Studies*, 35: 47-56, 1968.

(3) Hall, R., and D. Jorgenson, "Tax Policy and Investment
Behavior," *American Economic Review*, 57: 391-414, 1967 (plus
comments and responses in June 1969 and September 1970).

(4) Harford, J., "Adjustment Costs and Optimal Waste
Treatment," *Journal of Environmental Economics and
Management*, 3: 215-225, 1976.

(5) Koopmans, T., "Concepts of Optimality and Their Uses,"
American Economic Review, 67: 261-278, 1977.

(6) Stiglitz, J.E., *Lectures in Public Finance*, New York,
Norton, 1985.

(7) Weitzman, M. L., "Shiftable versus Non Shiftable
Capital," *Econometrica*, 39: 511-529, 1971.

37. Pure Public Goods with Many Private Goods[1]

In a seminal paper (3), Samuelson introduced the
concept of a pure public good -- a good that entered
everyone's utility in the same amount because everyone could
"consume" it at the same time [see Chapter 23]. Applying
his notion directly to reality has proven difficult because
there are very few pure public goods - goods for which the
cost of exclusion is high and the marginal social cost of
the last user is low (relative to the average cost of
provision). There are, however, many goods which exhibit
many of the properties of a pure public good to one degree
or another. Figure 37.1 on page 370 offers a schematic
catalog. It is useful, therefore, to analyze the equilibria
conditions that emerge from the pure case despite its
limited direct applicability.

Consider a group of m consumers each with utility
schedules depending upon n private goods and one public
good; i.e., for consumer j (j = 1,...,m),

$$u_j = u_j(\vec{x}_j, G),$$

---

[1] Material found in Chapter 23 is applicable here. This
problem will, in fact, replicate the analysis in Section
23.4 and provide the details of an alternative approach and
some illustrative geometry. Concepts introduced in Chapters
13, 17, and 18 will be employed.

where $\vec{x}_j = (x_j^1, \ldots, x_j^n)$ is a vector of private goods and G is the public good. Summarize the production possibilities available to the economy by

$$T\{(\sum_{j=1}^{m} x_j^1), \ldots, (\sum_{j=1}^{m} x_j^n), G\} = 0.$$

Questions:

(a) Characterize Pareto optimality in terms of marginal rates of substitution in consumption and marginal rates of transformation in production.

(b) Let there be two consumers, one private good, and one public good. Illustrate (a) graphically.

Suggested Solutions:

Pareto optimality can be viewed as the maximization of one person's utility subject to a feasibility constraint <u>and</u> holding everyone else's utility fixed at some prescribed level [see Section 13.9 beginning on page 225]. In terms of a Lagrangian, therefore, the problem is

$$\max \{u_1(\vec{x}_1, G) - \sum_{j=2}^{m} \lambda_j [u_j(\vec{x}_j, G) - \bar{u}_j] + t[T(\vec{X}, G)]\}$$

where

$$\vec{x}_j \equiv (x_j^1, \ldots, x_j^n)$$

is the jth person's consumption vector,

$$X^k \equiv \sum_{i=1}^{m} x_1^k$$

is total consumption of the kth good, and

$$\vec{X} \equiv (X^1, \ldots, X^n).$$

The first-order conditions include the requirements that

$$\frac{\partial u_1(\vec{x}_1^*, G^*)}{\partial x_1^k} = t \frac{\partial T(\vec{X}^*, G)}{\partial X^k}, \quad k = 1, \ldots, n; \tag{1}$$

$$-\lambda_j \frac{\partial u_j(\vec{x}_j^*, G^*)}{\partial x_j^k} = t \frac{\partial T(\vec{X}^*, G)}{\partial X^k}, \quad \begin{array}{l} k = 1, \ldots, n, \\ j = 2, \ldots, m; \text{ and} \end{array} \tag{2}$$

$$\frac{\partial u_1(\vec{x}_1^*, G^*)}{\partial G} = \sum_{j=2}^{m} \lambda_j \frac{\partial u_j(\vec{x}_j^*, G^*)}{\partial G} + t \frac{\partial T(X^*, G^*)}{\partial G}. \tag{3}$$

Rearranging equation (3), one finds that

$$\frac{1}{t}\frac{\partial u_1(\vec{x}_1^*,G^*)}{\partial G} - \sum_{j=2}^{m}\frac{\lambda_j}{t}\frac{\partial u_j(\vec{x}_j^*,G^*)}{\partial G} = \frac{\partial T(\vec{x}^*,G^*)}{\partial G} \cdot \qquad (4)$$

From equations (1) and (2), however,

$$\frac{1}{t} = \frac{\partial T(\vec{x}^*,G^*)}{\partial x^k} \Big/ \frac{\partial u_1(\vec{x}_1^*,G^*)}{\partial x_1^k} \qquad \text{and}$$

$$\frac{\lambda_j}{t} = \frac{\partial T(\vec{x}^*,G^*)}{\partial x^k} \Big/ \frac{\partial u_1(\vec{x}_1^*,G^*)}{\partial x_j^k} \cdot$$

As a result, equation (4) becomes

$$\frac{\dfrac{\partial T(\vec{x}^*,G^*)}{\partial x^k}}{\dfrac{\partial u_1(\vec{x}_1^*,G^*)}{\partial x_1^k}} \frac{\partial u_1(\vec{x}_1^*,G^*)}{\partial G} + \sum_{j=2}^{m} \frac{\dfrac{\partial T(\vec{x}^*,G^*)}{\partial x^k}}{\dfrac{\partial u_j(\vec{x}_j^*,G^*)}{\partial x_j^k}} \frac{\partial u_j(\vec{x}_j^*,G^*)}{\partial G}$$

$$= \frac{\partial T(\vec{x}^*,G^*)}{\partial G} \cdot$$

Rearranging once more, one finds a familiar result:

$$\frac{\dfrac{\partial u_1(\vec{x}_1^{\,*},G^*)}{\partial G}}{\dfrac{\partial u_1(\vec{x}_1^{\,*},G^*)}{\partial x_1^k}} + \sum_{j=2}^{m} \frac{\dfrac{\partial u_j(\vec{x}_j^{\,*},G^*)}{\partial G}}{\dfrac{\partial u_j(\vec{x}_j^{\,*},G^*)}{\partial x_j^k}} = \frac{\dfrac{\partial T(\vec{X}^*,G^*)}{\partial G}}{\dfrac{\partial T(\vec{X}^*,G^*)}{\partial x^k}}. \qquad (5)$$

Equation (5) holds for all $k = 1,\ldots,n$. It requires that for any private good x^k, the marginal rate of transformation between that good and G [the right-hand side of (5)] must equal the <u>sum</u> of the marginal rates of substitution between that good and G across the entire population [the left-hand side of (5)]. Moreover, equations (1) and (2) combine to show that

$$\frac{\dfrac{\partial u_1(\vec{x}_1^{\,*},G^*)}{\partial x_1^k}}{\dfrac{\partial u_1(\vec{x}_1^{\,*},G^*)}{\partial x_1^\ell}} = \frac{\dfrac{\partial T(\vec{X},G)}{\partial x^k}}{\dfrac{\partial T(\vec{X}^*,G^*)}{\partial x^\ell}} = \frac{\dfrac{\partial u_j(\vec{x}_j^{\,*},G)}{\partial x_j^k}}{\dfrac{\partial u_j(\vec{x}_j^{\,*},G^*)}{\partial x_j^\ell}}$$

for $j = 2,\ldots,m$; $k = 1,\ldots,n$; and $\ell \neq k = 1,\ldots,n$. The marginal rates of substitution between any two private goods are equal, for any individual, to the marginal rate of transformation between those goods.

Figure 37.1

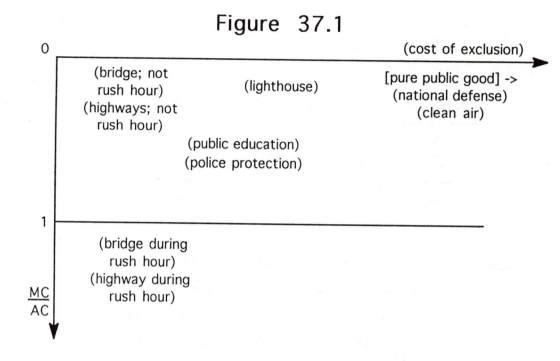

Figure 37.2

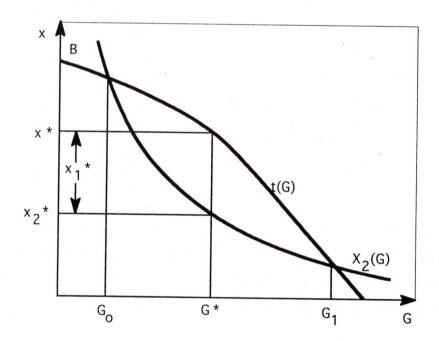

b. Maximizing $u_1(x_1,G)$ subject to producing on the production frontier $t(G)$ in Figure 37.2 and to holding $u_2(x_2,G)$ equal to some fixed level amounts to maximizing $u_1(x_1,G)$ subject to the vertical distance between $t(G)$ and the $u_2(x_2,G)$ indifference curve [denote $X_2(G)$ in Figure 37.2]. This distance is reflected as a composite constraint [denoted $\{t(G)-X_2(G)\}$] in Figure 37.3.

The solution to the maximization problem is, as usual, characterized by the tangency of the constraint and the highest attainable $u_1(x_1,G)$ indifference curve [denoted U_1^{max} in Figure 37.3} - a tangency which shows that the slope of the $u_1(x_1,G)$ indifference curve must equal the slope of the constraint. Since the slope of the constraint is, by its very definition, equal to the slope of the production frontier minus the slope of the constraining $u_2(x_2,G)$ indifference curve, it is clear the that

$$t'(G*) - X_2'(G*) = \{\partial U_1/\partial G\}$$

at $G*$; i.e.,

$$\{MRS_1 + MRS_2\} = X_2'(G*) + \{\partial U_1/\partial G\} = t'(G*),$$

the marginal rate of technical substitution. This is, of course, simply a restatement of equation (5).

A good deal more can be said about public goods. For the moment, the focus has been on the technique, within a

Figure 37.3

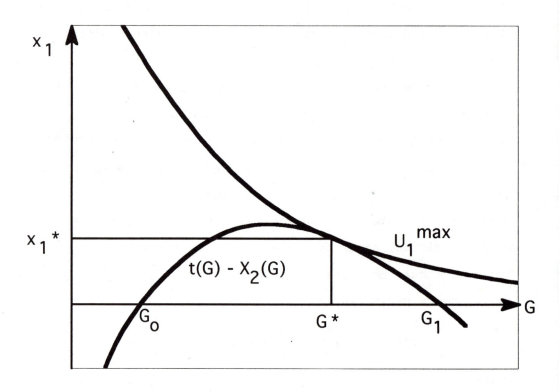

general equilibrium model, of characterizing Pareto optimality. It will become clear that the conditions derived here are identical to those that would evolve from maximizing a social welfare function that includes everyone's utility function in its argument. The interested reader is referred to Samuelson (3, 4, and 5) and Margolis (2) for a firm, historical introduction to the public goods literature.

References

(1) Buchanan, J.M., and M.Z. Kafoglis, "A Note on Public Goods Supply," *American Economic Review*, 53: 403-414, 1963.

(2) Margolis, J., "A Comment on the Price Theory of Public Expenditure," *Review of Economics and Statistics*, 37: 347-349, 1955.

(3) Samuelson, P.A., "The Pure Theory of Public Expenditure," *Review of Economics and Statistics*, 36: 387-389, 1954.

(4) _____, "Diagrammatic Exposition of the Theory of Public Expenditure," *Review of Economics and Statistics*, 37: 350-356, 1955.

(5) _____, "Aspects of Public Expenditure Theories," *Review of Economics and Statistics*, 40: 332-338, 1958.

38. Voting and the Provision of Local Public Goods[1]

One way to get people to reveal their true preferences for a public good, especially on a local level, is to set up a series of referenda in which they have an incentive to vote in accordance with those preferences [see Section 23.6 beginning on page 424]. The number of school districts that each year must face the electorate to pass their budgets serves as a reminder that such voting procedures are, in fact, employed.

Political devices are not necessarily the best solutions to economic problems, though, and an economist will always wonder about properties of their outcomes. With respect to the voting solution to a public goods problem, for example, one might ask if the series of referenda leads to a Pareto optimal allocation.

To observe the complexity of this concern, consider a series of referenda in which the proposed level of public good to be provided, and its price tag, starts high but is gradually reduced. Citizens of the community are expected, under such a scheme, to determine what level they think best and vote "no" only as long as the proposed level exceeds their choice; at that point, they will begin to vote

---

[1] Material found in Chapter 23 is applicable here. This problem will expand on Section 23.4 and provide some detail in the comparison of a voting solution with the Pareto optimal allocation of a public good.

374

"yes."   The idea is to undertake a series of votes that
stops only when the barest of majorities votes in the
affirmative.

Suppose, in this context, that G represents a public
good to be provided locally. Assume that it can be
purchased outside the community at a fixed rate from the
community's collected holdings of a second good y; the
marginal rate of transformation between G and y can
therefore be declared equal to 1 without loss of generality.
Suppose that the level of G to be provided is to be financed
by a proportional tax on the community's endowments of the
second good. Finally, assume that there are N people in the
community and that each has an initial endowment $\bar{y}_i$.

Questions:

(a) Characterize the level of public good that will
emerge from the referenda when an arbitrary $u(G, y_i)$
represents everyone's utility.

(b) Suppose that

$$u(G, y_i) = \ln (y_i) + V(G)$$

for the ith individual. Is the voting solution
characterized in part a Pareto optimal?

(c) Suppose that

PROBLEM 38

$$u(G,y_i) = -\frac{1}{\alpha} y_i^{-\alpha} + V(G), \quad \alpha \neq 0.$$

Under what conditions would the voting solution be Pareto optimal?

(d) You will have found in the last section that even a symmetric distribution of income is not enough to guarantee the Pareto optimality of the voting solution. Symmetry in the distribution of the preferred level of provision may, however, be enough. Suppose now that there are M types of people with

$$u^i(G,y_i) = (G_i^* - G)^2 + y_i + \alpha$$

representing the utility function for the $f(G_i^*)$ people of type i. Defining

$$R \equiv \sum_{k=1}^{M} \bar{y}_k f(G_i^*)$$

(the total endowment of the community), their combined resource constraint is then

$$R \geq G + \sum_{i=1}^{M} y_i f(G_i^*).$$

Show that symmetry in the distribution of G_i^* guarantees that the voting solution is Pareto optimal.

376

PROBLEM 38

Suggested Solutions:

(a)   For any individual, the problem is to

$$\max\ u(G, y_i) \tag{1}$$

$$\text{s.t.}\ y_i = (1-t)\bar{y}_i \tag{2}$$

$$t = G \Big/ \sum_{k=1}^{N} \bar{y}_k. \tag{3}$$

Substituting equation (3) into (2) and then (2) into (1), maximization with respect to G leads to the first-order condition that

$$\frac{\partial u}{\partial G} = u_1 - u_2\ (\bar{y}_i / \sum_k \bar{y}_k) = 0. \tag{4}$$

Equation (4) requires that the marginal utility generated by financing the last unit of G equal the marginal disutility of forgoing an individual's share of that financing.   Were we now to list voters in the (ascending) order of their preferences for G, the level chosen by the median voter would emerge as the winner in the referenda series, and it would satisfy (4) for the median endowment of y [this is the Bowen equilibrium of page 424].

(b) It is clear from equation (4) that the voting solution will be characterized for the median voter by

377

$$V'(\tilde{G}) - \{\frac{1}{(1-t)y_i}\} \{\bar{y}_i / \sum_k \bar{y}_k\}) = 0;$$

the reduced form of this condition is, however, independent of his endowment:

$$V'(\tilde{G}) [(1-t) \sum_k \bar{y}_k] = 1. \tag{5}$$

A Pareto optimal provision must, meanwhile, satisfy the condition that [pages 421-423]

$$\sum_{i=1}^{N} MRS_k = MRT = 1; \quad i.e.,$$

$$\sum_{k=1}^{N} V'(\hat{G}) (1-t)\bar{y}_k = 1, \tag{6}$$

since, for the ith person,

$$(u_1/u_2) = \{V'(G)/[1/(1-t)\bar{y}_i]\}.$$

Equation (6) duplicates (5), so $\hat{G} = \tilde{G}$ and so the voting solution is Pareto optimal.

(c) Appealing once again to equation (4), the voting solution will now solve

$$V'(\tilde{G}) (1-t)^{\alpha+1} \bar{y}_i^{\alpha} \sum_k \bar{y}_k = 1$$

while Pareto optimality requires that

$$\Sigma \text{ MRS}_i = \Sigma_k V'(\hat{G}) (1-t)^{\alpha+1} \bar{y}_k^{(\alpha+1)} = 1.$$

In this case, then, $\hat{G}$ and $\tilde{G}$ will be identical only if

$$\bar{y}_i^{\alpha} \Sigma_k \bar{y}_k = \Sigma_k \bar{y}_k^{(\alpha+1)}. \tag{7}$$

Equation (7) holds under two conditions: either when $\alpha = 0$ (a condition that is not allowed) or when $y_i = \bar{y}_k$ for all people (i.e., when all people are identical). To see this, note that

$$\Sigma_k \bar{y}_k^{\alpha+1} = \Sigma_k \bar{y}_i^{\alpha} \bar{y}_k - \Sigma_k [\bar{y}_k(\bar{y}_i^{\alpha} - \bar{y}_k)] \tag{8}$$

and observe that the second term in equation (8) disappears only when $\alpha = 0$ or when $y_i = \bar{y}_1$ for all $k = 1,\ldots,n$. Underprovision or overprovision of G will otherwise emerge from the voting depending on the sign of α and the distribution of the $\bar{y}_i$.

(d) An alternative, but equally appropriate, formulation of the Pareto optimality problem asks the government to choose a level $\hat{G}$ that solves [see Problem 37]

PROBLEM 38

$$\max \quad u^1(G,y_1)f(G_1^*)$$

$$\text{s.t. } u^j(G,y_j) = \bar{u}^j, \quad j = 2, \ldots, N,$$

$$R > \sum_{k=1}^{N} y_k f(G_k^*) + G.$$

Maximizing the utility of group 1 holding everyone else's utility constant certainly achieves a circumstance in which no group can be made happier without hurting someone else. The corresponding Lagrangian is

$$L(y_1,\ldots,y_N,G) = u^1(G,y_1)f(G_1^*)$$

$$+ \sum_{k=2}^{N} \lambda_k(u^k(G,y_k) - \bar{u}^k)f(G_k^*)$$

$$+ \lambda_R(G - \sum_{k=1}^{N} y_k f(G_k^*) - R) .$$

The following first-order conditions emerge:

$$\frac{\partial L}{\partial G} = f(G_1^*) \frac{\partial u^1}{\partial G} + \sum_{k=2}^{N} \lambda_k f(G_k^*) \frac{\partial u^k}{\partial G} + \lambda_R = 0 \qquad (9a)$$

$$\frac{\partial L}{\partial y_1} = f(G_1^*) - \lambda_R f(G_1^*) = 0 \qquad (9b)$$

380

PROBLEM 38

$$\frac{\partial L}{\partial y_j} = \lambda_j f(G_j^*) - \lambda_R f(G_j^*) = 0, \quad j = 2, \ldots, n. \tag{9c}$$

Equations (9b) and (9c) combine to require that

$$\lambda_R = \lambda_j, \quad j = 2, \ldots, N.$$

Since $(\partial u^j / \partial y^j) = 1$, equation (9a) collapses to a form that has a familiar interpretation:

$$- \sum_{k=1}^{N} \frac{\partial u^k}{\partial G} f(G_k^*) = 1 = MRT; \tag{10}$$

i.e., the sum of the marginal rates of substitution across the population must equal the marginal rate of transformation. Observing that

$$\frac{\partial u^k}{\partial G} = -2(G_k^* - G), \quad k = 1, \ldots, N, \tag{11}$$

equation (10) reduces to

$$\hat{G} = \sum_{k=1}^{N} G_k^* \left\{ \frac{f(G_k^*)}{\Sigma f(G_j^*)} \right\} + \frac{1}{\Sigma f(G_j^*)} \approx \mu_{G_k}^* .$$

It is clear from equation (11) that G_k* is considered the optimal level of G by people in group k, so $\mu_{G_k}^*$ is the mean

381

of the individuals' choices. Since the median G_k^* will
emerge from the series of referenda, the voting solution is
Pareto optimal if the mean equals the median; i.e., the
referenda achieve Pareto optimality if the distribution of
the preferred levels of the public good (not necessarily
income) is symmetric.

Attacking the "free rider" problem by devising schemes
that bring forth true individual preferences for public
goods has occupied a substantial portion of the literature
devoted to public finance. The present question has touched
briefly on but one version of one such scheme -- a voting
mechanism under proportional taxation. Among the references
listed below, Musgrave (5) provides an overview of the more
standard treatments of these solutions, while Arrow (1),
Inada (3), and Tullock (7) extend the analysis in a variety
of directions. The notion that Pareto optimality requires
provision of a (weighted) average of the individuals' "best"
choices is, however, well established.

Attention has also been focused here on a locally
provided public good for which a voting mechanism is most
applicable. While this perspective appears to have done
little more than specify the scope and shape of the resource
constraint (setting MRT = 1 is most consistent with using
local tax revenue to purchase public goods from outside the
community), it has, in fact, led the reader very close to

the Tiebout hypothesis [see (6)]. Roughly stated, Tiebout suggested that if towns were viewed simply as distinct bundles of public goods available at different prices (tax rates), then people reveal their true preferences for local public goods by the very act of choosing a place to live.

The other side of the hypothesis can emerge, at least suggestively, from the last part of this question. Suppose one were to look for a Pareto improving division of the community into two parts. Lapsing into a continuous density function for the G_k*, it is easily shown that such a division does exist, and that the very best boundary between what become high and low provision communities is a level $\bar{G}$ that is the average of the Pareto optimal provisions of these two new communities. Taking such division to the limit, however, it is seen that Tiebout can be correct only when there are at least as many towns as there are G_k*.

More sophisticated views of the local public goods problem raised by Tiebout have since been generated, though, and the interested reader is referred to Williams (6) and Brainard and Dolbear (2) for the foundations of research that is currently enjoying a resurgence.

References

(1) Arrow, K., *Social Choice and Individual Values,* New Haven, Conn., Yale University Press, 1951.

(2) Brainard, W., and F. Dolbear, "The Possibility of Oversupply of Local Public Goods: A Critical Note," *Journal of Political Economy*, 75: 86-92, 1967.

(3) Inada, K., "A Note on the Simple Majority Decision Rule," *Econometrica*, 32: 525-31, 1964.

(4) Johansen, L., "Some Notes on the Lindahl Theory of Determination of Public Expenditure," *International Economic Review*, 4: 346-358, 1973.

(5) Musgrave, R., *Theory of Public Finance*, New York, McGraw-Hill, 1959.

(6) Tiebout, C.M., "A Pure Theory of Local Expenditures," *Journal of Political Economy*, 64: 416-24, 1956.

(7) Tullock, G., "Some Problems with Majority Voting," *Journal of Political Economy*, 67: 571-79, 1959.

(8) Williams, A., "The Optimal Provision of Public Goods in a System of Local Government," *Journal of Political Economy*, 74: 18-33, 1966.

39. The Optimal Return to Government Investment[1]

The impact of various imperfections in the capital market on the optimal return to government investment have been the subjects of intense investigation. The distortion caused by corporate profits taxation has, for example, been extensively studied by Baumol (2 and 3), Sandmo and Dreze (6), Seagraves (7), and others. They have argued that under fifty percent taxation, the proper discount rate for public investment is some weighted average of the return to a riskless government bond (say r) and the return to private capital (2r in this case). Others have argued, in another context, that to the extent that a risk premium on private investment is a private cost and reflects the imperfect spreading of risk by a market, the government should ignore it; the pure rate of time preference is the appropriate discount factor [see Arrow and Lind (1), Samuelson (5), and Vickrey (8)]. These are, of course, contradictory answers to what is formally the same question: how should the government react when the private sector makes its investment decisions in a distorted capital market?

This problem will explore the basis for the contradiction as it was presented in Ogura and Yohe (4).

---

[1] Material found in Chapters 19 and 20 is applicable here. Basic constructions from utility and production theory will be employed, with social welfare represented by a well-behaved, direct utility function.

The answer will emerge from the interaction of public and private capital in the production process. Let $u(c_1,\ldots,c_T)$ be an intertemporal welfare function over the lifetime of potential projects wherein c_t is consumption in period t. Define total production in period t by $y_t = f(p_t, g_t)$ where p_t and g_t are the stocks of private and public capital existing in period t. Labor is not in the production function, but that is not too damaging; think of a steady state path and view everything in per capital terms, if necessary. Marginal products are positive but decreasing for all p_t and g_t, but the sign of $[\partial^2 f/\partial p, \partial g]$ depends on the interaction between the two types of capital; i.e.,

$$\frac{\partial^2 f}{\partial p \partial g} \quad \begin{matrix} > 0 \\ < 0 \end{matrix} \quad \begin{matrix} \text{if } p_t \text{ and } g_t \text{ are complements} \\ \text{if } p_t \text{ and } g_t \text{ are substitutes.} \end{matrix}$$

Without depreciation (a noncrucial assumption),

$$g_t = g_{t-1} + \Delta g_{t-1} \text{ and}$$

$$p_t = p_{t-1} + \Delta p_{t-1}$$

where investment in public and private capital [Δg_{t-1} and Δp_{t-1}, respectively] are taken out of consumption so that

$$c_t = y_t - \Delta p_t - \Delta g_t.$$

Finally assume that private capital is hired up to the point where its marginal product equals some cutoff point k_t which may or may not equal consumers' pure rate of time preference r_t [this can be taken to be the rate of interest paid on pure discount bonds; see page 363]; i.e.,

$$\frac{\partial f}{\partial p}(p_t, g_t) = k_t \gtrless r_t. \tag{1}$$

Questions:

(a) Show that the optimal return to government investment is a weighted sum of k_t and r_t.

(b) Use part (a) to analyze when the optimal return to government capital can exceed r_t, equal r_t, and fall below r_t. Explain each case intuitively in terms of the government's ability to counteract the distortion reflected in equation (1).

Suggested Solutions:

(a)   The appropriate Lagrangian is

$$u(c_1, \ldots, c_T) \ + \ \sum_{t=1}^{T} M_t [f(p_t, g_t) - c_t - \Delta p_t - \Delta g_t]$$

$$+ \ \sum_{t=1}^{T} V_t [p_t + \Delta p_t - p_{t+1}] + \sum_{t=1}^{T} W_t [g_t + \Delta g_t - g_{t+1}]$$

$$+ \ \sum_{t=1}^{T} \eta_t [\frac{\partial f}{\partial p}(p_t, g_t) - k_t].$$

For all but the last period, the first-order conditions require that

$$\frac{\partial u}{\partial c_t} - M_t = 0;$$

$$- M_t + V_t = 0;$$

$$- M_t + W_t = 0;$$

$$M_t \frac{\partial f}{\partial p}(p_t, g_t) + V_t - V_{t-1} + \eta_t \frac{\partial^2 f}{\partial p^2}(p_t, g_t) = 0; \text{ and} \qquad (2)$$

$$M_t \frac{\partial f}{\partial g}(p_t, g_t) + W_t - W_{t-1} + \eta_t \frac{\partial^2 f}{\partial p \partial g}(p_t, g_t) = 0. \qquad (3)$$

It is clear, therefore, that

$$M_t = V_t = W_t = \frac{\partial u}{\partial c_t}, \quad t = 1, \ldots, T - 1. \tag{4}$$

The shadow price of each (budgetary) constraint must equal the (marginal) impact on utility of releasing that constraint by one unit. Moreover, the marginal utility of adding one more unit of total production in period t must be independent of how that additional unit appears, be it public capital, private capital, or consumption. Combining equation (4) with (2) and (3) also reveals that

$$\eta_t \frac{\partial^2 f}{\partial p^2}(p_t, g_t) = \frac{\partial u}{\partial c_{t-1}} - [1 + \frac{\partial f}{\partial p}(p_t, g_t)] \frac{\partial u}{\partial c_t} \quad \text{and} \tag{5}$$

$$\eta_t \frac{\partial^2 f}{\partial p \partial g}(p_t, g_t) = \frac{\partial u}{\partial c_{t-1}} - [1 + \frac{\partial f}{\partial g}(p_t, g_t)] \frac{\partial u}{\partial c_t}. \tag{6}$$

Recalling equation (1) and letting $f_g^*(t)$ denote the best return to government investment, it is possible to combine equations (5) and (6):

$$f_g^*(t) = [\frac{\partial^2 f}{\partial p \partial g}(p_t, g_t) / \frac{\partial^2 f}{\partial p^2}(p_t, g_t)] \, k_t$$

$$+ \{ 1 - [\frac{\partial^2 f}{\partial p \partial g}(p_t, g_t) / \frac{\partial^2 f}{\partial p^2}(p_t, g_t)]\} \, r_t. \tag{7}$$

In writing equation (7),

$$r_t \equiv [(\partial u/\partial c_{t-1})/(\partial u/\partial c_t)] - 1$$

reflects the pure rate of time preference. Equation (7) therefore instructs us that the optimal rate of return should be a weighted sum of the marginal product of private capital and the consumers' rate of time preference.

(b) Simple manipulation of equation (7) reveals that

$$f_g^*(t) = r_t + [\frac{\partial^2 f}{\partial p \partial g}(p_t, g_t)/ \frac{\partial^2 f}{\partial p^2}(p_t, g_t)](k_t - r_t). \qquad (8)$$

Since

$$\frac{\partial^2 f}{\partial p^2}(p_t, g_t) < 0$$

and the cross partial $\{(\partial^2 f/\partial p \partial g)(p_t, g_t)\}$ can have either sign, the optimal marginal return to public capital can be greater or less than r_t depending upon the signs of the cross partial derivative of the production function and $(k_t - r_t)$. Equation (8) is, however, easily interpreted. Consider, for example, the case in which imperfect risk spreading in the private capital market creates an investment rule such that $k_t > r_t$ for all t. A misallocation of resources results. The economy provides too much current consumption at the expense of too little investment for the future. Equation (8) shows how much power the government can muster to optimally counterbalance this underinvestment with its own investment decisions.

In the extreme case, public and private capital might be perfect substitutes,

$$\frac{\partial^2 f}{\partial p^2} = \frac{\partial^2 f}{\partial p \partial g} ,$$

so that a unit increase in public investment would simply replace one unit of private investment; the government would then be powerless to correct the distortion. Equation (8) makes it clear that public investment should also return k_t on the margin under these circumstances.

If private and public capital were independent [as in the additive production function assumed by Arrow and Lind (1)], then $\partial^2 f/\partial p \partial g = 0$ and a unit increase in public capital would have no effect on the marginal product of private investment. The government should then act as if the distortion in the capital market did not exist and continue to invest until a marginal return of r_t could be achieved. Public and private capital might exhibit imperfect substitutability, of course; in this intermediate case, though, $k_t > f_g^*(t) > r_t$.

If private and public capital were complements,
finally, the one more unit of public investment would
actually induce an expansion in private investment by
increasing its marginal productivity. As a result, public
investment actually could become an effective vehicle with
which to reduce the tendency of the private sector to
underinvest. The optimal investment rule would therefore
call for public investment to continue beyond the point
where its marginal product equaled the rate of time
preference; i.e., equation (8) indicates that $f_g^*(t) < r_t$
because $\partial^2 f / \partial p \partial g > 0$.

The opposite conclusions are drawn, quite naturally,
when the market distortion provides extra incentives to
private investment. The intuition developed above about the
government's ability to counterbalance the effects of the
distortion is, nonetheless, accurate.

When there are no distortions, moreover, $k_t = r_t$ and
the second term of equation (8) disappears. The allocation
problem is then a first best question, and the optimal
marginal return to public capital is simultaneously equal to
the return to private capital and the rate of time
preference.

The general proposition that emerges from this
exercise states that the marginal return to publicly
provided capital will optimally exceed (fall below) the rate

of time preference if and only if one of these two
conditions is satisfied:

> (i)   public and private capital are substitutes
>   (complements) and the marginal return to
>   private capital exceeds the pure rate of
>   time preference, or
>
> (ii) public and private capital are complements
>   (substitutes) and the rate of time
>   preference exceeds the return to private
>   capital.

In addition, the marginal return to government capital
optimally equals the pure rate of time preference if and
only if (i) public and private capital are independent or
(ii) private capital returns the rate of time preference.

The key to the apparent confusion lies in different
characterizations of the underlying production structure.
Those who have studied the tax impact have assumed, at least
implicitly, that public and private capital are positive
substitutes in the Hicksian q-sense; i.e., increases in the
private (public) capital stock reduce the marginal product
of public (private) capital. Those who argue for ignoring
the private risk premium have meanwhile presumed that the
two types of capital are, on the margin, independent.

While these may be reasonable approximations of

reality in some cases, they exclude one important dimension
of government investment. There are, in particular, many
examples in which public and private capital actually
complement each other. The construction of an improved
highway system, for instance, often significantly increases
the productivity of private industry in a specified region.
An irrigation project will usually increase the agricultural
yields of the areas it services. A subsidy to scientific
research or education by the government can be considered
investment that can raise the productivity of private
capital. The list is virtually endless. The very reason
that the government chooses to intervene in these cases lies
in the external economies that such activities can create.

References

(1) Arrow, K., and R.C. Lind, "Uncertainty and the
Evaluation of Public Investment Decisions," *American
Economic Review*, 60: 364-378, 1970.

(2) Baumol, W., "On the Social Rate of Discount," *American
Economic Review*, 58: 788-802, 1968.

(3) Baumol, W., "On the Discount Rate for Public Projects"
in R. Haveman and J. Margolis (eds.), *Public Expenditure and
Policy Analysis*, Chicago, Markham, 1970.

(4) Ogura, S., and G. Yohe, "The Complementarity of Public
and Private Capital and the Optimal Rate of Return to

Government Investment," *Quarterly Journal of Economics*, 91: 651-622, 1977.

(5) Samuelson, P.A., "Principles of Efficiency - Discussion," *American Economic Review*, Papers and Proceedings, 54: 93-96, 1964.

(6) Sandmo, A. and J.H. Dreze, "Discount Rate for Public Investment," *Economica*, 38: 395-412, 1971.

(7) Seagraves, J.A., "More on the Social Rate of Discount," *Quarterly Journal of Economics*, 85: 317-329, 1971.

(8) Vickrey, W., "Principles of Efficiency - Discussion," *American Economic Review*, Papers and Proceedings, 54: 88-91, 1964.

40. Peak Load Pricing and the Structure of Demand Uncertainty[1]

Peak load pricing has been the topic of a series of papers since the publication of Oliver Williamson's seminal work in 1966. His was a linear, perfect knowledge model in which it was observed that price discrimination could be a socially optimal strategy: peak consumers should pay a price that covered not only variable cost, but also the entire fixed cost of providing enough capacity to cover their demand.

Price discrimination might not be feasible, though, and a branch of the literature has studied the second best problem of handling variable demand with a single price. This branch is, in fact, a specialized version of more general analyses of firms facing uncertain demand conducted by, among others, Leland (4) and Sandmo (5).

This problem will concentrate on the peak load studies typified by Brown and Johnson (1), Visscher (6), and Carlton (2). They have all noted that there must exist states of nature for which demand outstrips capacity whenever a single price is set -- even when that price is set optimally. Some type of rationing mechanism is thus required to deal with

---

[1] Material found in Chapters 10 and 12 is applicable here. The analysis presented will be based upon the theoretical structure of consumer surplus introduced in Chapter 8.

the resulting excess demand.

No surprises so far, right? Not so far, but it turns out that the profitability of a firm's offering the optimal capacity and charging the optimal price depends crucially upon the choice of this rationing mechanism. Depending upon the sign of expected profits, in fact, either a tax or a subsidy might be required to sustain the socially superior equilibrium.

As interesting as this observation might be, a second, potentially more important effect, can be lost if one pays to much attention to rationing. It is mentioned only in passing by Carlton [page 1009], but it is nonetheless the focus of this problem. Under a random rationing scheme (e.g.), it has been observed that expected profits evaluated at the optimum will be negative whenever demand uncertainty is additive. If demand uncertainty is multiplicative, however, positive profits can result at the optimum under the identical rationing mechanism. And so a second line of questioning: what underlying demand structure, altered by the way uncertainty effects demand, can create such a dramatic effect?

Consider the Williamson model. Offpeak and peak demand schedules are represented by

$$p = \alpha_1 - \delta_1 x_1 \text{ and} \tag{1}$$

$$p = \alpha_2 - \delta_2 x_2 \qquad\qquad (2)$$

respectively. Peak demand occurs $\pi_2 \cdot 100\%$ of the time; offpeak demand, $\pi_1 \cdot 100\%$ of the time; and $\pi_1 + \pi_2 = 1$. Capacity costs are fixed at β per unit, and variable costs are b per unit. Suppose, finally, that the income elasticity of demand is zero, so that consumer surplus can be the area under the given demand schedules [see Chapter 10].

Questions:

(a) Show that the socially optimal prices are $p_1 = b$ during the offpeak period and $p_1 = b + (\beta/\pi_2)$ during the peak. Characterize optimal capacity.

(b) Suppose now that the firm can charge only one price. Characterize the socially optimal price and capacity.

(c) Additive demand uncertainty is defined

$$p = f(x) + \theta,$$

where θ is a random variable. Restrict the Williamson model to reflect additive uncertainty. Characterize the socially optimal price and capacity and show that expected profits are negative.

(d)   Multiplication uncertainty is defined

$$p = \theta f(x).$$

Repeat part (c) for this case, but show that expected profits can be positive.

Suggested Solutions:

(a) Under the Williamson model, consumer surplus is

$$S = \pi_1 \int_0^{x_1} (\alpha_1 - \delta_1 s) \, ds + \pi_2 \int_0^{x_2} (\alpha_2 - \delta_2 s) \, ds$$

$$- \pi_1 \int_0^{x_1} b \, ds - \pi_2 \int_0^{x_2} b \, ds - \beta x_2$$

$$= \pi_1 \alpha_1 x_1 + \pi_2 \alpha_2 x_2 - (\pi_1 \delta_1 x_1 / 2)$$

$$- \pi_1 b x_1 - (\pi_2 \delta_2 x_2 / 2) - \pi_2 b x_2 - \beta x_2.$$

The first-order conditions for (x_1^*, x_2^*) are therefore

$$\alpha_1 - b - \delta_1 x_1^* = 0, \text{ and}$$

$$\alpha_2 - b - \delta_2 x_2^* - (\beta / \pi_2) x_2^* = 0$$

so that

$$x_1^* = [\alpha - b]/\delta \text{ and}$$

$$x_2^* = [\alpha_2 - (\beta/\pi_2) - b]/\delta_2.$$

Clearly, then,

$$p_1^* = b \text{ and}$$

$$p_2^* = b + (\beta/\pi_2) > b + \beta,$$

and expected profits are zero:

$$\pi_1 p_1^* x_1^* + \pi_2 p_2^* x_2^* - bx_1^* \pi_1 - bx_2^* \pi_2 - \beta x_2^*$$

$$= \pi_1 bx_1^* + \pi_2 bx_2^* + \beta x_2^* - bx_1^* \pi_1 - bx_2^* \pi_2 - \beta x_2^* = 0.$$

Offpeak consumers pay only for operating and delivery costs, while peak consumers pay operating costs plus more than 100% of the costs of providing the capacity they require.

(b) When only one price is allowed, consumer surplus is

PROBLEM 40

$$S(p) = \pi_1 \{ \int_0^{x_1(p)} (\alpha_1 - \delta_1 s) \, ds - bx_1(\bar{p}) \} +$$

$$\pi_2 \{ \int_0^{x_2(p)} (\alpha_2 - \delta_2 s) \, ds - bx_2(\bar{p}) - \beta x_2(\bar{p}).$$

The first-order condition that characterizes the best price is

$$\pi_1 [\alpha_1 - \delta_1 x_1(\bar{p})] \delta_1 - b\pi_1 \delta_1 + \pi_2 [\alpha_2 - \delta_2 x_2(\bar{p})] \delta_2 - b\pi_2 \delta_2 - \beta \delta_2 = 0. \tag{3}$$

Substituting equations (1) and (2) into (3) plus a little algebra now reveals that

$$\bar{p} = \frac{b[\pi_1 \delta_1 + \pi_2 \delta_2] + \beta \delta_2}{\pi_1 \delta_1 + \pi_2 \delta_2} = b + \frac{\beta \delta_2}{\pi_1 \delta_1 + \pi_2 \delta_2}. \tag{4}$$

Capacity is then read from the peak demand schedule, so

$$\bar{x}_{cap} = \frac{\alpha_2 - b - [\beta \delta_2 / (\pi_1 \delta_1 + p_2 \delta_2)]}{\delta_2} = \frac{\alpha_2 - b}{\delta_2} - \frac{\beta}{\pi_1 \delta_1 + \pi_2 \delta_2}. \tag{5}$$

(c) The Williamson two-period model can be made to reflect additive demand uncertainty by specifying that $\alpha_1 > \alpha_2$ <u>and</u>

401

$\delta_1 = \delta_2 = \delta$. From equations (4) and (5), therefore

$$\bar{p}^a = b + \frac{\beta\delta}{\delta(\pi_1 + \pi_2)} = b + \beta < p_2^* \text{ and}$$

$$\bar{x}_{cap}^a = \frac{\alpha_2 - b}{\delta} - \frac{\beta}{\delta(\pi_1 + \pi_2)} = \frac{\alpha_2 - b - \beta}{\delta} > x_2^* \text{ .}$$

Expected profits are negative because

$$\pi_1[\bar{p}^a - b]x_1(\bar{p}^a) + \pi_2[\bar{p}^a - b]\bar{x}_{cap}^a - \beta\bar{x}_{cap}^a$$

$$< \pi_1[\bar{p}^a - b]\bar{x}_{cap}^a + \pi_2[\bar{p}^a - b]\bar{x}_{cap}^a - \beta\bar{x}_{cap}^a = 0.$$

(d) The Williamson model reflects multiplicative demand uncertainty if $\alpha_1 = k\alpha_2$ and $\delta_1 = k\delta_2$ with $0 < k < 1$. From equations (4) and (5), then,

$$\bar{p}^m = b + \frac{\beta}{\pi_1 k + \pi_2} > b + \beta = \bar{p}^a \text{ and} \tag{6}$$

$$\bar{x}_{cap}^m = \frac{\alpha_2 - b}{\delta_2} - \frac{\beta}{(\pi_1 k + \pi_2)\delta_2} < \bar{x}_{cap}^a. \tag{7}$$

Capacity is not as high and the price is not as low; it is, in fact, possible that

$$\bar{p}^m > p_2^* \text{ and } \bar{x}_{cap}^m < x_2^*.$$

After noting from equations (6) and (7) that

$$\bar{x}_{cap}^m = \frac{\alpha_2 - \bar{p}^m}{\delta_2},$$

expected profits can be evaluated:

$$\pi_1 [\bar{p}^m - b] x_1^a (\bar{p}^m) + \pi_2 [\bar{p}^m - b] \bar{x}_{cap}^m - \beta \bar{x}_{cap}^m$$

$$= - [\frac{\pi_1}{\delta_1} + \frac{\pi_2}{\delta_2}] \frac{\beta \bar{p}^m}{\pi_1 k + \pi_2} + [\frac{\pi_1 \alpha_1}{\delta_1} + \frac{\pi_2 \alpha_2}{\delta_2}] \frac{\beta}{\pi_1 k + \pi_2} - \frac{\beta \alpha_2}{\delta_2} + \frac{\beta \bar{p}^m}{\delta_2}$$

$$= \frac{\beta \pi_1}{\delta_2 (\pi_1 k + \pi_2)} \{\alpha_2 [1 - k] - \bar{p}^m [(1/k) - k]\}. \tag{8}$$

The sign of (8) depends on k. When k = 1, peak and offpeak demand coincide and expected profits are zero. For values of k that make the bracketed term,

$$1 > k > [p^{-m}/(\alpha_2 - 1)]^{0.5}$$

positive, therefore, expected profits are positive. They are otherwise negative.

The rationale behind this exercise can now be discussed. When a single price solution is constructed for a variable demand problem in lieu of a multiple price solution, the socially optimal capacity increase is smaller the more inelastic peak demand is relative to offpeak demand. The associated increase in capacity cost is therefore muted by a significantly more inelastic peak demand schedule. This dampening works to keep the change in revenues from both peak and offpeak demand within the region where they increase faster than capacity costs; profits rise from zero.

If capacity were to rise more dramatically because peak demand was not sufficiently steeper, however, then revenues would run a higher risk of moving into regions where increased sales would increase revenues too slowly, or perhaps even cause them to fall; profits could fall below zero. Facing a peak demand schedule that is significantly more inelastic than the offpeak demand therefore serves to keep capacity from getting unprofitably large. Uncertainty which enters the demand side multiplicatively allows this as a possibility, but additive uncertainty does not.

It was also observed that there can be too much of a good thing. When peak demand is excessively inelastic, then the socially optimal capacity can even fall below the level that would be provided under a multiple price solution. Capacity costs would fall, in that case, but sales would be moving down into elastic regions of both demand schedules. Revenues would fall at an increasing rate and expected profits could again turn negative if peak demand were excessively inelastic. This is the genesis of the k^* below which the social optimum became unprofitable.

References

(1) Brown, G., and M.B. Johnson, "Utility Pricing and Output under Risk," *American Economic Review*, 59: 119-128, 1969.

(2) Carlton, D., "Peak Load Pricing with Stochastic Demand," *American Economic Review*, 67: 1006-1010, 1977.

(3) Dausby, R.E., "Capacity Constrained Peak Load Pricing," *Quarterly Journal of Economics*, 92: 387-389, 1978.

(4) Leland, H., "Theory of the Firm Facing Uncertain Demand," *American Economic Review*, 62: 278-291, 1972.

(5) Sandmo, A., "On the Theory of the Competitive Firm under Uncertainty," *American Economic Review*, 61: 65-73, 1971.

(6) Visscher, M., "Welfare Maximizing Price and Output with Stochastic Demand," *American Economic Review*, 63: 224-29, 1974.

(7) Williamson, O., "Peak Load Pricing and Optimal Capacity with Indivisible Constraints," *American Economic Review*, 56: 810-827, 1966.

Note: A Symposium on Peak Load Pricing published in the spring (1976) issue of the *Bell Journal of Economics*.

41. The Asymmetry of Taxes and Subsidies[1]

When a regulatory agency wants to design a set of
incentives that will elicit a particular behavior from a
given firm (or industry), it can choose either a "carrot" or
a "stick" by awarding either a subsidy for intended behavior
or charging a tax for inappropriate behavior. Despite a few
comments to the contrary [see Baumol and Oates (1) and
Mishan (3), e.g.], it can be observed that these
alternatives need not have symmetric effects. When the
firm(s) is not risk neutral, in particular, taxes and
subsidies are not equally effective.

This problem will explore the potential asymmetry in a
safety example provided by Just and Zilberman (2). It will
be a problem in manipulating and interpreting results, so a
good deal of rather tedious algebra will be subsumed in the
statement of the problem. While the careful reader might
want to do those computations, anyway, the thrust of the
treatment lies in deciphering the subsequent implications.

Consider a single firm that produces a good denoted x.
Let q represent safety in the production of x in the sense
that (1-q) is the probability that an accident will occur.
Production costs can therefore be represented by $c(x, q)$;

---

[1] Material found in Chapter 13 is applicable here. The
notion of risk aversion from Chapter 12 will be combined
with some of the fundamental constructions of Chapters 4 and
7 to investigate more fully the topic of Section 13.12.

PROBLEM 41

assume that

$$\frac{\partial c}{\partial x} > 0, \qquad \frac{\partial^2 c}{\partial x^2} > 0,$$

$$\frac{\partial c}{\partial q} > 0, \qquad \frac{\partial^2 c}{\partial q^2} > 0, \text{ and}$$

$$\frac{\partial^2 c}{\partial x^2} \frac{\partial^2 c}{\partial q^2} - \{\frac{\partial^2 c}{\partial x \partial q}\}^2 > 0$$

(i.e., the cost function is assumed to be convex in x and q [page 496]). Finally, suppose that the firm maximizes $u(\pi)$, where π represents profits and $u(\pi)$ represents a utility (objective) function with $du/d\pi > 0$ and $d^2u/d\pi^2 < 0$.

If the government were to pay a subsidy s when an accident did not happen and to charge a tax t when an accident did occur, then the firm would maximize expected utility,

$$Eu \equiv qu[px-c(x,q)+s] + (1-q)u[px-c(x,q)-t],$$

with respect to x and q. Defining, for the purpose of simplifying notation,

$$u_1 \equiv u[px-c(x,q)+s] \text{ and}$$

PROBLEM 41

$$u_1 \equiv u[px-c(x,q)-t],$$

the first-order conditions for that problem can be written:

$$\{q \frac{\partial u_1}{\partial \pi} (x^*,q^*;s) + (1-q) \frac{\partial u_2}{\partial \pi}(x^*,q^*;t)\}\{p - \frac{\partial c}{\partial x} (x^*,q^*)\}$$

$$= E\{\frac{\partial u}{\partial \pi} (x^*,q^*; s,t)\}\{p - \frac{\partial c}{\partial x} (x^*,q^*)\} = 0 \text{ and} \quad (1)$$

$$u_1(x^*,q^*;s) - u_2(x^*,q^*;t) = E \{\frac{\partial u}{\partial \pi}(x^*,q^*;s,t)\} \frac{\partial c}{\partial q}(x^*,q^*). \quad (2)$$

Totally differentiating equations (1) and (2) with respect to x^*, q^*, s, and t, carefully collecting terms, and taking notice of second-order conditions can then reveal that

$$\frac{dq^*}{ds} = \alpha[\frac{\partial u_1}{\partial \pi}(x^*,q^*;s) - q^* \frac{\partial^2 u_1}{\partial \pi^2}(x^*,q^*;s) \frac{\partial c}{\partial q} (x^*,q^*)] \text{ and} \quad (3)$$

$$\frac{dq^*}{ds} = \alpha[\frac{\partial u_2}{\partial \pi}(x^*,q^*;t) + (1-q^*) \frac{\partial^2 u_2}{\partial \pi^2}(x^*,q^*;t) \frac{\partial c}{\partial q}(x^*,q^*)]. \quad (4)$$

In equations (3) and (4),

$$\alpha \equiv \frac{\partial^2 c}{\partial x^2} (x^*,q^*) E\{\frac{\partial u}{\partial \pi}(x^*,q^*;s,t)\}/|M| > 0$$

408

because M is the matrix of second-order conditions.

Questions:

(a) Show that a subsidy increase always increases optimal safety but that a tax need not. Explain why.

(b) Show that risk aversion increases (decreases) optimal safety relative to risk neutrality when safety is already high (low). Explain both results in terms of reducing risk.

(c) Assume that absolute risk aversion is a decreasing function of profits. Show that a subsidy (tax) is then more effective in increasing safety when safety is initially low (high) [the results of part (b) will be helpful].

Suggested Solutions:

These exercises involve manipulation of equations (3) and (4). Part (a) follows rather straightforwardly from those equations and the definitions of absolute risk aversion [page 178]. Part (b) can be deduced from a comparison of the first-order conditions for optimal safety and output with and without risk neutrality. Part (b) will then play an integral part in interpreting the expression that results from subtracting (3) from (4).

(a) It is clear from equation (3) that $(dq^*/ds) > 0$.
Equation (4) meanwhile shows that a tax increases safety if
and only if

$$\alpha\{1 + (1-q^*)\ [\frac{d^2u_2}{d\pi^2}/\frac{du_2}{d\pi}]\ \frac{\partial c}{\partial q}\}\ \frac{du_2}{d\pi} > 0.$$

Given that an accident has occurred, the Pratt measure of
absolute risk aversion is

$$r(\pi) \equiv -\ \frac{d^2u_2}{d\pi^2}\ /\ \frac{du_2}{d\pi}$$

[page 178, again], and (dq^*/dt) is positive if and only if

$$1 > (1 - q^*)r_2(\pi)\ \frac{\partial c}{\partial q}\ . \tag{5}$$

The rationale behind equation (5) can be explained by
looking at the firm's possible reactions to a higher tax.
There is, first of all, an incentive to reduce the
probability of paying a high tax that tends to push q^* up.
Increasing q^* is costly, though, and it may pay to reduce q^*
instead. This second response would save money in either
state of nature, but those savings would have to be weighed

against the increased probability of paying the tax. The higher (lower) the optimal chance for an accident $[1-q^*]$, the higher (lower) the marginal cost of safety $[\partial c/\partial q]$, and/or the more (less) risk averse the firm $[r_2(\pi)]$, the more (less) likely it becomes that equation (5) will not be satisfied. A reduction (increase) in q^* would then result.

(b) The risk neutral firm solves

$$\max_{x;q} \quad \{px - c(x,q) + qs - (1-q)t\}$$

so that it considers first-order conditions which require that

$$\frac{\partial c}{\partial x}(\hat{x},\hat{q}) = t \text{ and} \tag{6}$$

$$\frac{\partial c}{\partial q}(\hat{x},\hat{q}) = t + s. \tag{7}$$

Since equation (2) can be rewritten

$$\frac{\partial c}{\partial q}(x^*,q^*) = \frac{u_1 - u_2}{E\{du/d\pi\}}, \tag{2'}$$

it is interesting to consider solutions to the following equations:

$$\frac{\partial c}{\partial x}(\bar{x},\bar{q}) = p \text{ and} \tag{8a}$$

411

$$\frac{\partial c}{\partial q}(\bar{x},\bar{q}) = k. \tag{8b}$$

What happens to $(\bar{x},\bar{q})$ when k is changed? The appropriate total derivatives of the two parts of equation (8) show that

$$\frac{\partial^2 c}{\partial x^2} \, d\bar{x} + \frac{\partial^2 c}{\partial x \partial q} \, d\bar{q} = 0 \quad \text{and}$$

$$\frac{\partial^2 c}{\partial x \partial q} \, d\bar{x} + \frac{\partial^2 c}{\partial q^2} \, d\bar{q} = dk.$$

Clearly, therefore

$$\frac{d\bar{q}}{dk} = \frac{(\partial^2 c/\partial x^2)}{[(\partial^2 c/\partial x^2)(\partial^2 c/\partial q^2) - (\partial^2 c/\partial x \partial q)^2]} > 0.$$

As a result, $q^* - \hat{q}$ will be strictly positive if and only if k defined by equations (7) and (2') is positive; i.e., $q^* > \hat{q}$ if and only if

$$\frac{u_1 - u_2}{E\{du/d\pi\}} > t + s. \tag{9}$$

To interpret equation (9), notice from Figure 41.1 that

Figure 41.1

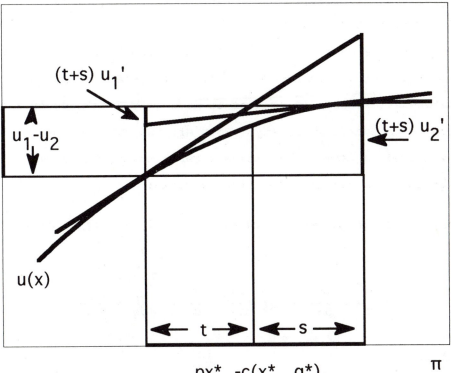

$$(t+s)(du_2/d\pi) > (u_1 - u_2) > (t+s)(du_1/d\pi); \qquad (10)$$

equation (10), in fact, follows from the mean value theorem. Suppose, then, that $q^* \to 1$. In that case, $E\{du/d\pi\} \to du_1/d\pi$ and equation (9) would be satisfied. When optimal safety is high, the risk averter moves toward reducing risk by increasing it even further.

On the other hand, $q^* \to 0$ means that $E\{du/d\pi\} \to du_2/d\pi$ and equation (9) is not satisfied. Low levels of optimal safety allow the risk averter to move away from risk by providing even less safety. Both effects can thus be explained in terms of a risk averter's moving the firm toward the certainty case that is closer.

(c) It can be observed from equations (3) and (4) that

$$\frac{dq^*}{dt} - \frac{dq^*}{ds} = \alpha\{ \left[\frac{du_2}{d\pi} - \frac{du_1}{d\pi}\right] + \frac{\partial c}{\partial q} E\left(\frac{d^2 u}{d\pi^2}\right) \},$$

where

$$E\left(\frac{d^2 u}{d\pi^2}\right) \equiv q^* \frac{d^2 u}{d\pi^2}(x^*, q^*; s) + (1-q^*) \frac{d^2 u}{d\pi^2}(x^*, q^*; t).$$

From equation (2), therefore

414

$$\frac{dq^*}{dt} - \frac{dq^*}{ds} = \alpha\{(u_1-u_2)\frac{E(d^2u/d\pi^2)}{E(du/d\pi)} - [\frac{du_1}{d\pi} - \frac{du_2}{d\pi}]\},$$

$$= \alpha\{(u_1-u_2)\frac{E(d^2u/d\pi^2)}{E(du/d\pi)} - \frac{(du_1/d\pi)-(du_2/d\pi)}{(u_1-u_2)}\}. \qquad (11)$$

In recording equation (11), it is defined that

$$E(du/d\pi) \equiv q^* \frac{du_1}{d\pi} (x^*,q^*;s) + (1-q^*) \frac{du_2}{d\pi} (x^*,q^*;t).$$

Now let $u(\pi)$ exhibit decreasing absolute risk aversion;
i.e., let

$$\frac{dr(\pi)}{d\pi} = - \{\frac{du}{d\pi}\frac{d^3u}{d\pi^3} - [\frac{d^2u}{d\pi^2}]^2\} / [\frac{du}{d\pi}]^2 < 0. \qquad (12)$$

The only way that equation (12) can happen is for $d^3u/d\pi^3 > 0$. For reasons paralleling the justification of equation (10), it is therefore necessary that

$$(t+s)(d^2u_2/d\pi^2) < [\frac{du_1}{d\pi} - \frac{du_2}{d\pi}] < (t+s)(d^2u_1/d\pi^2). \qquad (13)$$

Combining equations (10) and (13), then

$$\{\frac{d^2u_1}{d\pi^2} / \frac{du_1}{d\pi}\} > \frac{\{(du_1/d\pi) - (du_2/d\pi)\}}{(u_1-u_2)} > \{\frac{d^2u_2}{d\pi^2} / \frac{du_2}{d\pi}\}. \quad (14)$$

Now let $q^* \to 1$. The middle term in equation (14) does not vary. However,

$$\frac{E(d^2u/d\pi^2)}{E(du/d\pi} \to \frac{d^2u_1/d\pi^2}{du_1/d\pi} > \frac{(du_1/d\pi) - (du_2/d\pi)}{u_1 - u_2}$$

from the left-hand side of equation (14). When optimal safety is high, equation (11) therefore implies that

$$\lim_{q^*\to 1} \{\frac{dq^*}{dt} - \frac{dq^*}{ds}\} > 0;$$

a tax is more effective than a subsidy. On the other extreme, (14) shows that when $q^* \to 0$,

$$\frac{E(d^2u/d\pi^2)}{E(du/d\pi)} \to \frac{d^2u_2/d\pi^2}{du_2/d\pi_2} > \frac{(du_1/d\pi) - (du_2/d\pi)}{u_1 - u_2}$$

so that

PROBLEM 41

$$\lim_{q* \to 0} \quad \{\frac{dq^*}{dt} - \frac{dq^*}{ds}\} < 0.$$

A subsidy is thus more effective when optimal safety is low. To explain these results, observe that a subsidy moves the firm into a region of lower absolute risk aversion (under decreasing $r(\pi)$). The implications recorded in (b) can thus be applied. When q^* is high, for example, (b) shows that lower risk aversion means that less safety is provided. The tax must therefore be more effective because it avoids the lower risk aversion. When q^* is low, on the other hand, (b) shows that lower risk aversion means more safety and the subsidy works better.

Combining the results of (b) and (c), it is seen that in problems of low safety, risk aversion and a tax produce less safety than risk aversion and a subsidy, but both produce less safety than risk neutrality. When safety is too high, on the other hand, risk neutrality produces less safety than either scheme under risk aversion, and a tax produces the most. It should be emphasized, however, that decreasing (absolute) risk aversion is crucial for these conclusions to hold. An excellent description of decreasing (absolute) risk aversion can be found in Stiglitz (4). In the beginning of that paper, increasing, decreasing, and constant absolute and relative [page 116, Problem 3.29] risk

417

aversions are characterized and compared. To emphasize the
limited restriction placed on part (c) by assuming that
absolute risk aversion is decreasing, it is enough to state
one result from Stiglitz: decreasing absolute risk aversion
is equivalent to requiring that the absolute amount of
income devoted to investment in a risky asset increase with
income (it is consistent with decreasing, constant, and
moderately increasing relative risk aversion).

References

(1) Baumol, W.J., and W.E. Oates, *The Theory of
Environmental Policy: Externalities, Public Outlays and the
Quality of Life,* Englewood Cliffs, N.J., Prentice-Hall,
1967.

(2) Just, R.E., and D. Zilberman, "Asymmetry of Taxes and
Subsidies in Regulating Stochastic Mishaps," *Quarterly
Journal of Economics*, 92: 139-148, 1979.

(3) Mishan, E.J., "The Postwar Literature on Externalities:
An Interpretative Essay," *Journal of Economic Literature*, 9:
1-28, 1971.

(4) Stiglitz, J.E., "The Effects of Income, Wealth and
Capital Gains Taxation on Risk Taking," *Quarterly Journal of
Economics*, 83: 263-283, 1969.

42. Monopoly and the Extraction of an Exhaustible Resource[1]

It has been argued, by some who have observed that monopoly output is smaller than the competitive output, that it is reasonable to expect a monopolist to exploit exhaustible resources more slowly than a competitive firm. This problem will explore that conjecture along the lines presented by Stiglitz (4). It will prove the conjecture true under all but the most restrictive assumptions.

Let demand for an exhaustible resource x be represented by

$$p(t) = f(t) \ x(t)^{\alpha-1}, \ 0 < \alpha < 1. \tag{1}$$

The total amount of x available is R_0 and the interest (discount) rate is r.

Questions:

(a) Show that the price elasticity for the demand curve recorded in equation (1) is $[1/(\alpha-1)]$ and that marginal revenue equals $\alpha p(t)$.

(b) Suppose, for the sake of simplicity, that extraction of the natural resource is costless. Show that the monopolist and the competitive firm would both exploit x

---

[1] Material found in various sections of Chapters 13, 14, and 19 is applicable here.

at the same rate (use an infinite time horizon).

(c) Suppose that extraction per unit x (denoted g(t)) is constant during any period and declining over time. Show that the monopolist is then more of a conservationist, extracting less now and more later, than a competitive firm.

(d) Consider a two-period model geometrically and show that if demand becomes more elastic in period 2 (because, for example, substitutes are developed), then the monopolist again sells less than the competitive market early (period 1) and more later (period 2). Use the solution to (b) as a benchmark.

Suggested Solutions:

The solutions to parts (b) and (c) involve maximizing the present discounted value of x(t) under the two types of market structure. Analyzing rates of extraction and rates of price changes are two sides to the same coin, and it is useful to keep both in mind. Part (a) is computational, and part (d) is yet another example of how geometry can be used to (rigorously) suggest solutions to otherwise complicated problems.

(a) From the definition of elasticity,

PROBLEM 42

$$\varepsilon(x) \equiv \frac{d \ln [x(t)]}{d \ln [p(t)]}$$

Since equation (1) can be rewritten

$$\ln [x(t)] = \frac{1}{\alpha-1} \ln [p(t)] - \frac{1}{\alpha-1} \ln [f(t)]$$

it is clear that $\varepsilon(x) = [1/(\alpha-1)]$. Marginal revenue therefore equals

$$p(t)(1 + \frac{1}{\varepsilon(x)}) = p(x)(1 + \alpha - 1) = \alpha p(x).$$

(b) Consider the monopolist's problem:

$$\max \int_0^\infty p(s)x(s)e^{-rs}\, ds$$

$$\text{s.t. } \int_0^\infty x(s)\, ds \leq R_0.$$ (2)

Under the presumption of constant price elasticity of demand implicitly recorded in (1), the appropriate Lagrangian is

$$\int_0^\infty f(s)x(s)^\alpha\, e^{-rs}\, ds + \lambda \{ \int_0^\infty x(s)\, ds - R_0\},$$

so the first-order condition for (2) is

$$0 = \alpha f(t)x(t)^{\alpha-1} e^{-rt} + \lambda = \alpha p_m(t)e^{-rt} + \lambda. \tag{3}$$

Equation (3) therefore has the natural interpretation that the (discounted) marginal revenue earned each and every period [denoted $(\alpha p_m(t)e^{-rt})$] should equal some constant (denoted simply $-\lambda$). Differentiating (3) with respect to t also reveals that

$$-\alpha r p_m(t)e^{-rt} + \alpha e^{-rt}\dot{p}_m(t) = 0,$$

where $\dot{p}(t) \equiv \partial p(t)/\partial t$. As a result,

$$(\dot{p}_m(t)/p_m(t)) = r \tag{4}$$

and the monopolist is seen to increase his price at a rate equal to the rate of interest.

This is a familiar result for competitive markets, as well. To be in equilibrium, the own rate of interest must precisely equal the market rate of interest to keep people from entering or leaving the industry. Put another way, the price earned this period must equal the (discounted) price earned in any other period; i.e.,

$$p_c(t)e^{-rt} = \text{constant}. \tag{5}$$

Differentiating equation (5) with respect to t and

rearranging reveals, as promised, that

$$(\dot{p}_c(t)/p_c(t)) = r.$$

Production under both market structures must therefore satisfy

$$\frac{\dot{x}_m(t)}{x_m(t)} = \frac{\dot{x}_c(t)}{x_c(t)} = \frac{(df/dt)/f(t)}{\alpha-1}$$

as well as the resource constraint that

$$\int_0^\infty x_m(s)\ ds = \int_0^\infty x_c(s)\ ds = R_0.$$

The rates of extraction must, therefore, be equal. It must be emphasized, however, that this conclusion holds only if extraction is costless and the price elasticity of demand for the resource remains constant.

(c) The new problem is

$$\max \int_0^\infty [p(s)-g(s)]x(s)e^{-rs}\ ds \qquad (6)$$

$$\text{s.t.} \quad \int_0^\infty x(s)\ ds \le R.$$

Looking at the corresponding Lagrangian and computing the

first-order condition, it is seen that the solution to (6) satisfies

$$0 = [\alpha f(t)x(t)^{\alpha-1} - g(t)]e^{-rt} + \lambda$$

$$= [\alpha p_m(t) - g(t)]e^{-rt} + \lambda. \tag{7}$$

Differentiating equation (7) with respect to t, then,

$$0 = -r[\alpha p_m(t) - g(t)]e^{-rt} + e^{-rt}[\alpha \dot{p}_m(t) - \dot{g}(t)].$$

As a result

$$\frac{\dot{p}_m(t)}{p_m(t)} = r - \frac{rg(t)}{\alpha p_m(t)} + \frac{g(t)}{\alpha p_m(t)}$$

$$\equiv r[1 - \lambda_m(t)] + \frac{\dot{g}(t)}{g(t)} \lambda_m, \tag{8}$$

where $\gamma_m(t) \equiv [g(t)/\alpha p_m(t)]$ is the extraction cost per dollar of marginal revenue. Since $\gamma_m(t)$ need not exceed 1, the price set by the monopolist can actually decline for a while.

The competitive solution, meanwhile, requires that the net revenue earned one period equal the (discounted) revenue earned any other period (entry or exit ensures, otherwise). Notationally, the competitive solution thus requires that

$$[p_c(t) - g(t)]e^{-rt} = \text{constant}. \qquad (9)$$

Differentiating equation (9) with respect to t produces

$$-re^{-rt}[p_c(t) - g(t)] + e^{-rt}[\dot{p}_c(t) - \dot{g}(t)] = 0.$$

Along the competitive path, therefore,

$$\frac{\dot{p}_c(t)}{p_c(t)} = r - \frac{rg(t)}{p_c(t)} + \frac{\dot{g}(t)}{p_c(t)}$$

$$\equiv r[1-\lambda_c(t)] + \frac{\dot{g}(t)}{g(t)} \lambda_c.$$

The parameter $\gamma_c(t) \equiv [g(t)/p(t)]$ is the extraction cost per dollar of average revenue. Once again, the price could fall.

Comparing equations (8) and (10) can now produce the desired result. As long as $p_m(t) < p_c(t)$, $\gamma_c(t) < \gamma_m(t)$ and

$$[\dot{p}_c(t)/p_c(t)] > [\dot{p}_m(t)/p_m(t)] > 0$$

perpetuates the condition. It can be argued, then, that possible paths begin with $p_m(0) < p_c(0)$ and $g_m(0) < g_c(0)$. To see this, suppose that $x_m(0) < x_c(0)$. Monopoly production would then have to exceed the competitive level at some point along the path if both structures are to exhaust R_0. As soon as $x_c(t) < x_m(t)$, though, $p_m(t) < p_c(t)$

forever.   Were $p_m(0) < p_c(0)$, on the other hand, monopoly output would begin, and remain, higher than the competitive level because $p_m(t)$ could never catch $p_c(t)$.

Both paths could not then satisfy the exhaustion constraint.   Figure 42.1 illustrates the only possible paths, and shows that the monopolist more closely follows the conservationist policy.

(d) Consider, now, Figure 42.2. It illustrates a two-period model in equilibrium under the assumptions of part b; i.e., the competitive market chooses an allocation that equates (discounted) prices at point E while the monopolist equates (discounted) marginal revenue at point A.

If the price elasticity of demand were to increase in the second period, though, discounted marginal revenue at x^0 for period 2 would be higher than point A.   If it slopes down from B (e.g.), a new monopolistic equilibrium would occur to the left of x^0 and again show the monopolist to be more of a conservationist.

It should be noted that even though the monopolist has been shown to conserve the resource for a time, the resulting allocation is still dynamically inefficient. Present generations could be better off even if they were forced to compensate future generations for the higher prices that would be passed forward if a monopoly were eliminated.

Figure 42.1

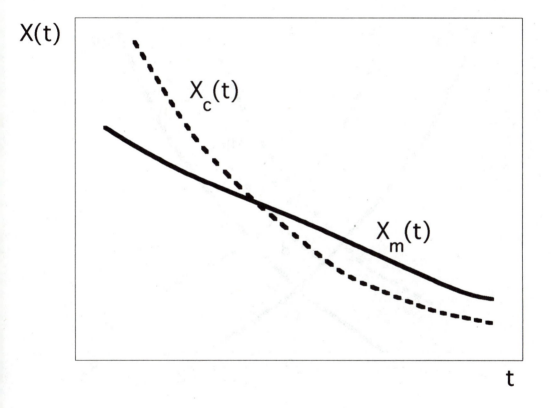

Figure 42.2

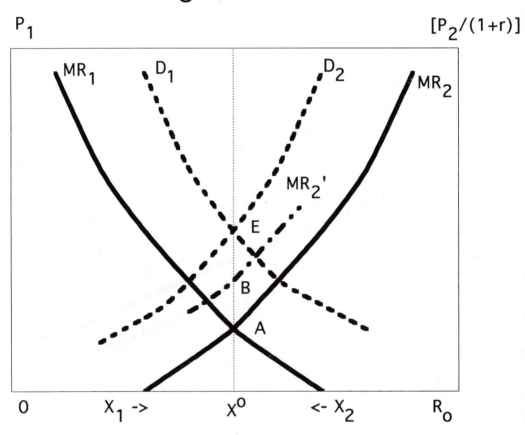

PROBLEM 42

The intuitive appeal of the monopolistic behavior here is based in a desire to hedge against uncertainty over future reserves by keeping substantial quantities of the resource around a little longer. It should also be observed that these have been simple models designed to produce interpretable results quickly. The interested reader is referred to Salant (2), Solow (3), Sweeney (5), Weinstein and Zeckhauser (6), and the footnotes in Stiglitz (4) for more realistic modeling.

Two comments on the Stiglitz paper appeared in the *American Economic Review* (March 1979). The first, contributed by Lewis, Matthews, and Burness, presents two special cases in which a monopolist would deplete a natural resource too quickly. These run counter to the Stiglitz result, but are derived from different assumptions. In the second, Tullock criticizes some of the more fundamental assumptions contained in the Stiglitz piece. His major point is that it is the fixed time period assumption of (at least) the two-period model and not the character of monopoly that produces the result.

References

(1) Phelps, E., and S. Winter, "Optimal Price Policy Under Atomistic Competition," in E. Phelps (ed.), *Microeconomic Foundations of Employment and Inflation Theory*, New York,

Norton, 1970.

(2) Salant, S., "Nash-Cournot Equilibrium for an Exhaustible Resource Like Oil," Federal Reserve Board mimeo, 1975.

(3) Solow, R., "The Economics of Resources on the Resources of Economics," *American Economic Review - Papers and Proceedings*, 64: 1-14, 1974.

(4) Stiglitz, J.E., "Monopoly and the Rate of Extraction of Exhaustible Resources," *American Economic Review*, 66: 665-671, 1976.

(5) Sweeney, J. L., "Economics of Depletable Resources: Market Forces and Intertemporal Bias," *Review of Economic Studies*, 44: 125-141, 1977.

(6) Weinstein, M., and R.J. Zeckhauser, "The Optimal Consumption of Depletable Natural Resources," *Quarterly Journal of Economics*, 89: 371-392, 1975.

43. Alternative Mechanisms for Controlling Pollution[1]

Effluent charges have long been favored by many economists as a means of controlling pollution. They, and their quota/standard equivalents, suffer, however, from one significant shortcoming. In work by MacAvoy (1) and others, it has been noted that the inability to measure effluent effectively has undermined the ability to enforce standards and/or to assess the appropriate emissions fee without significant self-monitoring efforts. Questions of moral hazard are thus raised [see page 455]. This problem will explore the efficacy of an effluent charge in achieving optimal emissions _and_ input mixes in contrast with the workings of an alternative mechanism that does not require effluent monitoring.

To generate a useful context for this comparison, let $B_y(y)$ represent a schedule of benefits generated by the consumption of some good y. Production is summarized by a well-behaved function

$$y = f(K_y, \ L, \ \sum_{i=1}^{n} \alpha_i m_i) \tag{1}$$

---

[1] Material found in Chapter 24 is applicable here, but the motivation of the problem also finds it roots in the "who knows what and when" issues of information raised in Chapter 25. Properties of competitive equilibrium described in Chapter 13 will be employed to define context.

PROBLEM 43

where most of the arguments of equation (1) are
identified with standard notation:

K_y = capital employed in production elastically
supplied at price r,

L = labor employed in production elastically
supplied at price w, and

m_i = material input employed in production of
which α_i represents the proportion of useable
input.

Let m_i be available along a supply schedule $C_i(m_i)$, and let
λ_i represent the proportion of m_i that produces some
deleterious pollutant z. As a result, the total potential
pollution is

$$z = \sum_{i=1}^{n} \lambda_i m_i.$$

To get an idea of the sort of application that this
framework might portray, think of m as coal, so that the α_i
might index the Btu content of various grades of coal and
the λ_i might index its corresponding sulfur content.

Since pollutant z might be potentially valuable if
delivered in a pure state z_c, (e.g., purified sulfur), a
schedule $B_z(z_c)$ is required to reflect its potential benefit
in that form. Let

PROBLEM 43

$$z_c = g(K_z, \sum_{i=1}^{n} \lambda_i m_i)$$

represent the production possibility of this potential joint product with K_z reflecting capital involved in the "purifying" process; it is also available at unit cost r. Unpurified pollution will be emitted, however, according to

$$z_e = \sum_{i=1}^{n} \lambda_i m_i - z_c$$

and will cause social harm according to

$$S = S(z_e).$$

Assume that all of these schedules have the usual shapes and are twice differentiable.

Questions:

(a) Characterize optimality for this configuration.

(b) Show that optimality could be achieved even if $S(z_e)$ were ignored by producers in a competitive market if the government imposed an appropriate effluent charge on z_e.

(c) Show that a system that charged a fee t_i for the employment of m_i and paid a subsidy τ for z_c delivered to its market could also achieve optimality.

PROBLEM 43

(d) Contrast the informational requirements of these alternative systems (i.e., the regulative structures embodied in parts (b) and (c)).

Suggested Solutions:

Insight into the comparative results required here follow directly from first-order conditions and the efficiency properties of competitive equilibrium.

(a) To characterize optimality, consider maximizing

$$\{B_y(y) - rK_z - rK_y - wL - \sum_{i=1}^{n} C_i(m_i) - S(z_e) + B_z(z_c)\},$$

with respect to K_z, K_y, L and the m_i with

$$y = f[K_t, \ L \ \sum_{i=1}^{n} \alpha_i m_i], \tag{2a}$$

$$z = \sum_{i=1}^{n} \lambda_i m_i, \tag{2b}$$

$$z_c = g[K_z, \ \sum_{i=1}^{n} \lambda_i m_i], \text{ and} \tag{2c}$$

$$z_e = \sum_{i=1}^{n} \lambda_i m_i - g[K_z, \ \sum_{i=1}^{n} \lambda_i m_i]. \tag{2d}$$

The appropriate first-order conditions are recorded below:

434

PROBLEM 43

L: $B'_y(y^*)f_l[K^*_y,L^*,\Sigma\alpha_i m^*_i] - w = 0,$ (3a)

K_y: $B'_y(y^*)f_K[K^*_y,L^*,\Sigma\alpha_i m^*_i] - r = 0,$ (3b)

K_z: $[B'_z(z^*_c)+S'(z^*_e)]g_K[K^*_z,\Sigma\lambda_i m^*_i] - r = 0,$ (3c)

m_i: $\alpha_i B'_y(y^*)f_m[K*_y,L*,\Sigma\alpha_i m^*_i] + \lambda_i B'_z(z^*_c)g_m[K^*_z,\Sigma\lambda_i m^*_i]$

$- C_i(m^*_i) - \lambda_i S'(z^*_e)[1-g_m(K^*_z,\Sigma\lambda_i m^*_i)] = 0$ (3d)

Each has an obvious interpretation with the possible exception of the last. There, however, equality of the marginal benefit generated by employing each grade of input is simply required to equal its complete marginal social cost [see Chapter 24].

(b) It is perhaps a miracle of modern economic theory that a single effluent charge can be shown to guarantee that the social optimum just characterized will be produced by a competitive economy. To see why, let t represent the efficient charge so that maximizing

$$\{B_y(y) - rK_z - rK_y - wL - \sum_{i=1}^{n} C_i(m_i) - tz_e + B_z(z_c)\}$$

with respect to K_z, K_y, L, and the m_i given the conditions recorded in equations (2a) through (2d) models the competitive economy's equilibrium behavior [see the First

435

and Second Theorems of Welfare - Chapters 17 and 18]. The outcome, indicated by that notation, is then the solution to a new set of first-order conditions:

L: $\quad B'_y(\hat{y}) f_L[\hat{K}_y, \hat{L}, \Sigma \alpha_i \hat{m}_i] - w = 0,$ (4a)

K_y: $\quad B'_y(\hat{y}) f_K[\hat{K}_y, \hat{L}, \Sigma \alpha_i \hat{m}_i] - r = 0,$ (4b)

K_z: $\quad [B'_z(\hat{z}_c) + t\hat{z}_e] g_K(\hat{K}_z, \Sigma \lambda_i \hat{m}_i) - r = 0,$ and (4c)

m_i: $\quad \alpha_i B'_y(\hat{y}) f_m(\hat{K}_y, \hat{L}, \Sigma \alpha_i \hat{m}_i) + \lambda_i B'_z(\hat{z}_c) g_m(\hat{K}_z, \Sigma \lambda_i \hat{m}_i)$

$\qquad - C_i(\hat{m}_i) - \lambda_i t[1 - g_m(\hat{K}_z, \Sigma \lambda_i \hat{m}_i)] = 0.$ (4d)

Setting $\hat{t} \equiv S'(z^*_e)$, however, equations (4a) through (4d) duplicate equations (3a) through (3d). As a result

$$\hat{K}_z = K^*_z, \qquad\qquad \hat{z}_c = z^*_c,$$

$$\hat{K}_y = K^*_y, \qquad\qquad \hat{z}_e = z^*_e,$$

$$\hat{L} = L^*, \qquad\qquad \hat{y} = y^*, \text{ and}$$

$$\hat{m}^*_i = m^*_i.$$

(c) Giving a subsidy τ for the sale of z_c and input charges t_i collected for the purchase of the various grades m_i, the competitive solution maximizes

$$\{B_y(y) - rK_z - rK_y - wL - \sum_{i=1}^{n} c_i(m_i) + \tau z_c - \sum_{i=1}^{n} t_i m_i\}$$

with respect to K_z, L, K_y, and the m_i; conditions (2a) through (2d) still hold, and the first-order conditions characterize a third vector of solutions:

L: $B'_y(\tilde{y})f_L(\tilde{K}_y, \tilde{L}, \Sigma\alpha_i\tilde{m}_i) - w = 0,$ (5a)

K_y: $B'_y(\tilde{y})f_K(\tilde{K}_y, \tilde{L}, \Sigma\alpha_i\tilde{m}_i) - r = 0,$ (5b)

K_z: $[B'_z(\tilde{z}_c)+\tau]g_K(\tilde{K}_z, \Sigma\lambda_i\tilde{m}_i) - r = 0,$ and   (5c)

m_i: $\alpha_i B'_y(\tilde{y})f_m(\tilde{K}_y, \tilde{L}, \Sigma\alpha_i\tilde{m}_i) + \lambda_i B'_z(\tilde{z}_c)g_m(\tilde{K}_z, \Sigma\lambda_i\tilde{m}_i)$

         $- c_i(\tilde{m}_i) + \lambda_i\tau g_m(\tilde{K}_z, \Sigma\lambda_i\tilde{m}_i) - t_i = 0.$ (5d)

Setting

$$\tau = S'(s^*_e) \text{ and}$$

$$t_i = \lambda_i S'(z^*_e),$$

equations (5a) through (5d) duplicate equations (3a) through (3d), and

$$\tilde{K}_z = K^*_z, \qquad\qquad\qquad \tilde{z}_c = z^*_c,$$

$$\tilde{K}_y = K_y, \qquad\qquad\qquad \tilde{z}_e = z^*_e,$$

$$\tilde{L} = L^*, \qquad\qquad\qquad \tilde{y} = y^*, \text{ and}$$

$$\tilde{m}_i = m^*_i.$$

(d) Comparing the information required to enact the policies envisioned in parts (b) and (c), notice that both require some notion of the optimal, total level of emissions so that $S'(z^*_e)$ can be evaluated. For an effluent tax to work, moreover, individual emission levels must be observed so that the required individual pollution fees can be collected. Therein lies a significant informational problem, because effluent is a difficult commodity to monitor effectively. On the other hand, the subsidy/input charge mechanism of part (c) requires information about the quantity and grade of material inputs being employed (more easily measured than effluent, perhaps at the point of supply) and the quantity of useable, cleansed pollutant being sold (again an easier measurement).

Reference

(1) MacAvoy, P., *The Effectiveness of the Clean Air Act of 1970*, New York, Norton, 1983.

44. Regulating the Monopolistic Polluter[1]

The results of Problem 43 notwithstanding, there is no single Pigovian tax that will achieve a social optimum when an external cost is imposed on society by a firm that is a monopolist in the goods market -- even under favorable conditions of perfect information, convexity in the production set, and nonreciprocated externality. One response to this problem has been an attempt to devise a single tax instrument that satisfies the second best property of improving social welfare under certain conditions while not reducing welfare under others. It is, however, far better to design a combination of instruments that were not limited to such a second best optimum.

The basic deficiency of the single instrument approach is that it aims to use one policy instrument to overcome two sources of resource misallocation: the externality imposed on consumers by the exercise of monopoly power [see Chapter 14] and the externality imposed on society more broadly defined by the production process [see Chapter 24]. It is the point of this problem that the difficulty of controlling the two sources could be overcome, at least theoretically, by combining an emissions tax with an output subsidy. Tax

---

[1] Material found in Chapters 14 and 24 is applicable here. Social welfare will, as on page 240, be taken to be the sum of consumer surplus and profit.

revenues could, moreover, finance at least part of the subsidy.

This problem will explore these issues by considering a monopolist whose production possibilities for some good X are represented by $X = f(L,E)$ with L and E representing the quantities of labor and emissions employed respectively. Let $f(L,E)$ be linearly homogenous and twice differentiable, and assume that the marginal productivities of both inputs are diminishing [standard assumptions from Chapter 1].

The demand for the good X is represented by $P(X)$, and the labor supply price is constant at w. In addition, let $C(E)$ and $S(E)$, respectively, represent the private and additional external cost of emissions; both of the associated marginal cost schedules are assumed to be positive and increasing.

Questions:

(a) Characterize the social optimum using the given information and any further assumptions that might be required. Interpret the characterization.

(b) Denote the socially optimal level of emissions characterized in part (a) by E*. Show that the competitive Pigovian emissions tax, $t_1{}^* = S'(E^*)$, will not achieve optimality unless $P' = 0$; i.e., unless there is no monopoly power.

(c) Consider a modification of the tax which applies to the competitive case:

$$t_2^* = t_1^* - \{P'(X) - MR(X^*)\},$$

where X* represents the optimal output of X and t_2^* is designed to mitigate against the monopolist's proclivity to respond to an emissions tax by lowering his or her output from a level that is already suboptimally low. Argue that t_2^* cannot achieve the first best solution characterized in part (a) unless $f(L,E)$ represents a Leontief technology [see page 19].

(d) Solve for a combination emissions tax, t, and output subsidy, τ, that can achieve the first best optimum. Compare this emissions tax with the competitive solution.

(e) Provide some geometric indication behind why your answer to (d) works.

Suggested Solutions:

(a) Assuming a constant marginal utility of income, the appropriate welfare optimization problem is

PROBLEM 44

$$\max_{L,E} \ \{ \int_0^{f(L,E)} P(s) \ ds\} \ - \ wL \ - \ C(E) \ - \ S(E).$$

The result of this optimization is (L^*, E^*) satisfying first-order conditions

$$P[f(L^*,E^*)] \ f_1(L^*,E^*) \ - \ w = 0 \text{ and} \qquad (1a)$$

$$P[f(L^*,E^*)] \ f_2(L^*,E^*) \ - \ C'(E^*) \ - \ S'(E^*) = 0 \qquad (1b)$$

with

$$X^* = f(L^*,E^*).$$

Equation (1a) is, of course, the familiar requirement that the marginal revenue product of labor be set equal to the going wage rate. Equation (1b), meanwhile, requires that the marginal revenue product of emissions be set equal to their true, total marginal cost: marginal private cost $C'(E^*)$ plus marginal social costs in excess of private costs $S'(E^*)$.

(b) The monopolist's problem, given an arbitrary emissions tax t, is to solve

$$\max_{L,E} \ \{P[f(L,E)] \ f(L,E)\} \ - \ wL \ - \ C(E) \ - \ tE.$$

The appropriate first- order conditions, therefore, require

442

PROBLEM 44

that

$$\{P[f(\hat{L},\hat{E})] - f(\hat{L},\hat{E})P'[f(\hat{L},\hat{E})]\}f_1(\hat{L},\hat{E}) - w = 0 \text{ and} \qquad (2a)$$

$$\{P[f(\hat{L},\hat{E})] - f(\hat{L},\hat{E})P'[f(\hat{L},\hat{E})]\}f_2(\hat{L},\hat{E}) - C'(\hat{E}) - t = 0. \tag{2b}$$

The solution to these conditions given $t_1^* = S'(E^*)$ with E^* defined by equation (1) duplicates (L^*,E^*) only if $P'[--] \equiv 0$; i.e., only if the monopolist has no monopoly power to exert. Recall from Problem 43, though, that $t_1^* = S'(E^*)$ represents the Pigovian tax that would be appropriate if the firm were perfectly competitive.

(c)   Notice that

$$MR(X) = P(X) + XP'(X)$$

so that

$$t_2^* = t_1^* + X^*P'(X^*) < t_1^*$$

unless, as before, $P'(X) = 0$. Furthermore, t_2^* falls as monopoly power grows with no guarantee that $t_2^* > 0$. This type of emissions tax-subsidy mitigates against the output effect of the emissions tax, but can achieve optimality only if the production process can be described by a Leontief fixed coefficient schedule.

The intuitive reason why can be seen by looking at

443

equations (2a) and (2b). Since adjusting $t_2{}^*$ affects only (2b), it encourages output by encouraging only emissions. This will lead to a suboptimally large emissions to labor ratio unless that ratio is variant to changes in the input price ratio (i.e., unless all of the expansion paths for <u>all</u> input price combinations are the same ray through the origin). This is a description of production that fits only the Leontief specification.

(d) Facing a control pair (τ, t), the monopolist would solve

$$\max_{L,E} \{(1+\tau) \, P[f(L,E)] \, f(L,E) - wL - C(E) - tE\};$$

i.e., the monopolist would face the following first order conditions:

$$(1+\tau)\{P[f(\tilde{L},\tilde{E})] - f(\tilde{L},\tilde{E})P'[f(\tilde{L},\tilde{E})]\} \, f_1(\tilde{L},\tilde{E}) - w = 0 \quad \text{and}$$

$$(1+\tau)\{P[f(\tilde{L},\tilde{E})] - f(\tilde{L},\tilde{E})P'[f(\tilde{L},\tilde{E})]\} \, f_2(\tilde{L},\tilde{E}) - C'(\tilde{E}) - t = 0.$$

These conditions reduce to equation (1) only if

$$t_2{}^* = -S'(E^*) \quad \text{and} \tag{3a}$$

$$\tau^* = \frac{-X^* \, P'(X^*)}{P(X') - X^*P'(X^*)} > 0. \tag{3b}$$

Specifying $t_2{}^*$ and τ^* defined in equation (3) would ensure

that the monopolist would employ $\tilde{E} = E^*$ and $\tilde{L} = L^*$ to
produce $\tilde{X} = X^*$. The output subsidy τ^* is designed to set
marginal revenue plus subsidy equal to marginal private
cost. The producer therefore takes account of the full
social cost (including the net cost to consumers) of
reducing the production externality by cutting output. The
emissions tax is set equal to the level of external cost at
that level of emissions for which the marginal cost of the
least cost method of abatement is equal to marginal external
cost. The emissions tax is therefore of the standard
Pigovian type.

(e) The two tool combination described in part (d) allows
the policymaker to lead the monopolist to employ any
combination (L,E) - not just (L^*,E^*) - because it completely
covers the positive orthant. To see why, simply notice
that, given w, compensated manipulation of t generates
movement to any given point on a given isoquant. The
subsidy τ, meanwhile, can generate not only the compensation
just mentioned, but also movement to any point along any
given output expansion path. Much in the spirit of polar
coordinates, therefore, the positive orthant is thereby
spanned.

Two possible objections to this instrument combination
are easily uncovered: the entire system would require an
enormous amount of information <u>and</u> proposing a subsidy

component for a monopolist would likely carry enormous political cost. The emissions tax, t^*, would simply equal the Pigovian tax that a perfectly competitive firm would face if it generated a production external cost; but setting the output subsidy correctly would require a measure of the firm's market power, the corresponding marginal revenue and the opposing social cost of emissions. The political problem might be solved only if policy makers believed that their economists could accurately deduce the appropriate τ^* ... and that their constituents believed that, too. Any bets? The combination (t^*, τ^*) would not necessarily break even, but at least the combination would hold an edge over the single instrument proposals in that it would extract at least partial funding of the controversial subsidy from the monopolist.

References

(1) Asch, P., and Seneca, J.J., "Monopoly and External Cost: an Application of Second Best Theory to the Automobile Industry," *Journal of Environmental Economics and Management*, 3: 69-79, 1976.

(2) Barnett, A.H., "The Pigovian Tax Rule Under Monopoly," *American Economic Review*, 90: 1037-1041, 1980.

(3) Buchanan, J.M., "External Diseconomies, Corrective Taxes and Market Structure," *American Economic Review*, 59: 174-

177, March 1969.

(4) Burrows, P., "Controlling the Monopolistic Polluter:
Nihilism or Eclecticism?" *Journal of Environmental Economics
and Management*, 8: 372-380, 1981.

(5) Misiolek, W.S., "Effluent Taxation in Monopoly Markets,"
Journal of Environmental Economics and Management, 7: 103-
107, 1980.

45. The Incidence of Pollution Control[1]

Problem 32 presented the Harberger corporate profits tax analysis - a two-sector, two-factor model. It covered a general equilibrium analysis of incidence whose results have stood the test of time. When there are more than two factors, however, things become much more complicated because the elasticities of substitution are harder to define [recall Problem 5]. Batra and Casas have presented two-sector, three-factor models of international trade (1, 2, and 3) that make the extension. Yohe (4) has applied their modeling to a general equilibrium analysis of the incidence of stricter pollution controls. This problem will present the Yohe model because it lies between the Harberger and the Batra and Casas work

There will be a polluting sector employing three factors (x_1, x_2, and z - pollution) and a nonpolluting sector employing only two (x_1 and x_2). The problem will, in addition, take the linear system describing the interactions of factor prices and commodity prices as given. A good deal of algebra will thus be subsumed in the statement of the problem, and the reader is referred either to Yohe (4) or Batra and Casas (2) for a full delineation of the missing

---

[1] Material found in Chapters 1, 17, and 18 will be applied to issues raised in Chapter 24. Descriptions of competitive equilibria offered in Chapter 13 will also be employed to define theoretical context.

steps.   This will be an exercise in exploiting and deciphering the linear system that the algebra produces.

Let the polluting and nonpolluting sectors be represented by linearly homogeneous functions

$$y_1 = f_1(x_1, x_2, z) \text{ and}$$

$$y_2 = f_2(x_1, x_2),$$

respectively.   There are constraints on the availability of all factors:

$$x_{11} + x_{12} \equiv \alpha_{11}y_1 + \alpha_{12}y_2 \equiv \bar{x}_1,$$

$$x_{21} + x_{22} \equiv \alpha_{22}y_2 \equiv \bar{x}_2, \text{ and}$$

$$z \equiv \alpha_2 y_1 \equiv \bar{z}.$$

The α_{ij} parameters therefore represent the proportional demand for factor x_i in the jth sector.   The regulatory handle on pollution control is $\bar{z}$ - a command and control specification of maximum allowable emissions.

Notice, as well, that pollution is being modeled as a factor of production instead of a joint product.   These two concepts are, however, formally equivalent as long as the

y_1-isoquants are precluded from intersecting the pollution axis; y_1 can never be produced from z alone. Assume that only x_1 substitutes with z (x_2 can be considered labor which (hopefully) does not accomplish any substitution by breathing what would otherwise be emitted). The ease with which pollution can be cleaned up is then reflected by σ^1_{12}, the elasticity between x_1 and z in f_1. This is a partial elasticity in the sense of Allen and Uzawa [see Problem 5]. It has been assumed that $\sigma^1_{22} = 0$. The larger $|\sigma^1_{12}|$, therefore, the easier the cleanup.

A good deal of algebra will now be omitted. Some extensive notation is, however, unavoidable. Let

$$w_i = \text{the price of } x_i,$$
$$p_i = \text{the price of } y_i,$$
$$t = \text{the shadow price of } \bar{z},$$
$$\theta_{ij} = \alpha_{ij}w_i/p_j = \text{the share of output allocated}$$
$$\text{to } x_i \ (i = 1, 2) \text{ in sector } j,$$
$$\theta_{12} = \text{the share of output allocated to z in}$$
$$\text{sector 1, and}$$
$$\theta_s = \text{the share of total output derived from}$$
$$\text{sector s.}$$

Let starred notation designate "percentage change in" so that (e.g.)

PROBLEM 45

$$w_i^* \equiv dw_i/w_i, \text{ etc.}$$

Designate

$$R = E_1 w_1^* + E_2 w_2^* + E_t t$$

$$= \beta_{12} \bar{x}_2^* + \beta_{22} \bar{x}_1^* + \beta_{12} \bar{z}_i^*$$

where the E's and β's are parameters. Only one will come into play:

$$\beta_{12} \equiv \lambda_{21}\lambda_{12} - \lambda_{22}\lambda_{11},$$

where λ_{ij} is the proportion of total supply of the ith factor employed in sector j.

Questions:

(a) Sector j is said to use factor i intensively if and only if

$$(\alpha_{ij}/\alpha_{kj}) > (\alpha_{i1}/\alpha_{k1})$$

for all goods 1 ≠ j and all factors k ≠ i. Show that section 1 uses pollution intensively. Show that the sign of β_{12} depends upon whether sector 2 uses x_1 or x_2

451

PROBLEM 45

intensively.

(b)   It can be shown that

$$
\begin{vmatrix}
\theta_{21} & \theta_{11} & \theta_{21} \\
\theta_{22} & \theta_{12} & 0 \\
E_2 & E_1 & E_t
\end{vmatrix}
\begin{vmatrix}
w_2^* \\
w_1^* \\
t^*
\end{vmatrix}
\begin{vmatrix}
p_1^* \\
p_2^* \\
R
\end{vmatrix}
\qquad (1)
$$

fully describes the model. The determinant of the matrix (henceforth denoted D) is strictly negative when the f_i are strictly concave [see page 475]. Show that for $\bar{z}^* < 0$ (i.e., for tighter pollution controls),

(i) $w_2^* > 0$ and $w_1^* < 0$ if and only if y_2 employs x_2 more intensively than x_1, and

(ii) $t^* > 0$ regardless of the factor intensity of y_2.

(c) Argue intuitively why $\bar{z}^* < 0$ causes the polluting sector to contract and the nonpolluting sector to expand.

(d) Let $Y = w_1 \bar{x}_1 + w_2 \bar{x}_2 + t\bar{z} = p_1 y_1 + p_2 y_2$ be "national income." Show that

PROBLEM 45

$$Y^* = \theta_2 \bar{z}^*;$$

i.e, demonstrate that stricter pollution controls reduce GDP.

(e)   Now let

$$\varepsilon_i = y_i^*/p_i^* \qquad (2)$$

be the usual price elasticity of demand.   Use the linear approximation that $Y^* = \theta_z \bar{z}^*$ to deduce the effect of changes in p_i on the results recorded in part (b).

Suggested Solutions:

(a) Since

$$(\alpha_{z1}/\alpha_{11}) > (\alpha_{z2}/\alpha_{12}) = 0 \text{ and}$$

$$(\alpha_{z1}/\alpha_{21}) > (\alpha_{z2}/\alpha_{22}) = 0,$$

it is clear that sector 1 "uses" pollution intensively.
    The sign of β_{12} meanwhile depends upon whether sector 2 uses x_1 on x_2 intensively:

$$\beta_{12} = \lambda_{21}\lambda_{12} - \lambda_{22}\lambda_{11}$$

$$= (\alpha_{21}y_1/\bar{x}_2)(\alpha_{12}y_2/\bar{x}_1) - (\alpha_{22}y_2/\bar{x}_2)(\alpha_{11}y_1/\bar{x}_1)$$

$$= (\alpha_{21}\alpha_{12} - \alpha_{22}\alpha_{11})[y_1y_2/\bar{x}_1\bar{x}_2].$$

The sign of β_{12} therefore turns on whether

$$(\alpha_{21}\alpha_{12} - \alpha_{22}\alpha_{11}) \gtrless 0;$$

i.e., it turns on whether

$$(\alpha_{21}/\alpha_{11}) \gtrless (\alpha_{22}\alpha_{12}).$$

As a result,

$$\beta_{12} \quad \begin{matrix} > 0 & \text{if } y_2 \text{ uses } x_1 \text{ intensively} \\ \\ < 0 & \text{if } y_2 \text{ uses } x_2 \text{ intensively.} \end{matrix}$$

(b)   Using Cramer's rule, one sees, first of all, that

$$w_2^* = \begin{vmatrix} 0 & \theta_{11} & \theta_{z1} \\ 0 & \theta_{12} & 0 \\ R & E_1 & E_t \end{vmatrix} D^{-1} = -(\theta_{12}\theta_{21}/D)B_{12}\bar{z}^*, \quad (3)$$

$$w_1^* = \begin{vmatrix} \theta_{21} & 0 & \theta_{z1} \\ \theta_{22} & 0 & 0 \\ E_2 & R & E_t \end{vmatrix} D^{-1} = + (\theta_{22}\theta_{21}/D)B_{12}\bar{Z}^*, \quad (4)$$

$$t^* = \begin{vmatrix} \theta_{21} & \theta_{11} & 0 \\ \theta_{22} & \theta_{12} & 0 \\ E_2 & E_1 & R \end{vmatrix} D^{-1} = \frac{\theta_{21}\theta_{12} - \theta_{22}\theta_{11}}{D} B_{12}\bar{Z}^*. \quad (5)$$

because $R = \beta_{12}\bar{Z}^*$ when $x_1^* = x_2^* = 0$.

Notice that w_1^* and w_2^* have opposite signs. It is seen, in particular, that w_2 (or alternatively w_1) moves in the same direction as $\bar{Z}$ if and only if the production of y_2 employs x_1 (or, again, x_2) intensively. If, for example, pollution standards become more restrictive so that $\bar{Z}^* < 0$ and y_2 employs x_1 intensively, then w_2 falls, and w_1 rises when y_2 employs x_1 intensively. Finally, since

$$(\theta_{21}\theta_{12} - \theta_{22}\theta_{11}) = (\alpha_{21}\alpha_{12} - \alpha_{22}\alpha_{11})[w_1 w_2 / P_1 P_2]$$

has the same sign as β_{12},

PROBLEM 45

$$(t^*/\bar{z}^*) < 0;$$

in words, then, a decrease in allowable emissions always leads to an increase in t.

(c) Since $t^* > 0$ when $\bar{z}^* < 0$, it is not surprising that the y_1 sector contracts; the supply of input it uses "intensively" has been reduced, and so its price is driven higher. The factors released by that contraction must be picked up by section 2 in a full employment model, so that sector expands.

(d) National income, when payment for pollution is put back into the economy, is simply

$$Y = w_1\bar{x}_1 + w_2\bar{x}_2 + t\bar{z}. \tag{6}$$

Totally differentiating equation (6), then,

$$dY = (w_1\,d\bar{x}_1 + \bar{x}_1\,dw_1) + (w_2\,d\bar{x}_2 + \bar{x}_2\,dw_2) + (t\,d\bar{z} + \bar{z}\,dt),$$

so

$$Y^* = \frac{w_1\bar{x}_1}{Y}\left(\frac{d\bar{x}_1}{\bar{x}_1} + \frac{dw_1}{w_1}\right) + \frac{w_2\bar{x}_2}{Y}\left(\frac{d\bar{x}_2}{\bar{x}_2} + \frac{dw_2}{w_2}\right) + \frac{t\bar{z}}{Y}\left(\frac{d\bar{z}}{\bar{z}} + \frac{dt}{t}\right)$$

$$\equiv \theta_1(\bar{x}_1^* + w_1^*) + \theta_2(\bar{x}_2^* + w_2^*) + \theta_z(\bar{z}^* + t^*)$$

$$= \theta_1\bar{x}_1^* + \theta_2\bar{x}_2^* + \theta_z\bar{z}^* + \{\theta_1 w_1^* + \theta_2 w_2^* + \theta_z t^*\}. \qquad (7)$$

From equations (3), (4), and (5), however, it is clear that the bracketed term in equation (7) equals

$$[\theta_1\theta_{11}\theta_{22}\theta_{z1} + \theta_2\theta_{12}\theta_{22}\theta_{z1} - \theta_1\theta_{21}\theta_{12}\theta_{z1}$$

$$- \theta_2\theta_{22}\theta_{12}\theta_{z1} + \theta_1\theta_{z1}\theta_{21}\theta_{12} - \theta_1\theta_{z1}\theta_{22}\theta_{11}] \, [B_{12}\bar{z}^*/D] \quad = 0.$$

because

$$\theta_j = \theta_1\theta_{j1} + \theta_2\theta_{j2} \quad (j = 1, 2) \text{ and } \theta_z = \theta_1\theta_{z1}.$$

For $\bar{x}_1^* = \bar{x}_2^* = 0$, therefore,

$$Y^* = \theta_z\bar{z}^*.$$

Looking at

$$Y = p_1 y_1 + p_2 y_2$$

in the light of equation (2), one sees that

$$Y^* = \frac{dY}{Y} = \frac{1}{Y} \{P_1 y_1 [P_1^* + y_1^*] + P_2 y_2 [P_2^* + y_2^*]\}$$

$$= \theta_1 y_1 [1 + \frac{1}{\varepsilon_1}] + \theta_2 y_2 [1 + \frac{1}{\varepsilon_2}]. \tag{8}$$

Making the first-order approximation that

$$Y^* \approx \theta_z \bar{z}^*,$$

one sees from equation (3), for example, that

$$\theta_{z_1} \bar{z}^* = - \frac{Dw_2^*}{\beta_{12}\theta_{12}} = \frac{\theta_z \bar{z}^*}{\theta_1} \approx Y^*/\theta_1. \tag{9}$$

Combining (8) and (9),

$$w_2^* \approx - \frac{\beta_{12}\theta_{12}}{D\theta_1} Y^*$$

$$= \frac{\beta_{12}\theta_{12}}{D\theta_1}(\theta_1 y_1^* + \theta_2 y_2^*) - \frac{\beta_{12}\theta_{12}}{D\theta_1} \{\frac{\theta_1 y_1^*}{\varepsilon_1} + \frac{\theta_2 y_2^*}{\varepsilon_2}\}. \tag{10}$$

$$= - \frac{\beta_{12}\theta_{12}}{D\theta_1}(\theta_1 y_1^* + \theta_2 y_2^*) - \frac{\beta_{12}\theta_{12}}{D\theta_1}\{\theta_1 p_1^* + \theta_2 p_2^*\}. \tag{10'}$$

The term $(\theta_1 y_1^* + \theta_2 y_2^*)$ is, however, Y^* when $p_1^* = p_2^* = 0$.

458

From part (d), therefore,

$$(\theta_1 y_1^* + \theta_2 y_2^*) = Y^* \Bigg|_{p_1^* = p_2^* = 0} = \theta_z \bar{z}^*,$$

and so equation (10') reduces immediately:

$$w_2^* \approx -\frac{\beta_{12}\theta_{12}}{D} \frac{\theta_z}{\theta_1} \bar{z}^* - \frac{\beta_{12}\theta_{12}}{D\theta_1} \{\theta_1 p_1^* + \theta_2 p_2^*\}. \tag{11a}$$

The first term in equation (11a) coincides with (3), so the second term captures the entire price effect. It can be observed, in fact, that equation (10) reduces directly to equation (3) when $\varepsilon_1 = \varepsilon_2 = -\infty$ so that $p_1^* - p_2^* = 0$,

Precisely the same reasoning leads to the conclusions that

$$w_1^* \approx \frac{\beta_{12}\theta_{22}}{D} \frac{\theta_z}{\theta_1} \bar{z}^* + \frac{\beta_{12}\theta_{22}}{D\theta_1} \{\theta_1 p_1^* + \theta_2 p_2^*\} \text{ and} \tag{11b}$$

$$t^* \approx \frac{\theta_{21}\theta_{12} - \theta_{11}\theta_{22}}{\theta_{z1}D} \frac{\theta_z}{\theta_1} \bar{z}^* + \frac{\theta_{21}\theta_{12} - \theta_{11}\theta_{22}}{\theta_{z1}\theta_1 D} \{\theta_1 p_1^* + \theta_2 p_2^*\}. \tag{11c}$$

PROBLEM 45

In every case, since $\bar{z}^* < 0$ implies (from (c)) that $p_1^* > 0$ and $p_2^* < 0$, the second terms in (11) can either amplify or diminish the constant price effects.

Suppose, for the sake of argument, that sector 2 were intensive in x_2. In that case, $\beta_{12} < 0$ and $w_2^* > 0$. If the percentage increase in p_1 (weighted by θ_1 - the polluting sector's share of total income) exceeded the percentage reduction in p_2 (weighted by θ_2,), then the second term in (11a) would be positive; the price effect would, in such a circumstance, work <u>against</u> the increase in w_2.

The reason behind this result is simple. The same low elasticity that would make p_1^* large would also make the contraction of the y_1 sector small. Changes in the employment of the other factors would be muted, therefore, and less dramatic change in w_2 and (w_1) would be observed. Other effects are similarly explained.

The interested reader may now want to investigate the circumstances under which these incidence effects are large and small. Yohe (4) observed that each of the following could have an effect:

(i) the degree of factor intensity, in either direction, of the y_2 sector (i.e., the size of $|\beta_{12}|$),

(ii) the ease with which the polluting sector can be cleaned up (i.e., the size of $|\sigma_{12}^1|$), and

460

(iii) the degree of productivity substitutability between

x_1 and x_2 in both sectors.

These observations can all be discerned from the mathematics recorded above, but it is more important to explore the underlying economics. The key there lies in the size of the x_1 - x_2 response necessary to accommodate $\bar{z}^* < 0$. The details are left to the reader.

It has been demonstrated that stronger pollution controls do have a backward incidence onto the other factors of production. The direction of that incidence depends upon the relative factor intensity of the nonpolluting sector, and its magnitude depends upon (among other things) the relative (and weighted) price elasticities of demand in both sectors. The parameters that require empirical investigation to determine actual incidence are therefore quite clear. It should be emphasized, though, that this has been a long-run equilibrium analysis. Contraction of the polluting sector would certainly cause some short-run unemployment of both factors which would persist until the long-run adjustments were completed - even if those long-run adjustments would turn out to favor labor.

References

(1) Batra, R.N., *Studies in the Pure Theory of International*

Trade, New York, St. Martin's Press, 1973.

(2) _____, and F.R. Casas, "A Synthesis of the Heckscher-Ohlin and the Neoclassical Models of International Trade," *Journal of International Economics,* 6: 27-38, 1976.

(3) Casas, F.R., "The Theory of Intermediate Products, Technical Change, and Growth," *Journal of International Economics,* 2: 189-200, 1972.

(4) Yohe, G.W., "The Backward Incidence of Pollution Control - Some Comparative Statics in General Equilibrium," *Journal of Environmental Economics of Management,* 6: 197-198, 1978.

46. Efficient Markets and Transactions Costs[1]

Despite fairly widespread belief in various forms of the efficient market hypothesis, some researchers believe that systematic trends in (e.g., stock, bond, commodities) prices go unexploited because of transactions costs. Specifically, it is argued that profitable buy/sell opportunities may be ignored because the commissions that brokers charge are too high [see, for example, Alexander (1 and 2), Fama (3), and Levy (4 to 6)]. This problem will construct an overly simple model to investigate this possibility.

Suppose, to begin to construct the model, that the path of a stock's price over time can be represented by

$$p(t) = \{p_0(1+g)^t\} + a \cos [\pi+(2\pi t/L)] + \eta(t) \qquad (1)$$

where the first term reflects a constant growth trend at rate g starting at p_0, the second term reflects a pattern of predictable variation around that trend [with an amplitude equal to a and a period set at L], and $\eta(t)$ reflects some uncertainty distributed somehow around a zero mean.

Figure 46.1 displays a representative price path with

---

[1] Material found in Chapters 19 and 20 is applicable here, but reference to discussions of uncertainty in Chapter 11 and of information in Chapter 25 may also pay dividends.

Figure 46.1

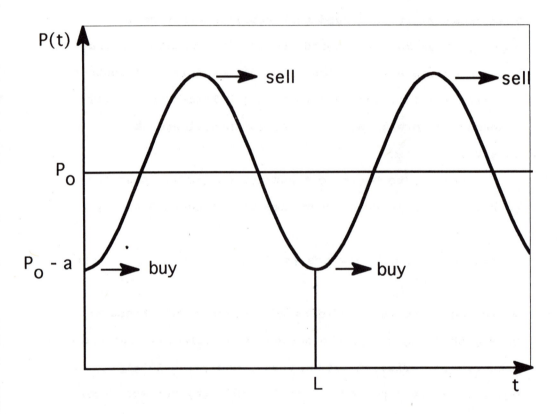

$\eta(t) \equiv 0$ and $g = 0$; Figure 46.2 provides a second example with $\eta(t) \equiv 0$ and $g > 0$. Note that both figures clearly identify the buy "low" and sell "high" patterns that are to be investigated here.

Assume that information is imperfect so that it takes two periods for any investor to determine when a critical point in a price time trajectory has been passed; i.e., assume that the price must increase (or fall) for two successive time periods before any investor will send off a buy (or sell) order. Finally, let r represent the appropriate interest rate/discount factor.

Questions:

(a) Suppose that brokers charge a commission equal to $c \cdot 100\%$ on either a buy or a sell order. Assume that Figure 46.1 applies so that $g = 0$ and $\eta(t) \equiv 0$. If investors consider only potential profits in making their buy and sell decisions, characterize their decision rule.

(b) Show that larger amplitudes in the price cycle increase the likelihood that a buy/sell program might be profitable even as the percentage commission climbs.

(c) Show that higher interest rates and/or longer periodicity in the cycle require lower commissions for the cycle to be profitably exploited.

Figure 46.2

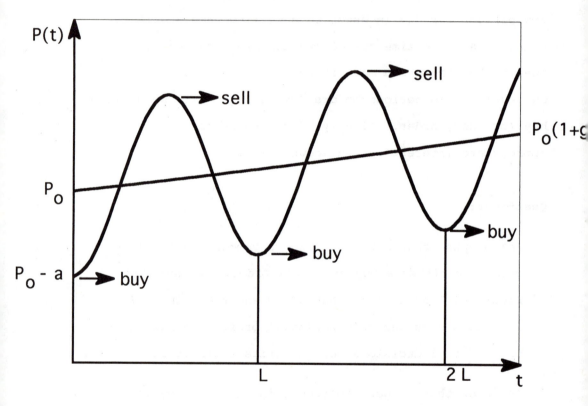

(d) Trace the effect on the breakeven commission of a fundamental time trend $g \neq 0$.

(e) Suppose that investors maximizes utility based on potential profits. Does allowing $\eta(t) \sim N(0, \sigma)$ change anything in your answers to parts (a) through (d)?

Suggested Solutions:

(a) For $g \equiv 0$ and $\eta(t) \equiv 0$, the relevant present value for an opportunity in which some asset might be purchased (in two time periods) at price $P(2)$ and sold in period $T_0 = [(L/2) + 2]$ at price $P(T_0)$ is

$$PDV = \frac{y[\% \text{ of } P(T_0) \text{ after commission}}{(1+r)^{T_0}}$$

$$- [P(2) \text{ plus commission}]$$

$$= \frac{(1-c)P(T_0)}{(1+r)^{T_0}} - (1+c)P(2).$$

Substituting from (1), then,

$$PDV = \frac{(1-c)}{(1+r)^{T_0}} \left\{ a \cos [2\pi + \frac{4\pi}{L}] - (1+c)[a \cos [\pi + \frac{4\pi}{L}] \right\}.$$

$$(2)$$

The prospective opportunity would be profitable as long as PDV $\geq$ 0.

To evaluate the effect of c on the likelihood that this condition might be met, consider the effects on $\hat{c}$, the commission rate that sets PDV = 0, of changes in r, a, and L. The total derivative of (2) with PDV $\equiv$ 0 is required:

$$0 = dPDV = -a \left\{ \frac{\cos [2\pi+(4\pi/L)]}{(1+r)^{T_0}} + \cos [\pi+(4\pi/L)] \right\} d\hat{c}$$

$$+ \left\{ \frac{(1-\hat{c}) \cos [2\pi+(4\pi/L)]}{(1+r)^{T_0}} - (1+\hat{c}) \cos [\pi+(4\pi/L)] \right\} da$$

$$- \frac{4\pi a}{2} \left\{ \frac{(1-\hat{c}) \sin [2\pi+(4\pi/L)]}{(1+r)^{T_0}} - (1+\hat{c}) \sin [\pi+(4\pi/L)] \right\} dL$$

$$- \frac{(1-\hat{c})(L/2)a}{(1+r)^{T_0-1}} \left\{ \pi \cos [2\pi+(4\pi)/L] \right\} dr. \tag{3}$$

(b) Evaluating equation (3) with dr = dL = 0,

$$\frac{dc}{da}\bigg|_{dr=dL=0} = - \left\{ \frac{(1-\hat{c})\cos[2\pi+(4\pi/L)]}{(1+r)^{T_0}} - (1+\hat{c})\cos[\pi+(4\pi/L)] \right\} /D,$$

where

PROBLEM 46

$$D \equiv \frac{a \cos [2\pi+(4\pi/L)]}{(1+r)^{T_0}} + \cos [\pi-4\pi/L] < 0 .$$

The sign of D follows from

$$\left| \cos [2\pi + (4\pi/L)] \right| = \left| \cos [\pi + (4\pi/L)] \right|$$

and $r > 0$.

Similarly, the numerator can be seen to be positive so that

$$\left. \frac{d\hat{c}}{da} \right|_{dr=dL=0} = - \frac{(+)}{(-)} > 0 ;$$

an increase in the amplitude of the cycle (i.e., its the size of the systematic variation) increases the commission consistent with an investor's exploiting the pattern.

(c) The identical procedure shows that

$$\left. \frac{d\hat{c}}{dr} \right|_{da=dL=0} = \left\{ \frac{(1-\hat{c})(L/2)}{(1+r)^{T_0}}a \cos [2\pi+(4\pi/L)] \right\} /D \qquad (4)$$

$$= \frac{(+)}{(-)} < 0 \text{ and}$$

469

$$\left.\frac{d\hat{c}}{dL}\right|_{da=dr=0} = -\frac{4\pi}{L^2} \left\{ -\frac{(1-\hat{c}) \sin [2\pi + (4\pi/L)]}{(1+r)^{T_0}} \right.$$

$$\left. + (1+\hat{c}) \sin [\pi + (4\pi/L)] \right\} / D$$

$$= -\frac{(-)}{(-)} < 0.$$

Ceteris paribus, then, increases in either the length of the cycle or the discount factor cause the affordable commission rate to fall.

(d) To include $g \neq 0$, note that

$$PDV = P_0 \left\{ \frac{1 + g}{1 + r} \right\}^{T_0} - \left. P_0 + PDV \right|_{g=0}$$

so that

$$dPDV = \frac{T_0 P_0 (1+g)^{T_0-1}}{(1+r)^{T_0}} dg - \frac{T_0 P_0 (1+g)^{T_0}}{(1+r)^{T_0+1}} dr + \left. dPDV \right|_{g=0} . \qquad (5)$$

Clearly, therefore,

$$\frac{d\hat{c}}{dg}\Bigg|_{da=dr=dL=0} = -\left\{\frac{T_0 P_0 (1+g)^{T_0 - 1}}{(1+r)^{T_0}}\right\} \Big/ D = -\frac{(+)}{(-)} > 0 \ ;$$

higher growth rates mean higher acceptable commissions. Meanwhile, working with equation (5) instead of (3) effects only (4) -- increasing the numerator and making $\hat{c}$ more sensitive to changes in the interest rate.

(e) If the investor were risk neutral, then the operative utility schedule would be linear and the expected value operator would distribute through both the utility function and the return calculation. As a result, the effect of uncertainty would evaporate and (a) through (d) would still apply.

If the investor were risk averse, however, then uncertainty would lower the expected value of the utility derived from a given opportunity and lower $\hat{c}$.

The model explores the impediment that transactions costs might put in the way of a market process. It is a simplistic model in the sense that uncertainty enters in a very superficial way. Still, there was an effect. More serious, though, is the background ghost of the efficient market hypothesis. Depending upon the version believed, lowering of the commission rate to make the pricing cycle profitable might simply increase demand at the trough, increase supply at the peak, and thereby reduce the amplitude of the cycle just enough to preclude profitability.

References

(1) Alexander, S., "Price Movements in Speculative Markets: Trends or Random Walks," *Industrial Management Review,* 2: 726, 1961.

(2) Alexander, S., "Price Movements in Speculative Markets: Trends or Random Walks, Number 2," *Industrial Management Review,* 5: 25-46, 1964.

(3) Fama, E.F., "Efficient Capital Markets: A Review of Theory and Empirical Work," *Journal of Finance* 25: 383-417, 1970.

(4) Levy, R., "Relative Strength as a Criterion for Investment Selection," *Journal of Finance*, 22: 595-610, 1967.

(5) Levy, R., "The Principle of Portfolio Upgrading," *The Industrial Management Review,* 7: 82-96, 1967.

(6) Levy, R., "Random Walks: Reality or Myth—Reply," *Financial Analysts Journal,* 5: 129-132, 1968.

47. **Plea Bargaining Arrangements as Social Insurance**[1]

It has been shown that nearly 90% of convictions obtained in criminal cases in the United States are the result of negotiated plea bargains. For that reason alone, perhaps, the tools of economics have been applied to an analysis of plea bargaining in an attempt to understand precisely what has been going on. Do plea bargains improve welfare, or are they simply a practical solution to the problems of judicial backlogs? Do they put unfair pressure on the innocent and/or the guilty to "cop a plea"? This list of impersonal, academic questions goes on and on; but behind them all, there are cases like the one in Virginia where a defendant got nervous during the third day of jury deliberation in his trial for murder and negotiated a plea of guilty to a lesser charge -- 30 minutes before the jury found him not guilty. Was that fair? Was it just?

This problem will be drawn from a paper published by Grossman and Katz (2). These authors took the efficiency arguments of previous authors, Landes (4) and Adelstein (1), as given and wondered about the social implications of plea bargaining. They found that plea bargaining could, if done correctly,

---

[1] Material found in Chapter 25 is applicable here, although the analysis will build upon some of the fundamental concepts presented earlier in Chapter 11.

(1) operate as an insurance policy to reduce risk and improve welfare and

(2) serve as a (partial) screening [i.e., signaling] device with which to differentiate guilty and innocent defendants.

We begin by reconstructing their model.

Let p represent punishment and u(p) represent every defendant's utility (separable) function based upon the domain of potential punishment; $u'(p) < 0$ and $u''(p) < 0$ for all p, so the defendant is assumed to be risk averse [see Section 11.7 beginning on page 177]. Society's loss in punishing an innocent citizen is then also u(p).

Social welfare derived from punishing a guilty citizen is meanwhile assumed to be the form $V = V(p-p_0)$, where p_0 is the most appropriate penalty that "fits the crime". Assume further that $V'(p-p_0) < 0$ for all p. Let λ reflect the (known or estimated) proportion of guilty defendants in the pool of accused so that, for example,

$$W = \lambda V(p-p_0) + (1 - \lambda)u(p)$$

would be the expected welfare of assigning a penalty p to all defendants. Finally, represent by θ_j (j = i,g) the probability that an innocent (i) or guilty (g) defendant is actually convicted. If we believe that the judicial system works at all, we can assume that $\theta_i < \theta_g$.

Questions:

(a) Suppose that only the guilty are accused; i.e., assume that $\lambda = 1$. Show, in terms of the certainty equivalent of a trial punishment, that a plea bargain can <u>always</u> be found that improves social welfare over the circumstance in which an arbitrary case is actually tried.

(b) Now let $\lambda < 1$. Construct a screening plea bargain (one accepted by the guilty and rejected by the innocent), and show that employing it dominates sending everyone to trial in terms of social welfare (under the assumption that the guilty defendants certainty equivalent penalty does <u>not</u> exceed p).

(c) Show that a screening plea bargain mechanism maximizes welfare when every defendant is the same.

(d) Make some accurate statements, based entirely upon your answers to parts (a) through (c), about the construction of a screening plea bargain mechanism if their exist two types of defendants -- one more risk averse than the other. (Hint: Segregate the two types according to certainty equivalent penalties for a given trial punishment.)

PROBLEM 47

Suggested Solutions:

(a) The expected utility of a trial, given $\lambda = 1$, is

$$EW_t = \text{[expected welfare of guilty convicted in trial]}$$

$$+ \text{[society's loss of guilty found innocent]}$$

$$= \theta_g V(pt - p_0) + (1 - \theta_g)V(-p_0)$$

$$< V[\theta_g(pt - p_0) - (1 - \theta_g)p]$$

$$= V[\theta_g pt - p_0] \tag{1}$$

for any trial penalty p_t. A defendant will accept a plea bargain p_b only if the certainty equivalent of the trial, c_j such that $u(c_j) = \theta_j u(p_t)$ for $j = g, i$,

exceeds the bargain; i.e., only if

$$c_j \geq p_b \text{ for } j = g, i.$$

Since only guilty defendants are indicted in this case ($\lambda = 1$), though, it matters here only that $c_g > p_b$.

It is necessary to consider two cases:

(i) Let p_t be set so that $c_g > p_0$ and consider setting $p_b = c_g$. Then,

$$u(c_g) = \theta_g u(pt) \text{ [by definition]}$$

476

$$< \quad u(\theta_g pt) \quad \text{[by concavity]}$$

and $c_g > \theta_g p_t$. In words, the certainty equivalent penalty exceeds the expected trial penalty. Nonetheless, expected social welfare generated by the plea bargain is

$$EW_b = \text{[certain utility of guilty bargain]}$$

$$= V(c_g - p_0)$$

$$> V(\theta_g pt - p_0)$$

$$> EW_t.$$

because $|c_g - p_0| < |\theta_g pt - p_0|$.

(ii) Now let pt be so high that $c_g > p_0$. In that case, $p_b = p_0$ will extract the most appropriate penalty from all (guilty) defendants without trial because

[defendants expected utility in trial]

$$= \theta_g u(pt)$$

$$= u(c_g) \quad \text{[by definition]}$$

$$< u(p_0).$$

PROBLEM 47

> Social welfare <u>must</u> therefore be improved
> by the plea bargain.

The intuition, here, is that the trial generates only
uncertainty around the certainty equivalent expected utility
of punishment. The plea bargain, in acting as an "insurance
policy" against that uncertainty, necessarily improves
social welfare [see page 180].

(b) The plea bargain structure will serve as an effective
screening device only if

> (i) the guilty always take the bargain <u>and</u>

> (ii) the innocent always take the trial.

Only bargains p_b contained in the open interval (c_i, c_g) will
be effective screens, therefore, because

$$u(p_b) < u(c_i) = \theta_i u(p_t)$$

implies that the innocent will opt for trial and

$$u(p_b) > u(c_g) = \theta_g u(p_t)$$

implies that the guilty will opt for the bargain.

For $p_b < c_i$ (or, alternatively, $p_b > c_g$), both guilty
and innocent would opt for the bargain (or a trial).
Moreover, it is easily argued that the best screening
bargain will be as close to the upper extreme c_g as

possible. Why? Because

(i)   increases in p_b above c_i do not effect the
utility of the innocent and

(ii) increases in p_b toward c_g bring the bargain
penalty closer to the appropriate penalty p.

To consider the social desirability of such a screening plea
bargain $p_b = c_g$, note that it would produce expected social
welfare amounting to

EW_s = [expected welfare generated by guilty taking

$$p_b \approx c_g]$$

+ [expected utility of innocent convicted in

trial]

$$\approx \lambda V(c_g - p) + (1 - \lambda)\theta_i\, u(pt).$$

If all those indicted go to trial, on the other hand,

EW_t = [expected welfare of guilty convicted]

+ [expected loss of guilty not convicted]

+ [expected loss of innocent convicted]

$$= \lambda\theta_g V(p_t - p_0) + \lambda(1-\theta_g)V(0-p_0) + (1-\lambda)\theta_i u(p_t).$$

But since c_g is arbitrarily close to p_b and $p > c_g > \theta_g p_t$,

$$EW_t < V[\theta_g p_t - p_0] + (1 - \lambda)\theta_i u(p_t)$$

PROBLEM 47

$$< V[c_g - p_0] + (1 - \lambda)\theta_i u(p_t)$$

$$\approx EW_s,$$

and the screening bargain that approximates c_g improves welfare over the case in which everyone goes to trial.

(c) It has already been demonstrated that the screening plea bargain produces higher welfare than the case in which everyone goes to trial. Now compare the screening case against the situation in which everyone takes the plea bargain. The best screening policy of bargain cum trial penalty solves

$$\max_{p_b; p_t} \quad \{\lambda V(p_b - p_0) + (1 - \lambda)[\theta_i/\theta_g]u(p_b)\}$$

subject to the constraint that the screening works:

$$\theta_g u(p_t) \underset{<}{\approx} u(p_b) < \lambda_i u(p_t);$$

i.e., the guilty take the bargain $[\theta_g u(p_t) < u(p_b)]$, the bargain extracts the highest penalty accepted $[\theta_g u(p_t) < u(p_b)]$, and the innocent accept the risk of a trial $[u(p_b) < \theta_i u(p_t)]$. Substituting, then, the problem is to maximize

$$\{V(p_b - p_0) + (1 - \lambda)[\theta_i/\theta_g]u(p_b)\} \qquad (2)$$

with respect to p_b. A nonscreening bargaining policy would maximize

$$\{V(p_b - p_0) + (1-\lambda)u(p_b)\} \qquad\qquad (3)$$

subject to the constraint that

$$u(p_b) < \theta_i u(p_t).$$

But since $u(p_b) < 0$ and $[\theta_i/\theta_g] < 1$, the maximand for equation (2) must always exceed the maximand for (3) for any p_b.

(d)   Notice, first of all, that if

$$c_{g_h} > c_{g_1} > c_{i_h} > c_{i_1},$$

then p_b within the open interval between the middle two terms screens innocent from guilty perfectly, and so the previous analysis works. There is a problem, however, if

$$c_{g_1} > c_{i_h} > c_{g_1} > c_{i_h}.$$

Application of part (c) shows that a plea bargain should at least be arranged so that guilty people who are highly risk averse accept it while innocent people with low aversion to risk reject it. Beyond that, little can be said.

References

(1) Adelstein, R., "The Plea Bargain in Theory: A Behavioral Model of the Negotiated Guilty Plea," *Southern Economic Journal*, 44: 488-503, 1978.

(2) Grossman, G.M., and M.L. Katz, "Plea Bargaining and Social Welfare," *American Economic Review* 73: 749-757, 1983.

(3) Hostrom, B., "Moral Hazard and Observability", *Bell Journal of Economics,* 10: 74-91, 1979.

(4) Landes, W., "An Economic Analysis of the Courts," *Journal of Law and Economics,* 14: 61-108, 1971.

(5) McCoy, T., and Mirra, M., "Plea Bargaining as Due Process in Determining Guilt," *Stanford Law Review,* 32: 887-941, 1980.

(6) Newman, J., *Conviction: Determination of Guilt or Innocence Without Trial,* Boston, Little, Brown, 1966.

(7) Shavell, S., "Risk Sharing and Incentives in the Principal and Agent Relationship," *Bell Journal of Economics,* 10: 55-73, 1979.

(8) Stiglitz, J., "Monopoly, Non-linear Pricing and Imperfect Information: The Insurance Market," *Review of Economic Studies,* 44: 407-430, 1977.

48. Education as an Economic Signal[1]

Aside from the more noble goals of producing an intelligent population that is equipped to deal with a complex world, education is useful for the signals it provides. Signals are generated throughout an individual's schooling, and reveal aptitudes, interests, and other types of information that help individuals sort themselves out during that period in their lives. They are also germane to the labor markets people enter after their schooling, since they provide potential employers with information that helps them judge the relative abilities of a wide range of applicants. The employer's knowledge is not made perfect by recognizing the signal, but it is typically used in lieu of expensive interviewing, testing, or probationary hiring.

While this observation is not new, it has been the focus of a good deal of discussion, especially since Michael Spence published his dissertation (4) in 1974. The reader is referred to Arrow (1), Fields (2), and Thurow (6) for earlier work, but this problem will be drawn from Stiglitz (5). The Stiglitz piece is a complete treatment of the educational signaling literature through 1975, so this exercise captures only a small part of it. The interested reader is encouraged to consult the original paper for a

---

[1] Material found in Chapter 25, particularly in Sections 25.10 and 25.11, is applicable here.

PROBLEM 48

more thorough presentation.

For present purposes, let $h(\theta)$ be the distribution of ability (θ) across the population and let λ reflect the "intensity" of education received. Productivity will depend upon both λ and θ; represent it multiplicatively by $m(\lambda)\theta$, where $(dm/d\lambda) \geq 0$ and $(d^2m/d\lambda^2) \geq 0$. Screening can be reflected stochastically by $e(\theta,A,\lambda)$, the probability that someone of ability will be judged to have ability A in an educational system of intensity λ. Define

$$e(\theta,A,\lambda) \equiv f[(\theta-A),\lambda] \equiv f(\varepsilon,\lambda). \tag{1}$$

The variable ε thus reflects any error made in assessing ability. Assume that ε has a mean of zero and a variance of $\sigma^2(\lambda)$ with $(d\sigma^2(\lambda)/d\lambda) \leq 0$. It is thereby presumed that higher levels of education decrease the dispersion in the errors. Finally, let the cost of education, represented by $c(\lambda)$, be increasing at an increasing rate; i.e., assume that $(dc/d\lambda) > 0$ and $(d^2c/d\lambda^2) > 0$.

Questions:

(a) Suppose that everyone whose productivity were perceived to be A received a wage $w(A)$ equal to his or her expected productivity. Show that

PROBLEM 48

$$w(A) \approx m(\lambda) \ \{\frac{h'(A)\sigma^2(\lambda)}{h(A)} + A\}. \tag{2}$$

Use equation (2) to argue that an individual with an ability θ will be overpaid (or, alternatively, underpaid) if $h'(\theta) < 0$ (if, in the other case, $h'(\theta) > 0$). In other words, people below (above) the mode of a single-peaked ability distribution are overpaid (underpaid).

(b) Characterize the output maximizing provision of educational intensity λ^*.

(c) Show that citizens whose abilities lie below (or above) the mode prefer levels of education that lie below (above) λ^*.

Suggested Solutions:

The solutions follow fairly straightforwardly from the definition of the wage recorded in (a) and a first-order Taylor expansion of $h(\theta)$ [see page 480]. The only snag lies in remembering how to formalize a conditional distribution. Finally, the conditions derived in part (b) are necessary to evaluate the expression that emerges in (c).

(a) According to the specification of the problem, an individual with a perceived ability A will receive a wage equal to his or her average marginal product; using the definition of conditional probability, then

$$w(A) = m(\lambda) \int_{\theta} \theta e(\theta, A, \lambda) h(\theta) \, d\theta \, / \int_{\theta} e(\theta, A, \lambda) h(\theta) \, d\theta. \qquad (3)$$

The expected wage for somebody with ability θ is then

$$w(\theta) = \int_{A} w(A) e(\theta, A, \lambda) \, dA. \qquad (4)$$

It is now convenient to recall equation (1) and the assumptions that $\varepsilon \equiv \theta - A$ has zero mean and variance $\sigma^2(\lambda)$. In addition, a first-order Taylor expansion of $h(\theta)$ around A is useful:

$$h(\theta) \approx h(A) + h'(A)(\theta - A) = h(A) + h'(A)\varepsilon.$$

Equation (3) can now be written

$$w(A) \approx m(\lambda) \left\{ \frac{\int_{\varepsilon} (A + \varepsilon) f(\varepsilon, \lambda)[h(A) + h'(A)\varepsilon] \, d\varepsilon}{\int_{\varepsilon} f(\varepsilon, \lambda)[h(A) + h'(A)\varepsilon] \, d\varepsilon} \right\}$$

$$= m(\lambda) \frac{Ah(\theta) + h'(A)\sigma^2(\lambda)}{h(A)}$$

$$= m(\lambda) \left\{ \frac{h'(A)\sigma^2(\lambda)}{h(A)} + A \right\} \qquad (5)$$

because

$$E(\varepsilon) = \int_{\varepsilon} \varepsilon f(\varepsilon, \lambda) \, d\varepsilon = 0$$

for all λ. As a result, equation (5) implies that

$$w(\theta) \approx m(\lambda) \int_A \left\{ \frac{h'(\theta)\sigma^2(\lambda)}{h(A)} + A \right\} f(\theta-A),\lambda) \, dA.$$

Changing variables according to $\varepsilon \equiv \theta - A$,

$$w(\theta) \approx m(\lambda) \int_\varepsilon \left\{ \frac{h'(\theta-\varepsilon)\sigma^2(\lambda)}{h(\theta-\varepsilon)} + (\theta-\varepsilon) \right\} f(\varepsilon,\lambda) \, d\varepsilon$$

$$\approx m(\lambda) \left\{ \theta + \frac{h'(\theta)\sigma^2(\lambda)}{h(\theta)} \right\} \qquad (6)$$

if the errors reflected by ε are not too large. Depending upon the size of $h'(\theta)$, therefore, a person with true ability θ will be overpaid or underpaid.

If, for example, $h'(\theta) > 0$, then $w(\theta) > m(\lambda)\theta$ and the individual is overpaid. The person in question would then be averaged together with more people whose abilities were higher. Assuming that $h(\theta)$ is unimodal, this is clearly illustrated in Figure 48.1 by θ_1. Notice simply that the area under $h(\theta)$ from θ_1 to $(\theta_1 + \varepsilon)$ is larger than the area within θ_1 and $(\theta_1 - \varepsilon)$.

If $h'(\theta) < 0$, though, then $w(\theta) < m(\lambda)\theta$ because more people with inferior abilities would be included in $w(\theta)$. This case is shown by θ_2 in Figure 48.1 - illustrative of an individual who would be underpaid.

Figure 48.1

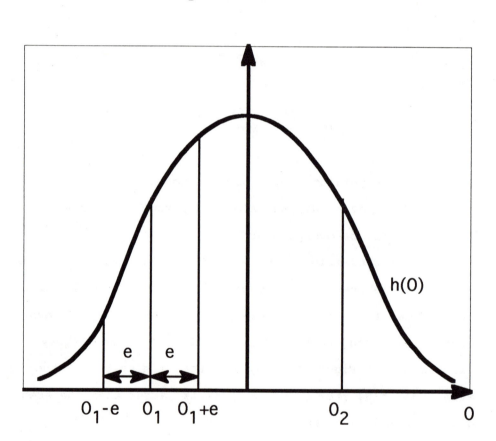

PROBLEM 48

Uncertainty produces similar results with respect to the worker's perceived ability. From equation (6), notice that a worker will be paid more (or, alternatively, less) than his or her perceived marginal product when $h'(A) > 0$ ($h'(A) < 0$) because the employer would correct for a tendency to underestimate (overestimate) actual ability in that range of the distribution.

(b) Maximizing national output in this context amounts to solving

$$\max_{\lambda} \quad \{m(\lambda) \int_{\theta} \theta h(\theta) \, d\theta - c(\lambda)\}.$$

The appropriate first-order condition is therefore

$$\frac{dm(\lambda)}{d\lambda} \, \bar{\theta} = \frac{dc(\lambda)}{d\lambda} \quad \text{or} \quad m'(\lambda^*)\bar{\theta} = c'(\lambda^*), \tag{7}$$

where $\bar{\theta} \equiv \int \theta h(\theta) \, d\theta$ is the mean ability of the working population.

(c) With a proportional tax rate, the government's budget constraint requires that

$$c(\lambda) = \int_{\theta} \tau m(\lambda) \theta h(\theta) \, d\theta = \tau m(\lambda)\bar{\theta}. \tag{8}$$

The average after-tax wage offered to someone with ability θ

is meanwhile

$$(1-\tau)w(\theta) \approx (1-\tau)m(\lambda)\{\theta + \frac{h'(\theta)\sigma^2(\lambda)}{h(\theta)} \} \qquad (9)$$

from equation (6). Combining equations (8) and (9),

$$(1-\tau)w(\theta) = \{\theta + \frac{h'(\theta)\sigma^2(\lambda)}{h(\theta)} \}(1-[c(\lambda)/m(\lambda)\bar{\theta}])m(\lambda)$$

$$= \{\theta + \frac{h'(\theta)\sigma^2(\lambda)}{h(\theta)} \}\{m(\lambda) - \frac{c(\lambda)}{\bar{\theta}}\}. \qquad (10)$$

Differentiating equation (10) in light of equations (8) and (9) will now provide the answer:

$$\frac{d[(1-\tau) w(\theta)]}{d\lambda} = \{\theta + \frac{h'(\theta)\sigma^2(\lambda)}{h(\theta)} \}\{(1-\tau)m'(\lambda)$$

$$- \frac{m(\lambda)}{\bar{\theta}} [\frac{m(\lambda)c'(\lambda)-c(\lambda)m'(\lambda)}{(m(\lambda))^2}]\}$$

$$+ (1-\tau)m(\lambda)\{ \frac{h'(\theta)}{h(\theta)} \frac{d\sigma^2(\lambda)}{d\lambda} \}$$

$$= \frac{w(\theta)}{m(\lambda)} \; \{(1-\tau)m'(\lambda)m(\lambda) \; - \; \frac{1}{\theta} \; [m(\lambda)c'(\lambda)$$

$$- \; \tau m(\lambda)\bar{\theta}m'(\lambda)]\} \; + \; (1-\tau)m(\lambda)\{\; \frac{h'(\theta)}{h(\theta)} \; \frac{d\sigma^2(\lambda)}{d\lambda} \; \}$$

$$= \; w(\theta)\{m'(\lambda) \; - \; \frac{c'(\lambda)}{\bar{\theta}} \; \} \; + \; (1-\tau)m(\lambda)\{\frac{h'(\theta)}{h(\theta)} \; \frac{d\sigma^2(\lambda)}{d\theta} \}.$$

$$(11)$$

This expression depends on both λ and θ, but does yield some information. Suppose that the optimal λ^* characterized by equation (7) were provided. In that case, with $\lambda = \lambda^*$,

$$\frac{d[(1-\tau) \; w(\theta)]}{d\lambda} \; = \; (1-\tau)m(\lambda^*)\{\; \frac{h'(\theta)}{h(\theta)} \; \frac{d\sigma^2(\theta)}{d\lambda} \; \} \qquad (12)$$

because the first term in (11) disappears at λ^*. For those with ability above the mode, $h'(\theta) < 0$ and equation (12) shows a positive sign because $[d\sigma^2(\lambda)/d\lambda] \leq 0$. These citizens would thus prefer a higher λ - a level of education above the optimum - that would increase their expected after-tax wage. Others with ability below the mode show $h'(\theta) > 0$ and would prefer less education.

As part of the more thorough discussion of education and signaling presented by Stiglitz (5), this model suggests that majority rule will produce an excessive investment in education if the wage effect dominates people's educational preferences. To see this, recall that the median votes dictates the majority voting solution [see page 424]. Equation (6) meanwhile shows that voters whose abilities lie above the mode prefer too much education. If ability is distributed lognormally like income, then the median exceeds the mode. The voting solution therefore yields an investment in education that exceeds the λ^* defined in part (b). There are obvious limitations to this model (like the assumption that everyone knows his or her ability exactly), but it is extremely suggestive.

References

(1) Arrow, K., "Higher Education as a Filler," *Journal of Public Economics*, 2: 193-216, 1973.

(2) Fields, G., "Towards a Model of Education and Labor Markets in Labor Surplus Economics," Yale University mimeo, 1973.

(3) Spence, M., "Job Market Signaling," *Quarterly Journal of Economics*, 87: 355-379, 1973.

(4) Spence, M., *Market Signaling*, Cambridge, Mass., Harvard University Press, 1974.

(5) Stiglitz, J.E., "The Theory of 'Screening,' Education and the Distribution of Income," *American Economic Review*, 65: 283-300, 1975.

(6) Thurow, L., "Education and Economic Equality," *Public Interest*, 20: 61-81, 1972.

49. **Multiple Price Equilibria**[1]

This problem will explore the potential that informational asymmetry might support multiple equilibria - an observation developed more fully in Salop and Stiglitz (4). It will culminate with the characterization of a condition that is necessary if a two-price equilibrium is to exist. It will lead the reader to conclude that excessively sloped average costs or too many informed consumers can preclude multiple price equilibria, at least in an informational model. Equilibrium prices and outputs will also be recorded.

The following notation will be employed. Let

c_i = search costs for consumer i (i = 1,2); $c_1 < c_2$;

L = total number of consumers (a large number);

α = proportion of L facing c_1 (0 ≤ α ≤ 1);

n = total number of firms;

p_h = price charged by high-priced firms;

p_1 = price charged by lower-priced firms;

AC(q) = average cost of producing q;

q^* = output that minimizes AC(q);

$p^* = AC(q^*)$ = the competitive price;

---

[1] Material found in Chapter 25 is applicable here; the notion that information is both valuable and, in some cases, costly will be explored.

PROBLEM 49

u = monopoly price; and

β = fraction of n charging p_1 ($0 \le \beta \le 1$).

There are many firms, some of which are perhaps charging lower prices for output than others. Salop and Stiglitz show, however, that there are only two possible prices, so that an average price $\bar{p}$ is simply

$$\bar{p} = \beta p_1 + (1-\beta) p_h.$$

Search for the low-price firms is, however, assumed to be costly. It will, in fact, cost c_i for consumers of type i, but search also holds the promise of identifying the lower-priced firms. All consumers who do not engage in a search choose a firm randomly, and pay p_h a total of $(1-\beta)$ 100% of the time.

Questions:

(a) Suppose that only C_1 consumers find it profitable to engage in search. Show that

$$p_h = p^* + C_2/(1-\beta)$$

if C_2 consumers are to be indifferent between search and no search.

(b) Characterize loci of (β, n) that satisfy zero profit constraints for both the high- and low-priced firms (one

495

locus for each type of firm).

(c) The intersection of the two loci derived in part (b) generates the two-price equilibrium; it is a pair $(\bar{\beta}, n)$ such that demand equals supply with zero profits for both high- and low-priced firms. Graph the loci and generate a condition that is necessary (and in fact sufficient under "well-behaved" assumptions) for the required intersection to exist. Explain the circumstances under which the condition will not be satisfied.

Suggested Solutions:

Part (a) outlines some of the major results of the Salop and Stiglitz model. Part (b) then evolves from the notion that price must equal average cost if profits are to be zero. Part (c) finally involves graphing the zero profit conditions found in part (b) for both types of firms. Total derivatives yield slopes, and end points are established. The necessary condition emerges from the end points.

(a) Under the assumption that some consumers (C_1 consumers) find it profitable to search and some (C_2 consumers) don't, it can be seen that

$$c_1 \leq \bar{p} - p_1 \leq c_2.$$ (1)

PROBLEM 49

From equation (1), therefore,

$$C_1 \le (1-\beta)(p_h - p_1) \le C_2. \tag{2}$$

Equation (2) plus the result competition supports

$$p_1 = p^*$$

and explains the genesis of

$$p_h = \min \{u; [p^* + C_2/(1-\beta)]\}.$$

To see why, note that the right-hand inequality of (2) must be an equality if C_2 consumers are to be indifferent between searching or not; i.e.,

$$(1-\beta)(p_h-p^*) = C_2.$$

Rearranging, then,

$$p_h = p^* + C_2/(1-\beta).$$

Notice that this is the highest price that the firms can charge without providing incentives for C_2 consumers to engage in search. If that were to happen, p^* would become the single-price equilibrium. Firms will continue to charge $p^* + C_2/(1-\beta)$ only until it reaches u, though, because higher prices would actually decrease profits.

(b) High-priced firms sell only to the $(1-\alpha)L$ uninformed consumers. Each of these firms therefore sells

$$q_h = (1-\alpha)L/n. \tag{3}$$

Low priced firms sell not only to their share of the uninformed consumers, but also to a proportion of the informed consumers. There are, in particular, βn low priced firms and αL informed consumers, so

$$q_1 + [(1-\alpha)L/n] + [\alpha L/\beta n] = [1 - \alpha + (\alpha/\beta)][L/n] > q_h. \tag{4}$$

Since these sales must yield zero profits, it must also be true that

$$p^* = p_1 = AC[1 - \alpha + (\alpha/\beta)][L/n]) \text{ and} \tag{5}$$

$$\min \{u; [p^* + C_2/(1-\beta)]\} = p_h = AC\{(1-\alpha)L/n\}. \tag{6}$$

Finally, given that $p^* = AC(q^*)$, equation (5) requires that

$$q^* = [1 - \alpha + (\alpha/\beta)][L/n], \tag{7}$$

where q^* is the output that minimizes average costs.

(c) Look first at equation (5). Totally differentiating this zero profit constraint with respect to n and β, one gets

$$0 = dAC(\sim) = - [1 - \alpha + (\alpha/\beta)][L/n^2] \, dn - [L/n][\alpha/\beta^2] \, d\beta.$$

Rearranging a bit reveals that

$$\frac{d\beta}{dn} = - \frac{\beta^2}{n\alpha} [1 - \alpha + (\alpha/\beta)] < 0$$

because $(\alpha/\beta) > \alpha$ when $\beta < 1$. The locus defined by equation (5) is thus downward sloping everywhere. It is asymptotic to $\beta = 0$ when $n \to 1$, and it associates $\beta = 1$ with $n = L/q^*$ [see (7)]. Figure 49.1 illustrates this locus, and correctly puts its leftmost limit at $n = L/q^*$; since $\beta \le 1$, the locus can never extend above $\beta = 1$, so it can never extend below $n = L/q^*$.

There are, however, two possibilities for equation (6). Suppose, first of all, that $u > p^* + C_2/(1-\beta)$. Then, $\beta < 1 - C_2/(u-p^*)$. In this region,

$$p^* + C_2/(1-\beta) = AC((1-\alpha)L/n)$$

defines the zero profit locus, and total differentiating produces

$$\frac{d\beta}{dn} = -\{(1-\beta)^2 \, L(1-\alpha) \, \frac{dAC(\sim)}{dq} \} \, / \, C_2 n^2. \qquad (8)$$

To evaluate the sign of equation (8), notice that equations

Figure 49.1

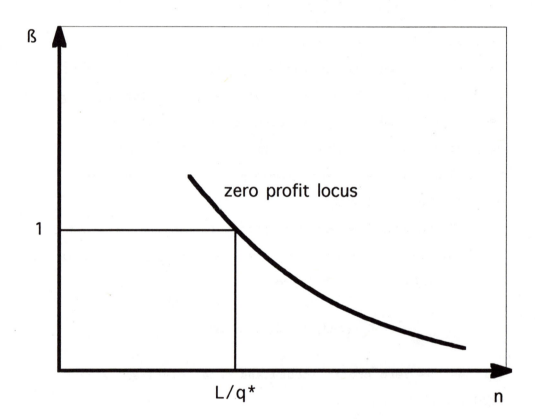

(3) and (4) reveal that

$$q_n < q_1 = q^*.$$

As a result, $dAC(\sim)/dq$ is evaluated in equation (8) at an output below the average cost minimizing q^*; it must therefore be negative. Clearly, then,

$$\frac{d\beta}{dn} > 0.$$

The positively sloped portion of the locus continues until $u \le p^* + C_2/(1-\beta)$ so that $\beta \ge 1 - C_2/(u-p^*)$. In this region,

$$u = AC((1-\alpha)L/n),$$

so that

$$q_u = (1-\alpha)L/n \qquad (9)$$

is always produced. Rearranging equation (9),

$$n_u \equiv (1-\alpha)L/q_u \qquad (10)$$

becomes the limit for the locus defined by equation (6). Figure 49.2 illustrates its entire range for $\beta > 0$; it is the thick line which turns vertical at $n = n_u$.

A two-price equilibrium will occur only when these

Figure 49.2

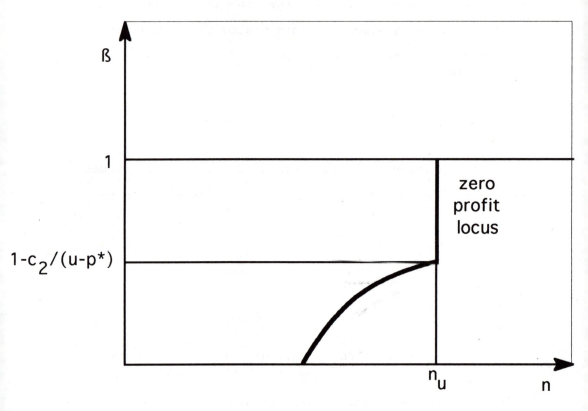

loci intersect. Since $n = L/q^*$ is the minimum allowed by equation (5) and $n_u = (1-\alpha)L/q_u$ is the maximum allowed by equation (6), a necessary condition for equilibrium is that

$$n_u = (1-\alpha)L/q_u > L/q^*.$$

In other words, a two-price equilibrium is possible only if

$$(1-\alpha) > q_u/q^*.$$

It will not exist for steeply sloped average cost schedules (for which $(q_u/q^*) \to 1$) or when the market consists mainly of informed consumers ($\alpha \to 1$). The first condition would make p_u so large that even C_2 consumers would search; and the second would destroy the dichotomy among consumers to the point at which there were too few uninformed consumers around for even one high priced firm to be profitable.

Notice that two "types" of equilibria are possible. If the two loci intersect on the vertical region of the $\pi_u = 0$ locus illustrated in Figure 49.2, then the higher price will be the monopoly price. If they intersect on the positively sloped portion, though, the higher price will fall short of the monopoly price.

Finally, note that all of this analysis presumes that consumers use only the information they can obtain by searching; they ignore signals with which they could differentiate firms without searching. If, for example, consumers were able to notice that the lower-priced firms captured larger shares of the market than the higher price firms (i.e., that $q_h > q_1$), then they could tell where to go without a search. This type behavior has been precluded; but it is suggestive because there will always be enough "noise" around for it to pay to become better informed [see Grossman and Stiglitz (2)]. Multiple price equilibria may then be possible.

References

(1) Diamond, P.A., "A Model of Price Adjustment," *Journal of Economic Theory*, 3: 156-168, 1971.

(2) Grossman, S., and J.E. Stiglitz, "Information and Competitive Price Systems," *American Economic Review - Papers and Proceedings*, 66: 246-253, 1976.

(3) Phelps, E., and S. Winter, "Optimal Price Policy Under Atomistic Competition," in Phelps, E. (ed.), *Microeconomic Foundations of Inflation and Employment Theory*, New York, Norton, 1970.

(4) Solop, S., and J.E. Stiglitz, "Bargains and Ripoffs: A Model of Monopolistically Competitive Price Dispersion," *Review of Economic Studies*, 44: 493-510, 1977.

50. The Value of Information[1]

Much of the discussion in Chapter 25 surrounds collecting and using information. This problem will address the value of that information. Consider an informational structure that allows one to distinguish between possible states of nature $\{x\}_{x \in X}$. If the signals from that structure are modeled as points on the real line, then the signals are simply functionals which map every state of nature in X into R. Represent an informational structure, taken to be a set of signals, by $\eta_i(x)$. If $\eta_i(x) = k$ for all possible $x \in X$, then no information is collected. If $\eta_i(x)$ is different for all possible $x \in X$, then information is complete. In between there are a multitude of structures that yield imperfect information. Each one, nonetheless, defines a partition of the set of all possible states of nature. If Y_i is the range of $\eta_i(x)$, in particular, then

$$\{\eta_i^{-1}(y) \equiv p_i(y)\}_{y \in Y_i}$$

is that partition.

Given this formalization of the information gathering process [devised by Marschak and Radner (3)], comparisons of

---

[1] Material found in Chapter 25 is applicable here. The exercise will draw heavily on a simple representation of expected utility.

informational structures are possible. One can, for example, say that structure i is "finer" than structure j if all of the partitions defined by $\eta_i(x)$ are contained inside those defined by $\eta_j(x)$ [i.e., if for every $y_i \in Y_i$ there exists a $y_j \in Y_j$ such that $p_i(y_i) \subseteq p_j(y_j)$].

A finer partition always yields more information, almost by definition; but that information may or may not be useful. For instance, knowing that 1000 1" nails and 500 2" nails have been delivered is more information than knowing at 1500 assorted 1" and 2" nails have been delivered. If you could use either nail interchangeably, though, the extra information would be useless. The notion of fineness is thus a straightforward concept with plausible assumptions.

The partitions defined by alternative structures do not have to nest, though, and comparisons become more difficult when they do not. It is, nonetheless, possible to make some comparative judgment, but only by looking at how the information can be used. One asks "What is the value of the information?" But to assess the relative values, one must know how a decision maker would respond to different types of information. This problem will explore an example found in Marschak and Radner (3) that illustrates a formal model of this comparison.

Let $\hat{a}_0$ represent the course of action that can be taken in the face of uncertainty to maximize expected utility with no <u>ex ante</u> information. Denote the

corresponding distribution of outcomes $\hat{x}_0$. The expected
utility generated over these states of nature is thus
$Eu(\hat{x}_0)$.

Now let $\eta_i(x)$ represent an informational structure
that provides some information on the possible outcomes.
The structure need not be complete. Let $\hat{a}_i[\eta_i(x)]$ be the
best set of actions that can be taken with that information,
and denote the corresponding outcome distribution $\hat{x}_i$. The
value of $\eta_i(x)$ can be thought to be

$$Eu(\hat{x}_i) - Eu(\hat{x}_0) \equiv V_1[\eta_i(x)], \tag{1}$$

the difference between the maximum levels of expected
utility obtainable with and without any information.

The difference identified in equation (1) is not the
only possible measure. One might, instead of (1), define
the value of $\eta_i(x)$ to be the solution to

$$E\{u(\hat{x}_i - V_2[\eta_i(x)])\} = Eu(\hat{x}_0). \tag{2}$$

In other words, $V_2[\eta_i(x)]$ is the cost that would allow $\eta_i(x)$
to produce a distribution of net outcomes that would
generate a maximal level of expected utility equal to the
level achieved with no information. Equation (2) assumes
that it is costless to collect no information.

Now, to provide the details of the example to be
considered here [see Chapter 3 in Marschak and Radner (3)

507

PROBLEM 50

Table 1 - Outcomes

States of Nature

Action	1	2	3	4	Expected Value
1	1	0	-100	-100	-49.75
2	-100	-100	1	0	-49.75
3	.4	-100	.4	-100	-49.8
4	-100	.4	-100	.4	-49.8
5	0	0	0	0	0

for a more complete description of the context of their illustration], let Table 1 summarize the outcomes of 5 possible actions in each of 4 equally probable states of nature. Consider, in the context of Table 1, three alternative informational structures. The first, designated η_1, amounts to no information at all. It translates each state of nature into the same signal:

$$\eta_1(x) = 0; \ x = 1,2,3,4.$$

The second differentiates states 1 and 2 from states 3 and 4; formally,

$$\eta_2(1) = \eta_2(2) = 0 \text{ and } \eta_2(3) = \eta_2(4) = 0.$$

The third differentiates states 1 and 3 from states 2 and 4:

$$\eta_3(1) = \eta_3(3) = 0 \text{ and } \eta_2(2) = \eta_3(4) = 0.$$

Structure 2 therefore partitions $\{1,2,3,4\}$ into $\{1,2\}$ and $\{3,4\}$; structure 3, into $\{1,3\}$ and $\{2,4\}$. Finally, suppose the utility function is of the form

$$u(y) = \begin{cases} y & \text{if } y \le .5 \\ .5 + .2(y-.5) & \text{if } y \ge .5. \end{cases} \tag{3}$$

Equation (3) is a piecewise linear schedule that displays risk aversion surrounding only the critical value .5.

Questions:

(a) Show that action 5 is best under $\eta_1(x)$. Characterize the best decision rules under $\eta_2(x)$ and $\eta_3(x)$.

(b) Compute $V_1[\eta_i(x)]$ and $V_2[\eta_i(x)]$ for $i = 1$, 2 and show that the relative values of $\eta_1(x)$ and $\eta_2(x)$ depend on which definition of value is used. Explain why.

Suggested Solutions:

(a) The rightmost column of Table 1 shows that action 5 achieves the highest level of expected utility with no information. Clearly, then,

$$Eu(\hat{x}_1) = 0.$$

PROBLEM 50

For the other structures, one can differentiate between
states of nature and make action decisions contingent on the
signals.

For $\eta_2(x)$, for example, there are two signals. When 0
is registered, states 3 and 4 are eliminated and one can
choose an action based on conditional expectations across
states 1 and 2. Action 1 maximizes that conditional
computation:

    Action 1 → (1/2) [.6 + 0] = .3
    Action 2 → (1/2) [-100 - 100] = -100
    Action 3 → (1/2) [.4 - 100] = -49.8
    Action 4 → (1/2) [-100 + .4] = -49.8
    Action 5 → (1/2) [0 + 0] = 0.

Similarly, a signal of 1 precludes states 1 and 2, so an
action can be chosen on the basis of a conditional
computation across states 3 and 4:

    Action 1 → (1/2) [-100 - 100] = -100
    Action 2 → (1/2) [1 + 0] = .5
    Action 3 → (1/2) [.4 - 100] = -49.8
    Action 4 → (1/2) [-100 + .4] = -49.8
    Action 5 → (1/2) [0 + 0] = 0.

Action 2 dominates. In the notation of the introduction,
then,

$$\hat{a}_2[\eta_2(1)] = \hat{a}_2[\eta_2(1)] = \hat{a}_2(0) = 1 \text{ and}$$

$$\hat{a}_2[\eta_2(3)] = \hat{a}_2[\eta_2(4)] = \hat{a}_2(1) = 2.$$

The level of expected utility achieved is simply computed from the utility function recorded in equation (3) because this strategy grosses 1, 0, 1 and 0 and utilities 0.6, 0, 0.6, and 0 in states 1, 2, 3, and 4 respectively:

$$E_u(\hat{x}_2) = .25 \{.6 + 0 + .6 + 0\} = .3.$$

Similarly, $\eta_3(x)$ differentiates states 1 and 3 from 2 and 4. Since $\eta_3(1) = \eta_3(3) = 0$, $\hat{a}_3(0)$ is computed across states 1 and 3. Action 3 is best. The other states are covered by $\eta_3(2) = \eta_3(4) = 1$, and $\hat{a}_3(1) = 4$. These computations are left to the reader. This strategy produces the highest level of expected utility possible under $\eta_3(x)$:

$$.25 \{.4 + .4 + .4 + .4\} = .4.$$

According to equation (1), therefore,

$$V_1[\eta_2(x)] = .3 < V_1[\eta_2(x)] = .4.$$

(b) Equation (2) provides an alternative measure of the value of information. Consider $\eta_2(x)$ first. Solving

$$E_u(\hat{x}_0) = .25\{[.5 + .2(1-V_2-.5)] - V_2$$
$$+ [.5 + .2(1-V_2-.5)] - V_2\} = 0$$

for V_2, one finds that

$$V^2[\eta_2(x)] = .5.$$

Since action on $\eta_3(x)$ yields the same outcome in all states, though,

$$V_2[\eta_3(x)] = .4 < V_2[\eta_3(x)] = .5,$$

and so, the rankings are reversed.

Risk aversion provides the explanation. For structure $\eta_3(x)$, the computation of both V_1 and V_2 took place entirely within the lower linear range of $u(--)$. As a result, only the mean outcome was important under both alternatives; in fact,

$$E\{u(\hat{X}_3 - V_2[\eta_3(x)])\} = E(X_3 - V_2[\eta_3(x)]\} = 0$$

requires that

$$V_2[\eta_3(x)] = E\hat{X}_3 \equiv V_1[\eta_3(x)].$$

Structure $\eta_2(x)$ produces some gross outcomes that lie in the upper segment of $u(--)$, however, and the concavity of the schedule (the risk aversion of the decision maker) comes into play [see Figure 50.1]:

Figure 50.1

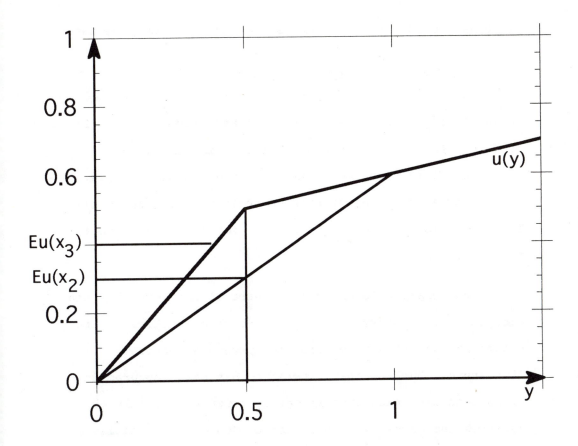

$$0 = E\{u(\hat{X}_2 - V_2[\eta_2(x)])\} < E(\hat{X}_2 - V_2[\eta_2(x)])$$

so

$$V_2[\eta_2(x)] < E(\hat{X}_2) = V_1[\eta_2(x)].$$

The observed reversal in rank is thus possible only because

$$V_1[\eta_3(x)] = E\hat{X}_3 < E\hat{X}_2 = V_1[\eta_2(x)].$$

It should be no surprise, then, that equations (1) and (2) produce identical rankings of arbitrary informational structures only when the utility function is linear (i.e., only under assumptions of risk neutrality; see Chapter 11). The reader is referred to Debreu (1) for a complete proof of this notion.

This example is but a small part of the work that has emerged on the theory of teams. That theory begins to study organizational structure, and has spawned an entire literature. Much of that literature has been captured in books, and the interested reader is referred not only to Marschak and Radner (3), but also to Groves (2), Montias (4 and 5), and Williamson (6). Aside from introducing that body of work, though, this example illustrates simply a crucial concern: what is the value of (this) information? Since information is costly, it should not be collected for the sake of collecting. It should be collected because having it allows one to perform better than not having it, net of the cost of collection, of course.

References

(1) Debreu, G., "Topological Methods in Cardinal Utility," in K. Arrow, et al. (eds.), *Mathematical Methods in the Social Sciences*, Stanford, Calif., Stanford University Press, 1970.

(2) Groves, T., "Incentives in Teams," *Econometrica*, 41: 617-633, 1973.

(3) Marschak, J., and R. Radner, *Economic Theory of Teams*, New Haven, Conn., Yale University Press, 1972.

(4) Montias, J.M., *The Structure of Economic Systems*, New Haven, Conn., Yale University Press, 1976.

(5) Montias, J.M., "The Aggregation of Controls and the Autonomy of Subordinates," *Journal of Economic Theory*, 15: 123-134, 1977.

(6) Williamson, O.E., *Markets and Heirarchies: Analysis and Antitrust Implications*, New York, Macmillan Co., 1975.